International Economic Adjustment

International Economic Adjustment

Small Countries and the European Monetary System

Edited by
MARCELLO DE CECCO

Published in cooperation with
the European University Institute, Florence

ST. MARTIN'S PRESS · NEW YORK

St. Martin's Press, Inc., 175 Fifth Avenue, New York, NY 10010
Printed in Great Britain
First published in the United States of America in 1983

Library of Congress Cataloging in Publication Data

De Cecco, Marcello.
International economic adjustment.

1. Foreign exchange problem – Europe – Addresses, essays, lectures. 2. Europe – Economic policy – Addresses, essays, lectures. 3. States, Small – Economic conditions – Addresses, essays, lectures. 4. Money – European Economic Community countries – Addresses, essays, lectures. I. Title.
HG3942.D4 1983 332.4'566'094 82-23164

ISBN 0-312-42050-1

Typeset by Unicus Graphics Ltd, Horsham
Printed in Great Britain by T. J. Press Ltd, Padstow

Contents

Introduction

MARCELLO DE CECCO
Professor of Economics, European University Institute, Florence

A study of the smaller countries of Europe – northern, central and southern – soon becomes a fascinating experience in economic analysis. Here, encompassed within a sample of scarcely more than 80 million people, we find 11 different sovereign countries, all run by democratic governments, some of them kingdoms, some republics, and involving all shades of geographical, geopolitical and economic situations. Within our sample we have the richest and the poorest countries of Western Europe: exporters of primary commodities, such as Finland; of temperate food, such as Denmark and Ireland; of Mediterranean agricultural products, such as Greece and Portugal; of oil and gas, such as Norway and Holland; of 'mature' industrial products (most of them); of technologically advanced industrial products (several of them). Among them we find neutral countries, such as Austria, Finland, Ireland, Sweden and Switzerland, and NATO members, such as Denmark, Norway, Portugal, Greece, Belgium and the Netherlands.

Economic conditions are equally disparate – domestic product per capita ranges from top of the world league, to medium, to low. Labour force participation rates go from extremely high to very low; unemployment rates from extremely low to extremely high.

The economic and political instances of these 11 countries show equally profound heterogeneity. Several of our countries were centres of colonial empires; others were centres of European empires. Some of them, such as Belgium, developed their industrial structures very early by world standards; some much later; others only recently.

Some of them have progressed very quickly from being extremely poor to being very rich – for instance Sweden and Switzerland, though they did so via extremely different paths of economic development. For others, such as Austria, prosperity was regained after a long geopolitical crisis. Some – Ireland and Finland, for example – have experienced very fast growth in the last decade. Others, such as Belgium and Sweden, have been recently declining, gently but surely. Still others have changed their export patterns – drastically in the case of Norway, very substantially in the case of Austria and Finland. Two – Greece and Portugal – have just started on the road to industrialization; both have high population growth rates, and are labour-exporters. Most of the others, with the exception of Finland, import labour from southern Europe and north Africa; these have experienced low or very low population growth, some for a long time, some for a much shorter time.

In the field of trade and exchange regimes we find equally heterogeneous experiences. Some countries have always had foreign trade control and strictly controlled capital movements; others have experienced traditionally free trade and capital movements; still others have switched from control to free trade and back to control.

Among our countries we have some traditional hard currencies (e.g., Switzerland); a former hard currency gone weak (Portugal); some new hard currencies, with a past of extreme weakness (e.g., Austria); petro-currencies (the Norwegian and the Dutch); and currencies that oscillate between a hard and a weak state most of the time, steering a middle course.

Several of the countries have pegged their currencies to another one – the mark in the case of former 'Snake' members, sterling in the case of Ireland up to the European Monetary System (EMS). Others, for example, Finland, have pegged to a trade-weighted currency basket. Still others, such as Belgium, have had a dual exchange market, while belonging to the 'Snake'. The two southern countries have had a more chequered recent exchange rate history. Portugal after 1971 first pegged to the mark until 1975, when it began to devalue against both mark and dollar. Dollar devaluation continues; devaluation against the mark was stopped at the end of 1979. Greece followed the dollar in its downward movement *vis-à-vis* the other hard currency until the middle of 1975; then a basket peg was adopted and the drachma started devaluing against the peg. Not until the end of the decade was the rapid depreciation against the European currencies interrupted.

At the start of the EMS, in March 1979, some countries joined formally, some stepped out but behaved as if they were in, while others stayed out and their currencies performed differently from the EMS's European Currency Unit (ECU).

To the list of heterogeneous features of our countries, we can add that some of them depend very heavily on big neighbours for their imports and exports while others have a much more diversified geographical distribution of trade.

One important unifying feature, however, is the very large percentage of gross national product (GNP) which the current account of the balance of payments represents in all those countries. With their 80 million people, in 1980 the small countries of Europe had over $200 billion of exports, compared to the $400 billion worth exported by the four big countries of Europe put together. And the latter have a population almost three times as large. If invisible trade is added, the comparison becomes even more persuasive.

Looking for other common features, one cannot fail to be struck by the central role these countries have played in recent years in stabilizing the international trade balance of Germany. If we take the 1980 trade figures, we see that these countries have absorbed about 39% of total German exports, and their total deficit with Germany was about $11 billion. It is useful to remember that the overall trade surplus of Germany was only $5 billion in 1980. It is also useful to note that in 1980 the German trade accounts registered massive deficit with both the United States and Japan: from the United States imports grew by 28%, while German exports to the United States grew by only 4%; from Japan imports grew by 23%, while German exports to Japan actually declined 3%.

The central role of the small countries of Europe in German visible and invisible trade is even better understood when individual country figures are examined. None of the countries in question, with the exception of Norway and Finland, takes less than 17% of her total imports from Germany. Austria takes 54%, Holland 30%, Portugal 21%, Greece 27% and Switzerland 26%.

If the relative specialization of German exports is respected *vis-à-vis* these countries, and we believe it is, and German exports to the 11 then consist mainly of investment goods and maintenance items for the same, it is easy to realize that these 11 small countries play a vital role in generating demand for the German investment goods industry. Since the percentages we have mentioned here were, if anything, larger in 1970 than they are at the close of the decade, it is fair to conclude that the integration of these countries' manufacturing sector with the German one is very high and has probably been very high for the whole postwar period. It is almost certain that we must look at intra-industry levels, if we want to get a meaningful picture of this interpretation, especially for what concerns the northern and central European countries; while in the case of Greece and Portugal, the exchange with Germany is one of Mediterranean agricultural commodities, light industrial goods, tourism and labour against investment goods and consumer durables.

Since the importance of these small countries is greater to Germany's trade balance than that of the German market for these countries' exports, it is easy to understand how basic it is that the Deutschmark (DM) remains fairly stable *vis-à-vis* their currencies.

In view of the performance of American and Japanese exports on these as well as on the German market, an up-valuation of the DM would mean disaster for German industry. Japanese and American penetration of these markets since 1975 has been truly phenomenal. It will be extremely interesting to see whether the renewed strength of both dollar and Yen in 1981 will lead to a fall of US and Japanese exports symmetrical to their growth following the weakness of these currencies. Our educated guess is that US exports will fall and that Japanese exports will grow by less but will keep growing, since high profit rates seem to be calculated by Japanese firms only over the long run, and especially through the continuous expansion of production, which determines the fall of fixed production costs.

In view of the absolute necessity that German exporters have of keeping their very high share of the small European countries' markets, it is necessary to consider the wisdom of creating an area of hard currencies that includes, around Germany, a good number of these small countries. With stable exchange rates, competitive conditions have remained stable between German industrial producers and industrial producers in these small countries. At the same time, however, competitive conditions have become extremely favourable for the two industrial giants, the United States and Japan, whose currencies have been depreciating against those of small countries for a good part of the most recent period. As a result, substantial market shares have been lost, in the small countries, by indigenous producers and by other European producers, and have been gained by American and Japanese producers. The formation of the EMS was considered as a treaty of non-belligerence between European industrial producers. In retrospect, it has so far served the purpose of integrating the United States and especially Japan with Europe, to a much greater extent than had happened before. Whether this is good or bad is debatable; what is certain is that it was not part of the strategy devised by the Europeans when the EMS scheme was hatched.

Passing on to examine the European small countries' reaction to the second oil shock of 1979, it is possible to detect a much greater uniformity in economic policies than was true when the same countries reacted to the first oil shock in 1973. The price increase of 1979 could be effected only because of the pressure of world demand for oil determined by the strong surge of world economic activity. The same had happened in 1973–74. This time, however, most of the small countries of Europe seemed to have reacted by adopting a strong contractionary policy, as they have obviously thought that the contractionary effect of a doubling in oil prices should be allowed to make itself felt on their respective economies.

As a result of the pick-up in economic activity, current account balances for these countries were deeply negative in 1979. They became even more negative in 1980, as oil was costing twice as much, and in spite of the fact that industrial production experienced a markedly reduced growth rate in 1980 and that unemployment surged in most of these countries.

Growing deficits were financed by short-term capital imports, mostly private or public borrowing on the Eurocurrencies market. This meant that interest rates had to be aligned, in these countries, to those ruling on the international financial market – or to exceed them, if anything, when exchange rate expectations were unfavourable to their individual currencies.

The dampening effect of high interest rates and, more generally, deflationary policies on imports, have necessarily meant a dampening effect on other countries' exports. Since a large share of total trade of small European countries is with Europe, it cannot be expected that exports grow while imports decline, when three of the four major European countries themselves are contracting. The only locomotive left in Europe in 1980 was Italy; it did all it could, but it is not a big locomotive anyway. Nor could small countries expect to redress their deficits by exporting more to Japan and the United States in view of the exchange rate levels we have described. Having stressed the uniformity of small response to the oil shock of 1979, I do not want to generate the impression that economic policy was the same in all these countries.

Structural and institutional characteristics that have existed for whole decades do not disappear in a couple of years. Thus, in 1980 unemployment remained much lower than elsewhere in Austria, Sweden and Switzerland, while it grew higher in traditional high-unemployment countries like Belgium. Growth rates have also differed markedly in 1980, as they had before. And traditional big public sector deficit countries have remained on top of this particular league.

As we approach the second half of 1981, economic prospects do not look particularly bright for any of these countries. The creation of massive unemployment, where it has taken place as a result of sticking to a hard currency policy, has merely transferred the cost of employment from the private to the government sector, thus rendering massive public borrowing indispensable. Reduction of imports, achieved by contractionary policies, does not seem to be able to generate more exports; for, given the high level of mutual integration of European economies, it only serves to depress European aggregate demand. Nor can outlets be easily found elsewhere: countries who look traditionally to developing countries will be faced by the latter's dangerous levels of foreign borrowing, with debt service payments inflated by high world interest rates. Countries who traditionally rely on the United States as an outlet can expect only modest gains from favourable exchange rates, as demand will probably remain weak in the United States well into 1982. Those who rely on the Eastern bloc will not fare much better, as the structural crisis that the Eastern economies have plunged themselves into does not seem capable of early solution and will certainly not induce higher imports; rather, the opposite will be more likely. OPEC countries, with demand for oil remaining slack, will not be able to buy as much as they have so far. The most profligate among them might even experience an external deficit in 1982.

In conclusion, the small European countries' prospects for 1982 and beyond must be disarmingly similar to those of large European countries: a mix of deflation, payments deficits and unemployment. In individual national instances, the existence of institutions conducive to social peace, or independence in the energy field, can reduce to a certain extent the severity of the recession; but it will be impossible for these countries to shield themselves more than to a modest extent against the vagaries of dominating variables, like the economic policy of the US Government, or price policy of OPEC.

The papers in this book were presented at the European University Institute Conference on International Adjustment, the EMS and Small European Countries held in Florence in March 1981.

External Shocks and Adjustment Policies in Finland, 1973-80

HANNU HALTTUNEN and SIXTEN KORKMAN
Bank of Finland, Helsinki, and
Labour Institute for Economic Research, Helsinki

Introduction

The 1970s were a period of violent fluctuations. Oil prices multiplied, world markets were severely depressed, exchange rate regimes were in a state of flux, and international financial markets were turbulent. For institutional reasons (relating mostly to Finnish foreign exchange policy), the direct macroeconomic effects of foreign financial developments were limited in the case of Finland. The real shocks, by contrast, were decisive to the economy's performance.

In this paper we briefly describe macroeconomic developments in Finland in the 1973–80 period. We also discuss the role played in the cyclical context by monetary and exchange rate policy.

The Finnish economy in the 1970s: an overview

In the 1970s about 30 per cent of total Finnish output was exported. In many instances the domestic effects of external disturbances have been magnified by certain structural characteristics of the Finnish economy and by economic policy.

The major external impulses are changes in trade prices and variations in export demand. Owing to the large share of timber, pulp and paper products in exports (about 50 per cent), price developments have been unstable and export earnings volatile, as the demand for these products is very sensitive and fluctuates much more than world trade on average. These fluctuations are illustrated in figures 1 and 2, which show the development of foreign and domestic prices as well as foreign demand and domestic output respectively.

Figure 1 demonstrates that Finnish export prices are highly correlated with/determined by prices of competitors' exports (in domestic

Fig. 1 Fluctuations in foreign and domestic export prices

currency). Moreover, it indicates the role of foreign trade prices for domestic inflation: inflation in Finland seems basically to be determined by the rate of increase of foreign trade prices (i.e., by foreign inflation and exchange rate changes), though there is scope for temporary deviations owing to gradual adjustment, changes in labour market conditions and in connection with comprehensive incomes policies.

Weakening demand for Finnish exports is quickly transmitted into reductions in domestic output (and vice versa) through multiplier effect (figure 2). The effects of foreign demand changes are aggravated by the fact that exports cannot be replaced by domestic consumption of these goods. On the other hand, Finland has often been able to compensate weakening demand in Western markets by increasing exports to the Soviet Union, which presently buys one-fifth of Finland's exports. Moreover, approximately two-thirds of Finland's total oil imports is from the Soviet Union, and trade takes place on a bilateral basis. This means that Finland is somewhat less exposed to oil price changes than most other OECD economies,

Fig. 2 Fluctuations in foreign demand and domestic output

since bilateral trade has made it easier to meet higher oil prices with increased exports.

Another reason why Finland's economic performance has deviated somewhat from the general pattern relates to the development of the terms of trade. Whereas the average deterioration in the terms of trade in the OECD area (measured by export unit values relative to import unit values) was some 10 per cent in 1974, Finland's terms of trade worsened only slightly and improved in 1975 (see figure 3), owing to favourable movements in the international price of paper, pulp and timber. In 1974 import prices went up by 41 per cent and export prices by 38 per cent. Thus the behaviour of trade prices and their effects on the whole economy resembled that of a devaluation of the Finnish markka (Fmk) by some 40 per cent (though the markka was kept fixed against a basket of currencies).

A consequence of the (unforeseen) terms-of-trade behaviour was that the Finnish economy experienced a boom when most of the other OECD countries went into recession. As the economy was already approaching the capacity ceiling, the external shock in combination with initially expansionary policies soon led to over-

Fig. 3 Terms of trade index (1970 = 100)

heating of the economy (in the course of 1974). This resulted in an acceleration of inflation (with, e.g., wage-drift becoming almost as large as negotiated wage increases – see figure 4), an erosion of relative cost positions and a substantial deficit in the current account.

In 1975 Finland's exports were badly hit by the recession in the rest of the OECD area, although GDP growth was still positive owing to the lagged reaction of domestic demand. As a first response to the growing external deficit (see figure 5), a strong credit squeeze embracing both domestic credit expansion and capital inflows was introduced late in 1975, when the option of accelerated foreign borrowing was not considered to be available any longer.[1] In the following year fiscal policy also became highly restrictive (figure 6); for instance, the share of taxes in GNP increased by 4 percentage points. The tax increases were motivated largely by concern about the government's debt position.

In 1977 international markets did not recover to the extent expected, and in 1978 the unemployment rate reached its post-war record ($7\frac{1}{2}$ per cent). Since Finland's international price competitiveness had remained weak, the emphasis in the policy stance now shifted to more direct means of restoring competitiveness and profitability in the exposed sector (consisting chiefly of manufactur-

Fig. 4 Earnings and employment trends in Finland, 1971–80

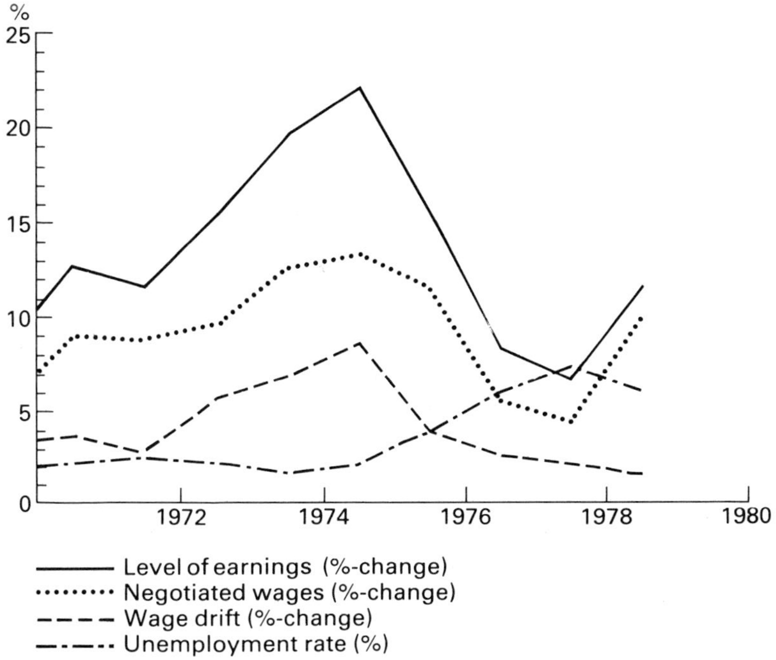

ing industry). Three devaluations lowered the external value of the markka in 1977 and 1978 by a total of some 18 per cent. Incomes policies and fiscal measures were also used to support moderation in domestic cost increases.[2]

In retrospect, the restrictive monetary and fiscal policies in 1975–77 can be seen to have had sizeable effects. For instance, inflation (in terms of consumer prices) decelerated in 1975–78 from 18 to 8 per cent and the current account surplus improved from −8 to +2 per cent of GDP. On the other hand, the average annual growth of GNP in those years was only 1 per cent, total employment fell by 5 per cent, and unemployment increased from 2 to 7½ per cent (in spite of a reduction in the participation rate and increased emigration).

The devaluations in 1977–78 were followed by more expansionary fiscal policies and the tight monetary policy was relaxed during 1978. These policy actions (in combination with the pick-up in foreign demand) again produced strong if somewhat delayed effects; output growth in 1979 and 1980 was 7.2 and 5.5 per cent respectively. However, the upswing in the international stock cycle and in

Fig. 5

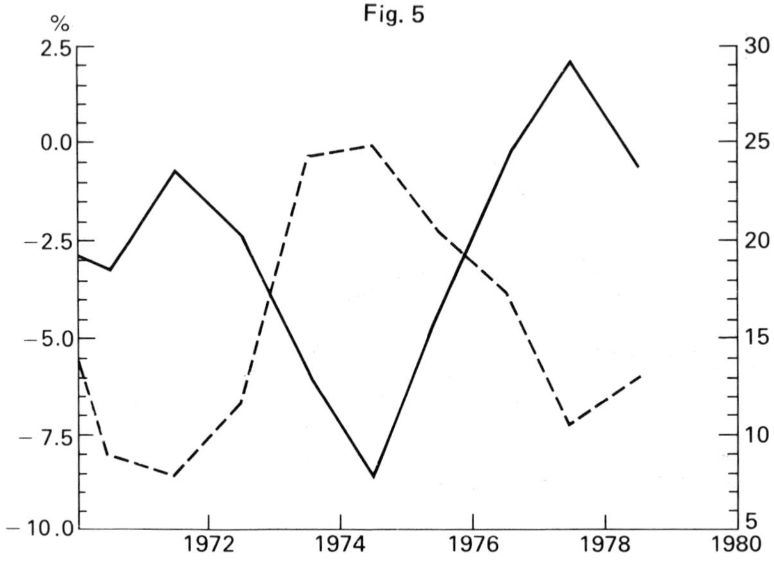

——— Current account surplus relative to GDP (%)
– – – – Indicator of monetary tightness (see figure 6)

Fig. 6 Finnish fiscal policy, 1972–80

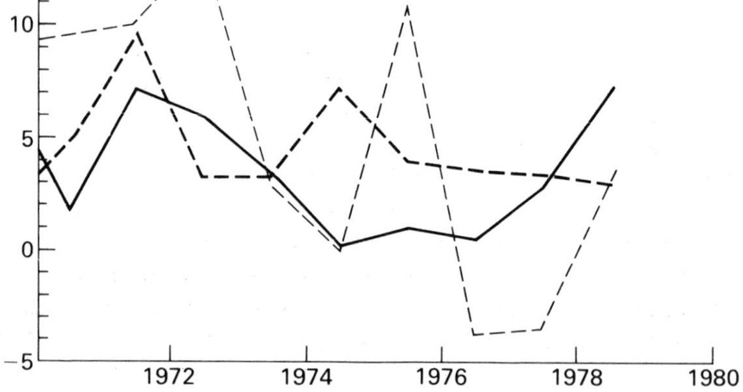

——— Real GDP (% change)
– – – – Real taxes (% change)
– – – – Real government expenditure (% change)

commodity prices in connection with the second oil crisis was smaller than during the first oil crisis. Thus, Finland's terms of trade weakened in 1980, which partly helped to dampen inflationary pressure. In spite of this, and of the revaluation of the markka by some 5 per cent in small steps in 1979 and 1980, domestic inflation accelerated. The external balance also deteriorated, but the weakening was partly cyclical and partly on a bilateral basis with the Soviet Union. The compensating exports associated with the latter presently helps soften the effects of low demand in the OECD markets.

Exchange rate changes and monetary policy were an essential part of the economic policies through which the authorities have sought to adjust the economy to rapidly changing international conditions. In the following sections we discuss the implications for the Finnish business cycle of the link from external balance to the stance of monetary policy (the 'monetary mechanism of adjustment') and the macroeconomic significance of some alternative strategies in exchange rate policy.

Monetary policy and the balance of payments

The Finnish financial system is characterized by the dominant position of deposit banks,[3] by the rigidity of nominal interest rates[4] and by the strategic role (from the point of view of the financial position of the private sector) of capital imports as well as commercial bank borrowing at the central bank. The banks' debt to the central bank is used not only as a major way of absorbing temporary liquidity changes, but also as a permanent source for financing bank lending. The importance of monetary policy is enhanced by the effective (regulative) means at its disposal as well as by its exceptional independence *vis-à-vis* the government.

The intermediate target of monetary policy has mostly been to control total credit expansion by influencing capital flows and the amount of central bank debt of banks. The instruments employed include relatively strict regulations of capital flows and manipulations of the terms at which commercial banks are permitted to borrow at the central bank. From data on the latter we have constructed a time series for the 'marginal interest rate' (the marginal cost) of central bank finance, which is in the following used as an indicator of 'monetary tightness'.[5]

The ultimate targets of monetary policy undoubtedly vary according to a lot of circumstances. Nevertheless, the relation between monetary tightness and external balance is particularly strong: a 'deterioration' in external balance has almost invariably induced monetary tightness and vice versa. For instance, in Halttunen and Korkman (1981) the following (reduced-form) equation was estimated for the marginal cost of central bank lending in 1961–79 (R_2 = coefficient of determination adjusted for degrees of freedom, DW = the Durbin–Watson statistic, t-values in brackets):

$$r = -\underset{(4.69)}{0.55}(B/M) - \underset{(2.62)}{0.13}(CB/M) + \underset{(2.50)}{0.68}r^* + \underset{(2.58)}{9.8}D_{67} \tag{1}$$

$$R^2 = 0.72 \quad DW = 2.25$$

where r = the marginal interest rate, r^* = the foreign interest rate (three-month Eurodollar rate), B = current account surplus, CB = cumulative current account surplus, M = value of total imports and D_{67} = dummy for devaluation expectations in 1967. The (volatile) behaviour of our indicator of monetary tightness would thus seem to be largely determined by the current account (cf. also figure 5) and by the foreign interest rate (affecting capital flows).

This link between external balance and monetary conditions is essential to the cyclical behaviour of the Finnish economy. Before discussing it, however, we shall report a very crude attempt at quantitative assessment of the relations involved in the determination of monetary tightness.

For this purpose we assume that the portfolio relevant for liquidity behaviour of the private sector (including private banks) can be taken to consist of commercial bank borrowing from the central bank (net of the banks' placements in the call money market) and short-term foreign debt.[6] The portfolio decision of interest in this context thus concerns the allocation of the total (net) short-term debt of the private sector as between central bank and foreign debt. This allocation will of course depend on the foreign interest rate and the (marginal) cost of central bank finance, and possibly on the level of income.

We thus assume that the portfolio behaviour focused upon may be characterized as follows:

$$Z = H(Z, r, r^*, Y) + F(Z, r, r^*, Y) \tag{2}$$

where

$Z = H + F$;

H = stock of central bank borrowing;

F = stock of net short-term debt of the private sector; and

Y = level of income.

(In view of the central bank's balance sheet, and considering that base money is aggregated into H, the counterpart to variations in H are changes in foreign exchange reserves.)

Next, define $f = F/Y$, $z = Z/Y$ and $b = B/Y$ and assume that the H- and F-functions are homogeneous (of degree one), so that F may be specified as

$$f = f(z, r, r^*). \tag{3}$$

Our *a priori* expectations are $0 < f_z < 1, f_r > 0$ and $f_{r*} < 0$.

Finally, assume that the foreign interest rate is exogenous and that the supply of central bank lending may be specified as follows:

$$r = \phi(h, b) = \phi(z - f, b) \tag{4}$$

for which $\phi_h < 0$ if the supply curve is rising,[7] while $\phi_{b2} < 0$ reflects our assumption about monetary policy reactions.[8] Linearizing and substituting, equations (3) and (4) may then be solved for r and f in terms of r^*, b and z:

$$f = \frac{1}{\alpha}[(f_z + \phi_h f_r) z + f_{r*} r^* + \phi_b f_r b] \tag{5}$$

$$r = \frac{1}{\alpha}[\phi_h(1 - f_z) z - \phi_h f_{r*} r^* + \phi_b b] \tag{6}$$

As the system (5)–(6) is exactly identified, we estimated the equations by ordinary least squares (sample period 1961–79). The results were as follows (Δ = difference operator; an additional dummy was introduced to count for the devaluation speculation at the end of 1977):

$$\begin{aligned} \Delta f = {} & \underset{(7.31)}{0.62\Delta z} - \underset{(3.62)}{0.0020\Delta r^*} - \underset{(0.79)}{0.060\Delta b} - \underset{(1.60)}{0.005\Delta D_{67}} \\ & - \underset{(3.45)}{0.01\Delta D_{77}} \end{aligned} \tag{7}$$

$R^2 = 0.93 \quad DW = 1.59$

$$r = \underset{(1.55)}{89.0z} + \underset{(2.52)}{0.80r^*} - \underset{(1.66)}{117.1b} + \underset{(2.73)}{11.4D_{67}} + \underset{(0.76)}{3.9D_{77}} \tag{8}$$

$R^2 = 0.64 \quad DW = 1.64$

Some of the estimates are not significant; in particular, strong multicollinearity between Δz and Δb is a source of difficulty. The implied structural coefficients are, however, all of 'right' sign and of 'reasonable' magnitude.[9]

According to the estimates, the marginal cost of central bank lending increases by approximately 2 percentage points for a 1 billion Fmk increase in central bank lending and by 1 percentage point for a 1 billion Fmk increase in the current account deficit (GNP in 1981 is something like 200 billion Fmk). Since the liquidity position of the private sector and the current account usually deteriorate simultaneously (both reflecting private investment in excess of saving), it stands to reason that fluctuations in monetary tightness are considerable (and closely related to the cyclical situation).

Another implication of the estimates is that a 1 per cent increase in the foreign interest rate (for a given r) will induce a capital outflow (stock shift) of approximately 500 million Fmk, while a 1 per cent increase in the marginal interest rate on central bank lending will induce only a 100 million Fmk inflow. This asymmetry is understandable in view of the fact that the marginal interest rate on central bank lending is not an 'interest rate' in the usual sense. In particular, it affects the public mainly through the credit rationing behaviour of banks.[10]

Our estimate of the effect of a change in the foreign interest rate on capital imports is fairly high,[11] though it is reduced somewhat when the induced effect on domestic monetary tightness is allowed for. Seldom, however, has Finnish monetary autonomy been compromised by capital mobility.[12] The main reasons for this are probably as follows.

First, variations in the foreign interest rate have usually been rather small (at least on an annual level). Second, long-term capital imports are of substantial size and strictly regulated by the Bank of Finland. Third, the foreign interest rate is positively correlated with the Finnish business cycle (both lagging somewhat with respect to the foreign business cycle). The effects of the foreign interest rate have therefore often been more than offset by the consequences for capital imports of the substantial fluctuations in private sector overall indebtedness.[13]

The relation between external balance and monetary tightness has definite cyclical implications. In particular, the link between the balance of payments and domestic monetary conditions, in combination with the time lag between changes in the stance of monetary policy and their ultimate effects on output and external balance, has tended to magnify cyclical fluctuations.

The mechanism at work may be set out most simply by abstracting from other influences and assuming both that monetary policy reacts on the balance of payments on current account with a lag and that it affects demand and output with a lag. The behaviour of the resulting system may then be described by figure 7. The $\bar{Q}$-curve shows the equilibrium dependence of the level of output Q on monetary tightness r, and the horizontal arrows show the direction of its gradual adjustment. The $\bar{r}$-curve correspondingly shows that a high level of income is in equilibrium associated with tight money (because the current account is negatively associated with the level of demand and output). As is seen, the equilibrium of the system is likely to be approached (if at all) in an oscillatory manner. The data for r and g (the logarithmic trend deviation of GNP) in figure 8 agree well with our reasoning (though the sequence could, of course, be due to other factors as well).

In an economy subject to exogenous shocks and with other endogenous feed-backs, the dynamic element just described need not be destabilizing. Simulations that we made with our empirical model indicate, however, that the externally oriented monetary policy in Finland has been cyclically destabilizing in the sense of increasing the variance of GDP (as compared with a policy of holding r constant; cf. Halttunen and Korkman, 1981, pp. 52–4).[14]

In sum, interest rate effects on capital flows have not – so far – seriously hampered the autonomy of Finnish monetary policy. This

Fig. 7

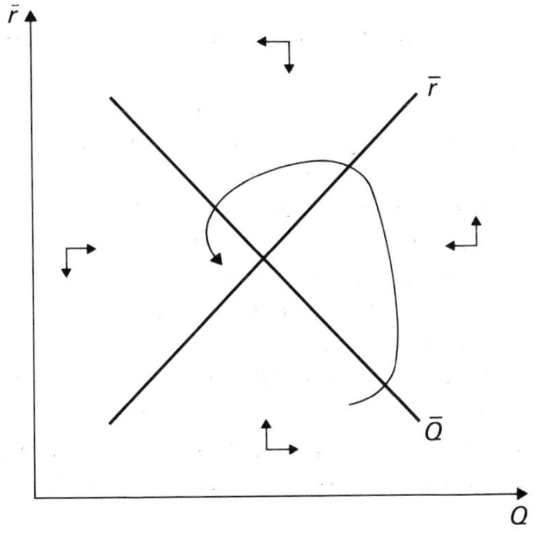

Fig. 8

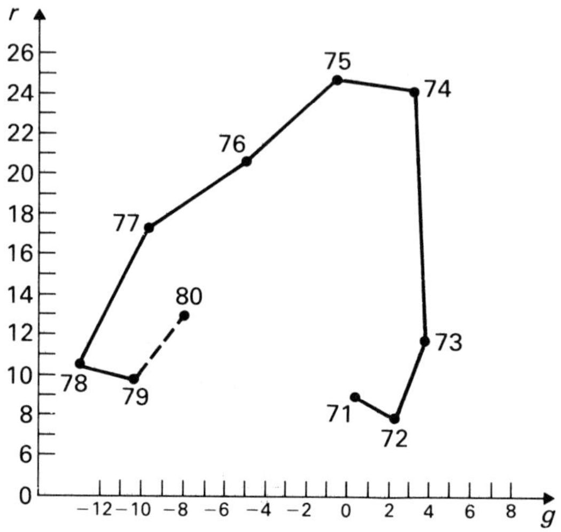

reflects the limited size of the effects, capital controls and the cyclically rather advantageous covariation between interest rates on the Eurodollar market and the Finnish business cycle. Nevertheless, developments in the balance of payments have largely determined monetary conditions – with often unfavourable cyclical consequences – because of their automatic money market effects as well as the policy reactions that current account imbalances induce.

Exchange rate policy, competitiveness and inflation

Freely floating exchange rates are not a feasible or practical alternative for a country that has chosen to maintain extensive regulations of capital flows and foreign exchange transactions. The exchange rate is then an instrument of policy, and some decisions about the use of it have to be made. In small economies the most common choice has been to peg to another currency or to a basket of other currencies.

The Finnish currency, the markka (Fmk) was tied to the dollar until February 1973 (until December 1971 within the par rate system and from 1971 to 1973 within the central rate system). Since then the regime adopted by the Bank of Finland has been to stabilize (within narrow margins) the external value of the markka in terms of a trade-weighted basket of foreign currencies.[15] Within this new

Fig. 9 Bank of Finland currency index (1974 = 100)

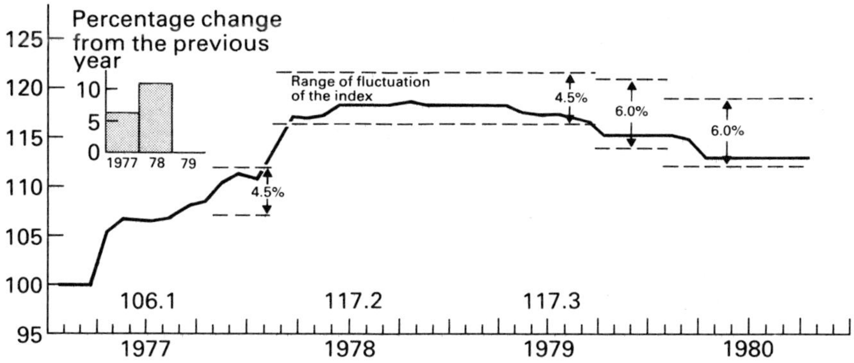

Fig. 10 Movements of the most important currencies against the markka (1974 = 100)

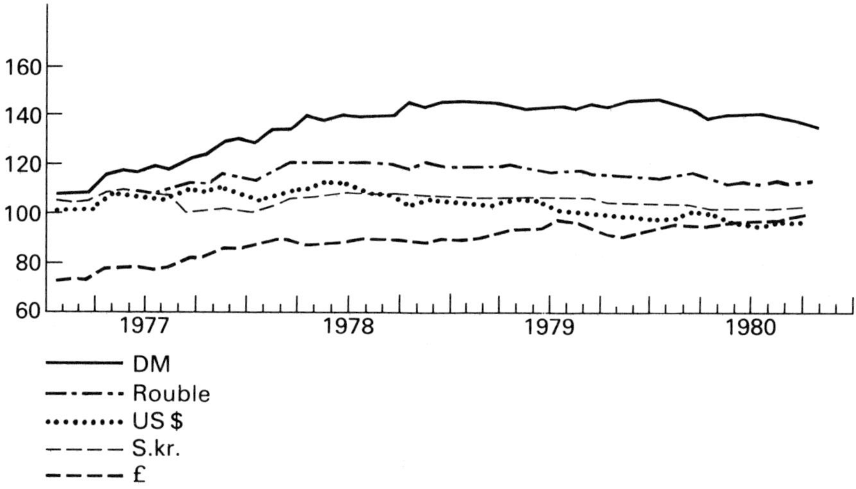

regime, however, there have already occurred a number of discretionary de- and re-valuations (see figure 9). The development of five most important bilateral rates is shown in figure 10.

The index remained rather stable through the years 1974–76, but the markka was devalued twice in 1977 (in April by 5.7 and in September by 3.0 per cent) and again in February 1978, by 8.0 per cent. In May–September 1979, by contrast, the Bank of Finland strengthened the external value of the markka by some 3 per cent, and in March 1980 by another 2 per cent.

The effects of the exchange rate changes undertaken are difficult to evaluate. This is due to their manifold short- and long-run effects. For the same reason, the appropriateness of different exchange rate strategies is a highly controversial issue.

The conventional strategy in Finland has been to devalue the markka when international competitiveness has been 'fundamentally out of line' in order to restore profitability and competitiveness of the exposed sector and to boost investment and growth (as in 1977–78). Incomes policies have been seen as the means to prevent sharp increases in profits from being shifted into domestic costs. Arguably, however, the occasional and large devaluations have caused a 'devaluation cycle', which will be illustrated in this section by means of a simulation experiment. The simulation also provides a reference point for a discussion of some exchange rate policy alternatives which have recently been the subject of much debate in Finland.

A devaluation situation

We shall now describe the effects of a 10 per cent devaluation by means of a simulation of a small empirical model of Finland (see Appendix). According to the simulation, the sequence of events initiated by the devaluation is broadly as follows (cf. figures 11 and 12). In the year when the devaluation is undertaken, the domestic price level will increase by 3.5 per cent and the relative current account will improve, while the level of output will be practically unchanged.[16] (The current account improved strongly in 1978 but slow growth continued and unemployment even increased.)

In the second year the level of output will increase by almost 2 per cent. The expansionary effect is due primarily to the improved competitiveness, but it is also somewhat strengthened by the fact that the initial improvement in external balance will reduce monetary tightness and thereby influence aggregate spending. (The devaluations in 1977–78 were one of the main factors explaining the rapid growth in 1979–80.) Owing to the higher level of demand and output as well as the partial restoration of original price ratios caused by the increasing domestic price level, the current account turns into a deficit.

In the third year the domestic price level already has increased by the full amount of the devaluation, but continues to rise more rapidly than foreign prices because of the relatively high level of economic activity. From this time on the level of output is falling,

Fig. 11 Dynamic effects of a 10 per cent devaluation at time t_0 on output and current account

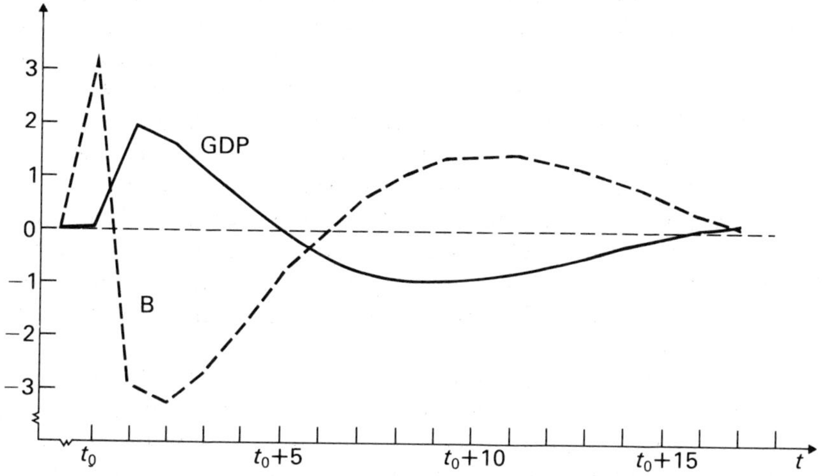

GDP = logarithmic trend deviation of real GDP; B = current account surplus relative to the value of total imports (%). GDP and B measure the devaluation effect as the absolute difference between the devaluation run and the control solution, while *p* and *C* in figure 12 measure the effect in terms of the percentage difference.

Fig. 12 Dynamic effects of a 10 per cent devaluation at time t_0 on the domestic price level and competitiveness

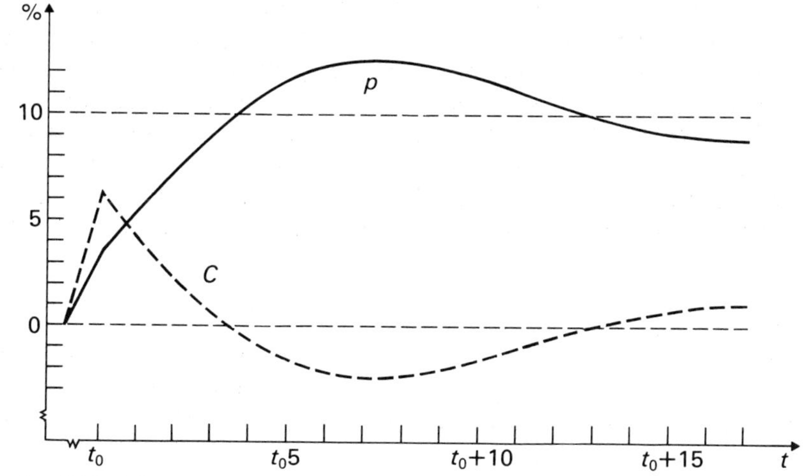

p = the GDP deflator; *C* = competitors' prices in Finnish markka divided by the GDP deflator.

however, both because the earlier gain in competitiveness is eroded through domestic inflation and because of the tightening of monetary conditions induced by the deterioration in the current account. (The presently strong inflationary pressure in Finland reflects not only oil prices, but also delayed effects of the devaluations, partly alleviated by the revaluations in 1979–80.)

Since the model is cyclical, there then emerges a phase during which the price level 'overshoots' its equilibrium level, while the dynamic output effect (somewhat later) turns negative. The relative current account largely reflects the evolution of domestic demand and output. In the 'long run' the output and current account effects will be zero and the only sustainable effect of the devaluation is a 10 per cent increase in the domestic price level.

While these results should not be taken too literally (they are 'stylized facts'), the main message conveyed by the simulation may nevertheless be relevant: a devaluation will temporarily change relative prices and will therefore have expansionary effects in the medium term. In the longer run, however, relative prices will be restored through a process of internal inflation. In a larger perspective the main outcome of the devaluation may thus turn out to be a permanently higher price level as well as the emergence of a relatively long cyclical movement associated with the devaluation.[17]

Alternative norms for exchange rate policy

Equally important as 'discretionary' exchange rate policies is the choice of the basic 'norm' or 'regime', which specifies the criteria according to which ordinary exchange rate policies are to be pursued. (Indeed, the distinction referred to is seldom an unambiguous one.) In the Finnish debate one may identify three principles or guidelines that have been focused upon. These are: pegging to a basket of other currencies; following a purchasing-power-parity rule to stabilize competitiveness; and the assignment of exchange rate policy to the control of inflation.

The currency basket

With generalized floating of the currencies of the large countries, the obvious solution for many small countries has been to peg the currency to a basket of other currencies (thus stabilizing the average price of foreign exchange).

The problem with such 'fixed-on-the-average' exchange rates is of course that the economy will be highly vulnerable to foreign price disturbances. Such shocks are an important source of macro-economic fluctuations in economies in which raw materials occupy an important position in both exports and imports (as in Finland). For such economies changes in the price of tradables may well be rapid and approximately balanced in the sense that major shifts in the terms of trade are not involved. A rapid increase in foreign prices will improve competitiveness, lower the real wage and initiate a process of domestic inflation which gradually restores original price and cost ratios (cf. figures 10 and 11, which indicated not only the effects of a devaluation but the effects of a 10 per cent increase in all foreign prices as well). The converse will happen in the case of a fall in foreign prices or a sudden reduction in foreign inflation (with the possible modification that downward price and wage rigidity may increase the real effects).

The problem of imported inflation can, of course, to some extent be diminished by increasing the weight given to 'hard' currencies in the currency basket pegged to.[18] The trade weights presently employed in Finland rest on the consideration that domestic price competitiveness should be protected against foreign exchange rate actions. Apart from the arbitrariness of the trade weights (even on competitiveness grounds), it may be argued that this gives too much weight to short-run considerations of competitiveness as compared with the longer-run consequences for the trend rate of inflation.

Tying to a 'hard' currency country may help to bring down the trend rate of inflation. It does not, however, alleviate the problem of price instability associated with large fluctuations in foreign trade prices (for instance, the increase in export and import price in 1974). Indeed, tying to a hard currency (setting ambitious targets for the trend rate of inflation) may not be feasible if foreign trade prices fluctuate strongly. This is arguably the case if rapid foreign price rises induce rapid domestic inflation while foreign price reductions do not correspondingly reduce domestic inflation (if there is downward rigidity of wages and prices). Pegging to a hard currency is then no substitute for occasional discrete revaluations to offset the domestic effects of sudden shifts in foreign trade prices.

Competitiveness

Obviously, a fixed exchange rate economy is vulnerable not only to foreign inflation but also to the harmful consequences of domestic in excess of foreign inflation. Rapid domestic cost increases and loss of competitiveness will lower profitability and market shares and sooner or later induce a deflationary process associated with unemployment, etc. Because of the high costs of deflationary policies, it has often been suggested that exchange rate policy be geared to the maintenance of price competitiveness at an appropriate level. In particular, following a purchasing-power-parity rule[19] in exchange rate setting would imply that accelerations of foreign inflation would induce revaluations of the exchange rate (and thus not be transmitted to the domestic economy), while domestic inflation in excess of foreign would correspondingly induce devaluations (to safeguard competitiveness).

The basic rationale for a purchasing-power-parity rule in exchange rate setting resembles the case for indexing money wages to prices.[20] The basic problem is also similar: any policy that (rigidly) stabilizes a central price ratio is open to the objection that it will thereby inhibit desirable adjustments if underlying conditions are changing (as they always are).[21] Exchange rate policy according to a competitiveness norm might therefore result in an endless inflationary or deflationary process. (A particularly obvious case arises if there is 'real wage resistance' and if the real wage is above the level that is compatible with the level of competitiveness aimed at in exchange rate policy.)

The commodity basket

It is widely acknowledged that a revaluation is an appropriate means of (and practically the only means of) protecting the economy against the consequences of unexpected (and undesired) shifts in the price level of foreign goods.[22] This argument can be generalized into the proposition that exchange rate setting should be tied to a commodity basket (rather than a currency basket) and used to stabilize the domestic currency development of foreign trade prices (fixing their level or rate of increase). Such an 'inflation norm' would then constitute a useful benchmark for domestic wage and price setting, and thus enhance the achievement of stable and predictable inflation.

We have tried to illuminate the consequences of such a policy by an exchange rate policy simulation. In this simulation exchange rate policy was assumed to react to variations in trade prices (average of import and export prices) since 1974 by revaluing and devaluing the exchange rate so that the average of import and export prices in domestic currency develops steadily, and so that trade prices and the exchange rate in 1979 were at the same level as in the real world.[23] In addition, the domestic rate of interest was varied so that the 'real' rate of interest was unaffected by the choice of the exchange rate policy rule.

Given the foreign price developments actually experienced during this time period, the assumed policy would have implied the following percentage changes in the exchange rate (actual changes of the exchange rate index are given in brackets):

1974	−30 (−3)	1977	5 (6)
1975	8 (1)	1978	14 (10)
1976	4 (−3)	1979	1 (0)

The main difference is that the hypothetical policy would have caused a considerable revaluation in 1974 (to offset the extraordinary foreign price shock which at that time impinged upon the Finnish economy) and some devaluation of the exchange rate already in 1975–76.

The effects on output and inflation are shown in figures 13 and 14. As can be seen, the exchange rate policy assumed would have

Fig. 13

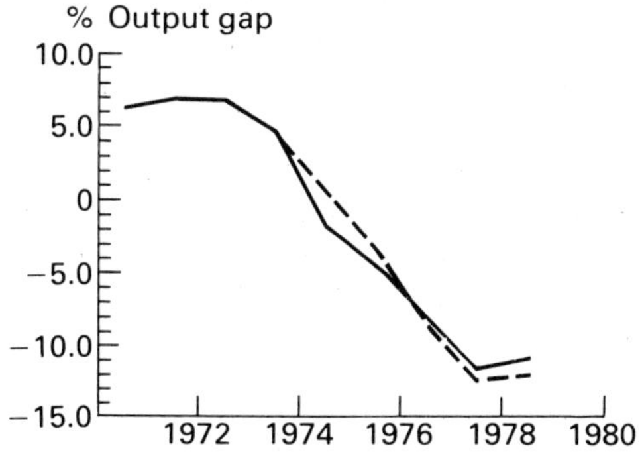

Fig. 14

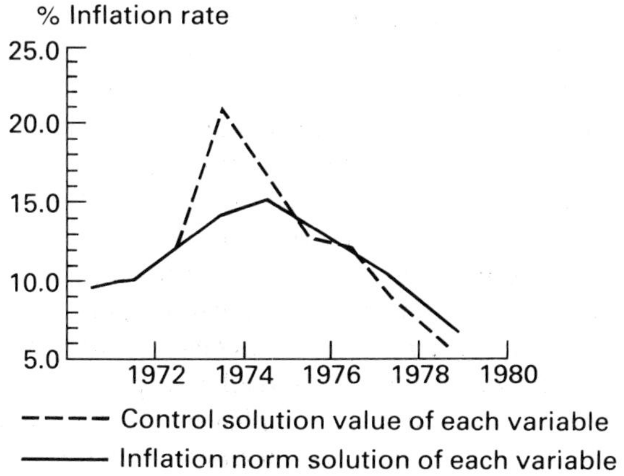

increased price stability considerably. It would have had a harmful effect on output mainly in 1975 (owing to the large appreciation of the Finnish markka in 1974 induced by the assumed policy rule). Actually, domestic prices would have been at a lower level in 1979, and thus the competitive position of the economy would have been better within this (restricted) time horizon. Thus, exchange rate policy according to an inflation norm would seem to be beneficial as a means of stabilizing inflation if price disturbances originate externally, as they did in Finland during the period under consideration.[24]

While inflation-oriented exchange rate policy would insulate the economy from foreign price level fluctuations, it would in other respects be much like fixed exchange rates. In particular, it would do nothing to offset the harmful effects of excessive domestic cost inflation or the consequences of fluctuations in the level of foreign demand. In case of import price rises associated with a falling terms of trade, the suggested exchange rate policy would even aggravate problems by leading to an appreciation of the exchange rate.[25]

Problems might also arise if price developments in the tradable sector are very uneven. A revaluation barely cutting 'excess profits' in one sector may then create a 'profitability crisis' in another. Considerations like these are not, however, necessarily arguments against the assignment of exchange rate policy to the control of inflation, but rather reflect the well-known fact that one instrument will (at best) solve one problem.

Some conclusions

The alternations between rapid growth and total stagnation experienced in Finland in the 1970s clearly were not only a consequence of external shock, but also were due to the unfortunate timing of economic policies. Simplifying somewhat, fiscal policy was generally passive,[26] monetary policy reacted to the balance of payments, and exchange rate policy was mainly geared to competitiveness. It was hoped that inflation would be held in check by incomes policies. These 'assignments' were often unsuccessful.

In particular, some conclusions with respect to exchange rate policy suggested by the experience reviewed above seem to us to be as follows. The devaluations improved competitiveness in the short run and increased growth and employment in the medium term. However, with domestic inflation sooner or later catching up (the speed of adjustment depending on the success of incomes policies), exchange rate policy in the longer run will mainly regulate the rate of inflation. In the conditions that prevailed in the 1970s in Finland, exchange rate policy might usefully have contributed to price stability (in addition to lowering average inflation) by offsetting the consequences of rapid movements in the foreign currency prices of tradables. In general, exchange rate changes have relatively stronger effects on the price level than on output (as compared with monetary policy). A case for inflation-oriented exchange rate policy may therefore be made on the basis of the comparative advantage of instruments.

Appendix

A small reduced-form model of the Finnish economy

This appendix briefly describes the structure and estimated equations of a reduced-form model of the Finnish economy, which was used in the simulations discussed above.[27]

The model is basically a conventional demand-oriented model which focuses on the role of central bank policy (monetary and exchange rate policy). The sectoral aggregation of the model makes a distinction between the central bank, the rest of the domestic economy and the rest of the world (the foreign sector). The domestic non-central bank sector finances its expenditures by its disposable income (GNP) or by net borrowing from the central bank and/or from abroad. With respect to commodity aggregation, it is assumed that the economy produces only one commodity, which may be either consumed or invested domestically (in addition to imports), or exported abroad.

The reduced form of the model (which was estimated) contains equations for the output gap (the logarithmic trend deviation of real GDP), the rate of inflation, the relative current account (the current account surplus relative to the value of total imports) and the marginal rate of interest on central bank finance. The model is recursive and was estimated, equation by equation, using the ordinary least squares. Annual data for the period 1961–79 were used except for the price equation, which uses the period 1956–79. The estimated equations are as follows.

Output gap

$$\begin{aligned} g = & \underset{(6.46)}{0.459} g_{-1} + \underset{(8.44)}{0.456} g^* - \underset{(4.55)}{0.141} r_{-1} + \underset{(2.30)}{0.184} \Delta \log p_{-1} \\ & - \underset{(4.87)}{0.185} \log p_{-1} + \underset{(4.55)}{0.173} (\log p^*_{-1} + \log e_{-1} \end{aligned} \qquad \text{(A1)}$$

$\bar{R}^2 = 0.966 \quad DW = 2.027$

Inflation rate

$$\Delta \log p = \underset{(5.50)}{0.352} + 0.5(\Delta \log p^* + \Delta \log e) + 0.5(\Delta \log p_m^* + \Delta \log e)$$
$$+ \underset{(7.27)}{0.611} \Delta \log p_{-1} + \underset{(2.85)}{0.285} g_{-1} \quad \text{(A2)}$$
$$\bar{R}^2 = 0.803 \quad DW = 1.911$$

Relative current account

$$b = -\underset{(6.27)}{2.670} \log y + \underset{(4.45)}{1.472} \log y^*$$
$$-\underset{(2.89)}{0.573}(\log p - \log p^* - \log e) + \underset{(2.03)}{0.024}\,\text{time} + \underset{(5.68)}{14.2} \quad \text{(A3)}$$
$$\bar{R}^2 = 0.675 \quad DW = 1.914$$

Marginal cost of central bank finance

$$r = -\underset{(4.69)}{0.553} b - \underset{(2.62)}{0.131} z + \underset{(2.50)}{0.682} r^* + \underset{(2.58)}{0.098} D_{67} \quad \text{(A4)}$$
$$\bar{R}^2 = 0.718 \quad DW = 2.252$$

The endogenous variables are:

$g = \log y - \log \bar{y}$

y = real gross domestic product

$\bar{y}$ = exponential trend of GDP (annual rate of growth = 4.8 per cent)

$\Delta \log p$ = domestic inflation rate; p = implicit GDP deflator

b = current account relative to the value of total imports

r = marginal rate of interest on central bank lending

The exogenous variables are:

$g^f = \log y^* - \log \bar{y}^*$

y^f = volume index of Finland's export markets (a weighted average of import volumes of Great Britain, Sweden, the Federal Republic of Germany, France, United States with 1974 export shares as weights)

$\bar{y}^*$ = exponential trend of y^* (annual rate of growth = 6.7 per cent)

p^* = competitors' prices in foreign currency (a weighted average of import prices of five OECD countries important for Finland's exports with 1974 export share as weights)

p_m^* = price index of imports of goods and services in foreign currency (calculated by dividing import prices in local currency by the currency index)

e = exchange rate index (domestic/foreign currency, calculated as a weighted average of five important bilateral rates with 1974 export shares as weights)

r^* = three-month Eurodollar rate

D_{67} = dummy variable (1967 = 1, otherwise 0) for devaluation expectations in 1967

The output gap equation (A1) is a reduced-form equation for the demand for domestic output by domestic and foreign residents. These demands are related positively to total domestic and foreign demands and negatively to the domestic price relative to the foreign price. The interest rate variable, the marginal rate of interest on central bank lending, and the 'expected inflation rate' (actual inflation lagged one year) enter the output gap equation through their effects on total domestic demand.

Equation (A2) gives the domestic inflation rate as a function of the foreign inflation rate (measured as an average of competitors' inflation rates and Finland's relative import price changes adjusted for changes in the exchange rate), the domestic inflation rate and output gap lagged one year. The sum of the coefficients of the 'foreign inflation rate' and the lagged domestic inflation rate is approximately one, implying long-run homogeneity. The (almost) full amount of an external price shock or of a change in the exchange rate is felt in the domestic price level within four or five years.

The current account equation (A3) is a reduced-form equation based on export and import equations where the export market share and the import share (out of GDP) respond to relative prices as well as to foreign and domestic demand pressures. The equation for the marginal interest rate (A4) is explained in the text (p. 14). In addition, the model contains a few technical relations.

Notes

1 In order to facilitate co-ordination of central bank measures regulating sources of finance to the private sector, the Bank of Finland started to make use of a financial framework or a 'credit budget', in which the net inflow of foreign capital together with central bank lending are key variables.

2 There is a long tradition in Finland of relying on incomes policies following big devaluations of the markka. For instance, its devaluation in the recession year of 1967 was accompanied by stabilization measures, the aim of which was to cut the wage–price spiral. Broad indexation was abolished, labour market organizations agreed on 'moderate' nominal wage increases, price control was imposed, and the government implemented tax reliefs.

3 Other financial institutions as well as the security market are, macroeconomically, of minor significance only. See the articles in the *Bank of Finland Monthly Bulletin* (1978).

4 As a consequence, equilibration of the bank loan market takes place through quantitative credit rationing variations rather than via price, and interest rate changes. See Oksanen (1977) and Tarkka (1979).

5 The banks' borrowing facility has typically been such as to imply an increasing (average and marginal) interest rate cost for each bank (or group of banks) according to the extent to which borrowing has exceeded a certain basic quota (within which the discount rate applies). In 1975 the Bank of Finland instituted an official (interbank) call money market. The interest rate on the call money market could then be regarded as measuring the marginal cost of finance for banks. Since 1980, however, the Bank of Finland has regulated the call money market and the system is again characterized by bank-specific quotas, penalty rate of interest for borrowing in excess of quotas, etc.

6 Long-term capital flows are strictly regulated. At times, short-term capital movements have also been affected by central bank regulations.

7 This follows from the institutional arrangements which have normally prevailed. Cf. n. 5 above.

8 We have experimented with many other conceivable target variables – such as unemployment and inflation – as well. The results were uniformly negative. Observe that since the balance of payments automatically affects monetary tightness (r is an increasing function of the net domestic assets of the central bank, i.e., a decreasing function of its net foreign assets), it is not possible in practice to identify 'discretionary' monetary policy reliably.

9 Estimation using the Cochrane–Orcutt autocorrelation correction gave very similar results. The structural coefficients implied by (7) and (8) are as follows: $f_r = 0.00055$, $f_{r*} = -0.00248$, $f_z = 0.72$, $\phi_h = 393.4$ and $\phi_b = 142.4$. It may be observed that f might depend on b also directly because of commercial credits associated with trade flows. If this is the case, our estimate of $|f_r|$ and $|f_{r*}|$ may be too large.

10 An increase in the marginal interest rate will often also induce the banks to raise the premium on forward exchange. This will diminish incentives for the non-bank public to increase its (covered) foreign debt even though the domestic credit market is getting tighter.

11 Provided that the relations are linear, an increase of the foreign interest rate by 10 percentage points would wipe out much of the foreign exchange reserves of the Bank of Finland (presently amounting to 7–8 billion Fmk). Our estimate is somewhat higher than those arrived at in most Finnish studies of capital flows.

12 A major exception is the large capital outflow associated with devaluation speculations in 1977, which forced the central bank to maintain a much higher interest rate on the call money market than deemed desirable on purely domestic grounds.

13 The covariation that has prevailed in the past need not repeat itself in the future. A high foreign interest rate (or devaluation speculations) in a situation in which the private sector is highly liquid might then strain the central bank's foreign exchange reserves and enforce an undesired credit squeeze. In face of this eventuality, it would seem desirable to develop a short-term money market through which monetary policy might more directly affect the liquidity behaviour of firms (to increase f_r).

14 The interaction between monetary conditions and the Finnish business cycle can be characterized crudely as follows. The (export-led) upswing is initially associated with an improved balance of payments, which puts downward pressure on the interest rate (within the same year). The effects of the fall in the interest rate strengthens the boom (in the following year), during which, on the other hand, the current account swings into deficit and the interest rate rises. This rise in the interest rate would be stabilizing if the export boom were 'long enough' or if the time lag between the rise in the interest rate and its demand-dampening effect were 'short enough'. However, the economy is typically hit by an export-led recession at approximately the same time as the contractive effects of the rise in the interest rate are gradually being felt. Later in the recession, a cyclical improvement of the current account occurs and the interest rate is lowered. This would be stabilizing, were it not for the fact that the fall in the interest rate typically adds to domestic demand primarily at the stage when a new export-led upswing is already well under way. The destabilizing effect is thus the outcome of export-led booms and recessions in combination with lagged monetary policy effects.

15 The concept of the currency index based on foreign trade weights was introduced as early as 1973 but received 'official' status only in November 1977 through a renewal of legislation concerning exchange rate policy. At this occasion the government fixed upper and lower limits to the currency index such that the band was 4½ per cent wide. The width of the band was increased to 6 per cent in September 1978. At present, 18 countries and 15 currencies (for Poland, Iran and Saudi-Arabia the US dollar is used) are used to calculate the index with the following weights in the basket: US$9.2%, £13.9%, Skr 17.5%, Nkr 3.9%, Dkr 3.8%, DM 13.4%, Hfl 3.8%, Bfr 2.2%, Sfr 2.2%, Ffr 4.2%, lira 2.3%, ÖS 1.3%, ptas 1.0%, yen 2.2% and Rbl 19.1%.

16 In our empirical experiments competitiveness turned out to affect output with only a one-year lag. This may reflect time lags associated with the multiplier processes, which make it reasonable that a devaluation should affect the trade balance more rapidly than the level of output. It is also possible that the expansionary substitution effect in the short run is counteracted if the increase in the profit share caused by the devaluation is deflationary (by decreasing the share of total income devoted to purchases of domestic goods).

17 Observe that the length of the cycle of output would seem to be a little more than ten years. The simulation thus agrees well with the Finnish literature on the so-called 'devaluation cycle'; cf. Korkman (1978) and references given there.

18 For an analysis of the effects of the choice of currency weights see, e.g., Branson and Papaefstratiou (1978).

19 Cf. the discussion in Thygesen (1978).

20 In the former case competitiveness is fixed, and this has definite consequences for the real wage; in the latter case the real wage is fixed, with implications for competitiveness. Both systems would prevent an increase in the price level of foreign goods from having real effects: the former by inducing an appreciation of the currency, and the latter by causing (speed-

ing up) domestic inflation so as to re-establish the real wage and relative prices.

21 The OPTICA proposal meets this objection because of the asymmetry of the intervention rule; cf. Basevi and de Grauwe (1977).

22 The role of exchange rate policy for inflation has been much debated by Swedish economists; see, e.g., Lundgren *et al.* (1974) and Bentzel *et al.* (1980).

23 Observe that there are in this context two different issues that should be separated. First, more or less continuous revaluations might be used to bring down the trend rate of inflation. During the transition period such a policy may have undesirable real effects, but in the longer run the only sustainable effect is likely to be a reduced average rate of inflation. Second, exchange rate changes might be used to even out fluctuations in the domestic currency development of foreign prices and thus to help stabilize the rate of inflation for any given trend rate. This may well be considered useful since it is probably unexpected changes in the rate of inflation that account for much of the costs of inflation. Our simulation focuses only on the second issue.

24 Our specifications impose a restriction according to which the domestic price level is equivalently affected by equi-proportionate changes in foreign prices and in the exchange rate. There are, however, some reasons to think that the speed of adjustment of domestic prices with respect to devaluations may have been slower than with respect to changes in foreign prices (in foreign currency), because incomes policy measured aimed at curbing inflation and safeguarding the positive effects on international competitiveness were implemented after the two big devaluations in 1957 and 1967 and also after the devaluations in 1977 and 1978. Consequently, a revaluation may dampen domestic inflation more rapidly (than implied by our estimates) and its real effects might be smaller.

25 The obvious conclusion is that prices of imported raw materials (lacking domestic substitutes) should be excluded from the index of foreign prices to which the exchange rate policy is geared. The foreign trade price index should also include only tradable goods, the prices of which reflect world market conditions (exogenous to the economy), rather than domestic costs.

26 This is particularly true of fiscal policy in the traditional demand management sense. Tax reductions and subsidies to strengthen competitiveness and increase firms' profitability were, however, an essential part of the strategy adopted in 1977.

27 A more detailed description of the model can be found in Halttunen and Korkman (1981).

References

Basevi, G. and de Grauwe, P. (1977), 'Vicious and virtuous circles: a theoretical analysis and a policy proposal for managing exchange rates'. *European Economic Review*, vol. 10, no. 3.

Bentzel, R. *et al.* (1980), 'Stabiliseringspolitik for 80 talet'. Konjunktursrådets rapport 1980–81.

Branson, W. H. and Papaefstratiou, L. (1978), 'Income instability, terms of trade and the change of exchange rate regimes'. Center Discussion Paper no. 277, Economic Growth Center, Yale University.

Halttunen, H. and Korkman, S. (1981), 'Central bank policy and domestic stability in a small open economy'. Bank of Finland, publication series, D:47.

Korkman, S. (1978), 'The devaluation cycle'. *Oxford Economic Papers*, vol. 30.

Lundgren, E., Lundgren, N., Mathiessen, L. and Ohlin, G. (1974), 'Kris eller Konjunkturuppgång?' Konjunkturrådets rapport 1974/75 (SNS, Stockholm), mimeo.

Oksanen, H. (1977), *Bank Liquidity and Lending in Finland* (Helsinki).

Tarkka, J. (1979), 'A test of credit rationing in Finland: an experiment with the data of 1967–1977', University of Helsinki, Department of Economics Discussion Papers, no. 130.

Thygesen, N. (1978), 'Inflation and exchange rates: evidence and policy guidelines for the European Community'. *Journal of International Economics*, vol. 8.

The Productivity Link between Exports and Domestic Demand: Sweden

SVEN GRASSMAN and HANS OLSSON
Stockholm University and Swedish Board of Industry

Introduction

The 1970s witnessed in vital respects the end of the Swedish model of economic and social policy, a model of harmonious growth and distribution that attracted much interest for several decades. Sweden was less successful than most other industrial countries in coping with the oil price increases and the concurrent international swings in inflation and activity. While the failure is partly of a political nature, certain concrete features of economic policy leading to the poor results are readily discernible.

In this paper we describe how a vigorous policy of domestic consumption restraint failed to create an export-led growth that had always been an important feature in Sweden's economic development.

The Swedish experience

With the dramatic change in terms of trade between OECD and OPEC, the industrial world was, in effect, left with a choice between lowering activity and imports to maintain the current account balance, or maintaining activity by allowing foreign finance of the necessary investment level. In the first oil shock the choice was somewhat in between: some borrowing and deep recession. Sweden's current account deficit was fairly typical or close to the average, while growth was among the slowest in the industrial world: GNP growth amounted to 20 per cent for the 1970s compared with 40 per cent for OECD. The external dissaving amounted to 0.5 per cent of GNP on average for the decade, not unlike the overall OECD pattern.

The Swedish performance on these two counts is an indication of a trade-off at a more uncomfortable level for the country as a whole. Given the preconditions as to the size of the terms-of-trade deterioration, this outcome can be interpreted as a less adequate Swedish economic policy. The fact that Sweden allowed itself only half of the OECD growth but scored a typical current account deficit points to one of the major qualifications to the borrowing/adjustment trade-off that has had particular serious consequences for Swedish policy: the low capacity utilization resulted not only in slow import growth, but also, via low productivity and high unit labour costs, in slow export growth.

This ambiguous, two-way relationship between income and current account balance has no doubt been prevalent in all countries. The reasons that Sweden suffered more from low capacity utilization and productivity are several. Domestic demand was actually allowed to rise at a slower path (partly owing to a bizarre statistical exaggeration of Sweden's current account deficit). In addition, government exerted considerable pressure on firms not to lay off labour as output stagnated.

A particular feature can also be found in Sweden's industry structure; Swedish industrial firms typically sell both abroad and at home. This means that it is largely the *same* firms and the *same* productive capacity that are affected by changes in export and domestic demand. Hence, when exports do not expand in pace with domestic restraint, the main result is a fall in overall capacity utilization and productivity. While the major result of this policy is a drop in income and domestic production, we also get the ironic side-effect that unit costs rise and international competitiveness is impaired.

Sweden was caught by both oil price increases in a quite favourable situation financially, and also with regard to inflation and the real terms of trade burden imposed on it. Until 1977 Sweden was a net creditor nation, and it still has a small foreign debt in relation to GNP. In 1973 the current account showed a surplus of 3 per cent GNP. In 1979, before the oil price hike, again there was a certain surplus, which in relative terms put Sweden in an almost as comfortable a current account situation as before the first oil shock.

The ratio of Sweden's inflation rate (consumer price index – CPI) to OECD's was 6:8 and 6:7 in 1973 and 1978, respectively. The country's terms of trade suffered less than most other countries in 1974 and 1980 owing to sharp export price increases, which were to only a minor degree of an internal cost-push nature. To round off the description of the ideal opportunity for a currency appreciation, twice sadly lost in Sweden, let us add that the Swedish labour movement on both occasions was sympathetic to a revaluation policy, agreeing, as it were, to accept lower imported inflation in exchange for nominal wage restraint.

Once the inflationary impulses from abroad penetrated the Swedish economy, the consequences were even more severe than in other countries. The combination of double-digit inflation and Sweden's highly progressive income taxes led to nominal wage demand increases of 20–25 per cent just in order to keep real disposable income at its previous level. Such nominal wage increases were actually negotiated in 1974, with the familiar results plaguing the Swedish economy for the rest of the 1970s. The basic harm, however, lays primarily in inflation *per se* and the over-all slow growth, not on competitiveness as conventional wisdom has it.

Sweden's relative unit labour costs rose by about 20 per cent between 1974 and 1976, but more than one-third of this can be explained in terms of productivity, and substantial parts were due to wage bill tax increases and a (now overdue) appreciation of the Swedish krona together with the Deutschmark bloc. While nominal wage increases were substantial in all countries after the first oil crisis, the productivity loss and exchange appreciation pushed unit labour cost up drastically. Thus, very little of the so-called cost crisis remains to be explained in terms of demand factors or a high capacity utilization.

The attempt to describe the basic macro-relationships of external and internal balance in terms of a two-sector model, where one sector sells on the home market and the other is an export sector under a technical transformation restriction, can of course be questioned at several levels.

First, it can be argued that, at a sufficiently low capacity utilization, one sector does not necessarily have to contract in order for the other to expand. There is always a link in the sense that overall demand for labour is correlated to wage development. But where factors are not truly scarce, government subsidizes most types of increases in employment, and when in the end it does not accept increased unemployment, the direct link via wages largely breaks down.

Second, there is both a supply and demand side to export. Freeing resources for exports will not result in increased exports unless there is a world demand for them. For the home country to win market shares, foreign exporters have to yield, and this can be accomplished only by lowered relative export prices (which seem highly dubious in a broader welfare context and difficult to bring about practically anyway).

Third, and this is what in combination with the two earlier factors makes the two-sector model inadequate as a policy tool for Sweden's economy, Swedish industry disposes of its output in roughly equal portions abroad and at home. This means that productivity, profits and investment are a function of total capacity utilization and sales. Reduction of domestic demand – both of non-tradables and in particular of tradables – in the absence of a parallel export expansion immediately results in lower capacity utilization and profits. Paradoxically, this also leads to higher unit costs and lower competitiveness. Exports, as it were, are hurt more by the fall in productivity than they are helped by the possibly dampened wage increases. In the following section we shall model this crucial effect explicitly.

A 'two-sector model' with common production capacity

The aim with the present, simplified model of the Swedish economy is to analyse how a certain change in the growth of final domestic demand (public consumption, private consumption or investment) affects the development of imports, exports and inflation.

Equations

In the model, increments in the *percentage change* of the different variables are defined in the following manner:

X	exports of goods and services (volume)
M	imports of goods and services (volume)
Q_{ind}	industrial output (volume)
Q_{other}	other corporate output (volume)
R_{ind}	productivity in industry
R_{other}	productivity in remaining corporate sector
W	labour cost per hour, whole corporate sector
K_{ind}	unit labour cost in industry
K_{other}	unit labour cost in remaining corporate sector
P_{ind}	price of industrial output
P_{other}	price of other output
XV	exports of goods and services (current prices)
MV	imports of goods and services (current prices)

These increments are determined as the result of given increments to the percentage changes in final demand components according to the following:

C_{publ} public use (volume)
C_{pri} private consumption (volume)
I investment

The percentage change of *export volume* is determined by price changes in industrial output in the following manner:

$$X = -\,1.70P_{ind}.$$

The price elasticity is thus assumed to be −1.7. Other factors determining export are assumed not to be affected by changes in domestic demand and do not enter into the equation.

The percentage change of *import volume* is affected both by the direct change in demand and indirectly as a result of the resulting changes in output by imports of intermediate goods. Further, the import volume is affected by price changes on Swedish goods:

$$M = 0.05\,C_{publ} + 0.22C_{pri} + 0.12I + 0.44Q_{ind} + 0.17\,Q_{other} + 1.30P_{ind}.$$

The price elasticity of imports is thus assumed to be 1.3. The other coefficients have been determined from input–output tables for 1975.

Industrial output is affected by the change in final domestic demand, by the change in output in the rest of the corporate sector, by the export change, and by the change in prices for industrial goods (the mirror image of price effects on imports):

$$Q_{ind} = 0.05\,C_{publ} + 0.36C_{pri} + 0.07I + 0.7\,Q_{other} + 0.35X - 0.40P_{ind}.$$

The price elasticity of −0.40 has been determined so as to have the change in output matched by the change in imports called forth by the price change. The other coefficients have been determined from the input–output table.

Other output is determined in a similar fashion:

$$Q_{other} = 0.07\,C_{publ} + 0.42C_{pri} + 0.25I + 0.18Q_{ind} + 0.08X - 0.10P_{ind}.$$

It should be observed – as is evident from the formulation of the import equation – that the limited part of output that is import-competing is assumed to conform to the price change of industrial output. The price elasticity thus is small owing to the smallness of imports in relation to total domestic production.

Productivity in industry is affected by the change in output. How much depends, *inter alia*, on the capacity utilization to start with. In the basic version of the model we assume that 0.7 of the output change results in changed productivity and that 0.3 thus gives rise to a change in the employment:

$$R_{\text{ind}} = 0.70 Q_{\text{ind}}.$$

Productivity in the rest of the corporate sector is affected in the same manner:

$$R_{\text{other}} = 0.70 Q_{\text{other}}.$$

Wages per hour in the total corporate sector are assumed to be affected by the productivity change. In the basic version we assumed that half of the productivity change has given rise to a change in hourly wages and that it is the productivity change in the industrial sector that determines wages:

$$W = 0.50 R_{\text{ind}}.$$

Unit labour costs in both industry and the remaining corporate sector are affected by the difference between hourly wage change and productivity change:

$$K_{\text{ind}} = W - R_{\text{ind}}$$

$$K_{\text{other}} = W - R_{\text{other}}.$$

Prices on industrial output are affected by the changes in unit labour cost and by the price change for intermediate non-industrial output. These two cost components account for 47 and 21 per cent, respectively, of variable costs in industry (explaining intermediate goods from the own sector). Two-thirds of the cost change assumed in the basic version give rise to a price change:

$$P_{\text{ind}} = 0.67(0.47 K_{\text{ind}} + 0.21 P_{\text{other}}).$$

Prices on non-industrial output are determined by the same mechanism, where wage costs make up for 61 and industrial output 27 per cent of variable costs (excluding intermediate goods from the own sector):

$$P_{\text{other}} = 0.67(0.61 K_{\text{other}} + 0.27 P_{\text{ind}}).$$

Exports in current prices are determined by the sum of the volume change of exports and the price change for industrial output:

$$XV = X + P_{\text{ind}}.$$

Imports in current prices are determined solely by the change in import volume, since import prices are assumed to be given:

$$MV = M.$$

In table A1 the basic version of the model is summarized in matrix form. Table A2 is a simplified input–output table for 1975 that has been used to determine several of the coefficients.

Simulation of the basic version

If the equation system is solved with the respect to the demand variable, and an increment of 1 percentage point is given to the growth in each of these variables at the same time, the incremental changes in the most pertinent variables of the model are given in table 1 (effects on all variables are given in table A3). With a 1 per cent increment in total domestic demand, we thus get an increase in imports of 0.73 per cent. Exports too increase somewhat, by 0.18 per cent in volume. This is due to the relative price decrease that takes place in the model – primarily as a result of the productivity improvement. The decrease of relative prices also seems to have a dampening effect on imports.

Table 1 Some incremental change in the model

	Public use	*Private use*	*Investments*	*All three components*
	%	%	%	%
Exports (volume)	0.02	0.12	0.04	0.18
Exports (current prices)	0.01	0.05	0.02	0.07
Import (volume) (=import, current prices)	0.08	0.45	0.20	0.73
Industrial output	0.07	0.52	0.14	0.74
Output in other corporate sector	0.09	0.53	0.28	0.90

As a result directly of the freezed demand and indirectly of the improvement in competitiveness, industrial output increases by 0.74 per cent. Non-industrial output increases even more, owing partly to the smaller 'import leakage'.

Alternative assumptions

The effects of an increase in demand are obviously dependent on the behaviour equations that make up the model. We shall now study how the results change with different assumptions concerning (1) price formation, (2) wage formation and (3) the determination of productivity. In the basic version we have assumed that price change will be 0.67 of the percentage change in cost, both for industrial and non-industrial output. If the cost change affects prices less, the effects on competitiveness will be smaller. If, for example, the price change is equal to the cost change, effects on competitiveness will be bigger.

Table 2 Effects on the current account of various cost changes on prices

	Pass-through on prices		
	0.67 (basic version)	*0.20*	*1.00*
	%	%	%
Exports (volume)	0.18	0.04	0.33
Exports (current prices)	0.07	0.02	0.14
Imports (volume = current prices)	0.73	0.79	0.66

In table 2 we show the effects on exports and imports with two alternative assumptions concerning the pass-through of cost changes on prices (same for industrial and non-industrial products), given an increment of 1 percentage point to change in all three components in domestic final demand. In the basic version of the model we assume that 0.5 of the productivity change also works out on wages per hour. If hourly wages would not at all be affected by the effects of unit labour costs, prices would be higher. With an increase in domestic demand exports would then increase more and imports less compared with the basic version of the model. Conversely, no change at all in competitiveness would occur if the productivity change would be fully absorbed by an increase in hourly earnings.

In table 3 we show the effects on exports and imports of the two alternative assumptions on the pass-through of productivity changes on wages, after an increment of 1 percentage point to all three components in final domestic demand. The fact that full pass-through of productivity on hourly wages, and thus unchanged unit labour costs

Table 3 Effects on the current account of various productivity changes on wages

	Pass-through on prices		
	0.70 (basic version)	*0.00*	*1.00*
	%	%	%
Exports (volume)	0.18	0.40	0.02
Exports (current prices)	0.07	0.16	0.01
Imports (volume = current prices)	0.73	0.63	0.80

in industry, does have a marginal effect on exports is due to the fact that prices on intermediate goods from the remaining corporate sector also change. Hourly wages in the total corporate sector are determined, it should be borne in mind, by the productivity development in industry alone.

The basic version assumed that 0.7 of the output change is reflected in improvement in productivity. If no productivity improvement occurred, however (and thus the whole increased output would lead to higher employment), then no effect on unit labour cost and competitiveness would follow. This case would then be similar to the case referred to above, where productivity changes are fully absorbed by higher hourly wages. On the other hand, if the whole output change gives rise to improved productivity, the effect on costs, prices and competitiveness will be greater than in the basic version.

In table 4 we show the effects of exports and imports with two alternative assumptions on the pass-through of the output change on productivity (same for industry and remaining part of the corporate sector) after an increment of 1 percentage point to the growth in all

Table 4 Effects on the current account of various output changes on productivity

	Pass-through on prices		
	0.70 (basic version)	*0.20*	*1.00*
	%	%	%
Exports (volume)	0.18	0.05	0.27
Exports (current prices)	0.07	0.02	0.11
Imports (volume = current prices)	0.73	0.79	0.69

three components of final domestic demand. A particularly favourable effect on the current account by an increased domestic demand occurs if (1) the whole increase in output leads to improved productivity, (2) hourly wages are not affected, and (3) the fall in costs is fully reflected in lower prices. This case is shown in table 5, again calculated after an increment of 1 percentage point to all three components in final domestic demand. In this case the current account thus would improve markedly with the increased domestic demand. To secure this result in practice may not prove easy but is altogether feasible, if wage-earners and firms can be persuaded to accept moderate wage and price increases in exchange for higher growth in real output.

Table 5 Effects on the current account of alternative pass-throughs

	Pass-through on prices	
	Basic version	*Very favourable version*
Exports (volume)	0.18	1.77
Exports (current prices)	0.07	0.73
Imports (volume = current prices)	0.73	0.02

Qualifications

Obviously, the model gives only a simplified picture of reality. For instance, we do not consider the time lapse between an improvement in competitiveness and effects on trade volume. The model also abstracts from important variables and mechanisms in the economy.

It should be stressed that a basic precondition of the model is that there exists unutilized capacity in the corporate sector, so that increased exports and import substitution would be made impossible by supply restrictions. For Sweden in the 1970s, however, such restrictions have been extremely mild and infrequent.

Further, it is assumed that the output of identical firms is disposed of both at domestic and export markets. Otherwise the improved productivity owing to increased domestic demand would not be beneficial to the production of exports through lower costs. This assumption is not completely fulfilled in reality, but in Sweden half of the exports emanate from firms with 37 per cent or more of its sales on the domestic market. The share of the domestic market in total industrial output is 65 per cent. Ideally, and to reap the full effects of the productivity effects modelled above, all exports would emanate from firms with such a high share of domestic sales. For manufacturing, which makes up the bulk of the Swedish export, the precondition does not hold very well: half of the exports come from firms that dispose of some 40 per cent or more of their output on the domestic market; the share of the domestic market and the total sales is 60 per cent. (The data refer to Sweden 1976, Central Bureau of Statistics SM 1978:12.)

Conclusions

It has been shown that the simple strategy of export-led expansion based on dampened domestic demand in a traditional two-sector substitution model has to be qualified in several respects. In an

Fig. 1 Private final consumption, 1970–79 (volume) (1970=100)

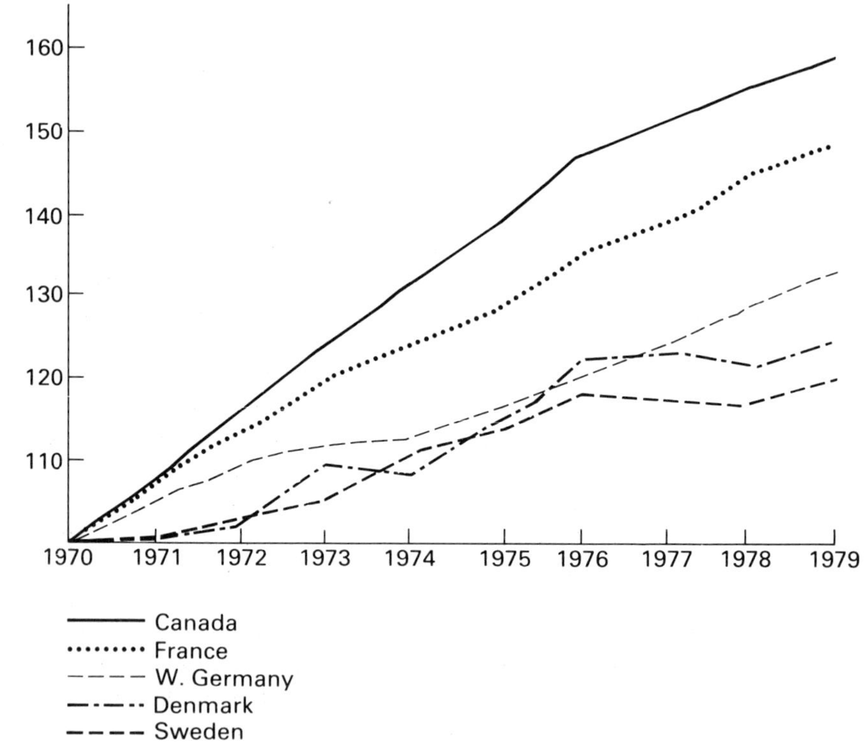

Source: OECD.

economy with a production structure like the Swedish one, where the available industrial capacity is common to sales abroad and at home, a too-low capacity utilization results in an overall fall in productivity and profitability, and thus in international competitiveness. In terms of unit labour costs, the productivity losses of a low capacity utilization tend to swamp possible gains in terms of low wage increases resulting from low activity levels.

As is shown in figure 1, private consumption rose in Sweden by only half the average rate in the industrial world. Some of the other industrial countries that had particular problems with international competitiveness also display a picture of low domestic demand. It is difficult to determine what is cause and effect in the observed correlation between poor export performance and low domestic activity. Some countries seem to have had chronic balance of payments problems owing to low competitiveness or an inept industrial structure and were thus forced to pursue a policy of low domestic activity. In the Swedish case it is obvious that causation has worked the other way, too, with an aggressive and costly strategy for export-led expansion leading not only to a slow domestic income development but also, ironically, to an erosion of competitiveness and export performance.

Appendix

(*overleaf*)

Table A1 The basic version of the model in matrix form

Explanatory variables		X	M	Q_{ind}	Q_{other}	R_{ind}	R_{other}	W	K_{ind}	K_{other}	P_{ind}	P_{other}	XV	MV
Exogenous														
Public use	C_{publ}		0.05	0.05	0.07									
Private consumption	C_{pri}		0.22	0.36	0.42									
Investments	I		0.12	0.07	0.25									
Endogenous														
Exports, volume	X			0.35	0.08								1	
Imports, volume	M													1
Industry output	Q_{ind}		0.44		0.18	0.70								
Output in other corporate sector	Q_{other}		0.17	0.17			0.70							
Industry productivity	R_{ind}							0.50	−1					
Productivity in other corporate sector	R_{other}									−1				
Labour cost per hour, whole corporate sector	W								1	1				
Unit labour cost in industry	K_{ind}										0.31			
Unit labour cost in remaining corporate sector	K_{other}											0.41		
Price of industrial output	P_{ind}	−1.70	1.30	−0.40	−0.10							0.18	1	
Price of other output	P_{other}										0.14			

Table A2 Simplified input–output table for 1975

Supply	Input: Industry	Input: Remaining corporate sector	Input: Total	Public use	Private consumption	Private investment	Public investment	Exports	Total
Industry products	92.3	44.5	136.8	11.9	85.9	22.8	1.6	70.4	329.4
Import	32.8	10.7	43.5	2.9	14.9	9.8		—	70.4
Domestic products	59.5	33.8	93.3	9.0	71.9	14.6		70.4	259.0
Other products	29.3	52.6	81.9	11.4	63.7	27.9	7.9	12.0	204.8
Import	4.4	3.5	7.9	1.5	4.0	0.2		—	13.6
Domestic products	24.9	49.1	74.0	9.9	59.7	35.6		12.0	191.2
Total	121.6	97.1	218.7	23.3	149.6	50.7	9.5	82.4	534.2
Import	37.2	14.2	51.4	4.4	18.2	10.0		—	84.0
Domestic products	84.4	82.9	167.3	18.9	131.4	50.2		82.4	450.2

Table A3 Effects on the model's endogenous variables of a 1 per cent increase of growth in final domestic demand (basic version)

	1% increase in:			
Effects on:	*Public use*	*Private consumption*	*Investments (percentage points)*	*All three components*
Exports (volume)	0.02	0.12	0.04	0.18
Imports (volume)	0.08	0.45	0.20	0.73
Industry output	0.07	0.52	0.14	0.74
Output in other corporate sectors	0.09	0.53	0.28	0.90
Industry productivity	0.05	0.36	0.10	0.56
Productivity in other corporate sector	0.06	0.37	0.20	0.63
Labour cost per hour (whole corporate sector)	0.03	0.18	0.05	0.26
Unit labour cost in industry	−0.03	−0.08	−0.05	−0.26
Unit labour cost in remaining corporate sector	−0.03	−0.19	−0.15	−0.37
Price on industrial output	−0.01	−0.07	−0.02	−0.10
Price on other output	−0.02	−0.09	−0.06	−0.17
Exports (current prices)	0.01	0.05	0.02	0.07
Imports (current prices)	0.08	0.45	0.20	0.73

Norwegian Economic Policy in the Past Decade and Some Thoughts on Policy in the Present One

ARNE JON ISACHSEN
Bank of Norway, Oslo

Introduction

Throughout the 1970s, the oil sector developed rapidly in Norway. Without the problem of energy shortage, and with the foreign exchange constraint relaxed through heavy taxation of foreign oil companies, the economic situation of Norway seems unique. However, there are certain problems connected with becoming 'nouveau riche', on the macro-level as well as on the micro-level.

Main economic events in the 1970s

A brief overview

In May 1972 Norway joined the 'Snake' to become a member of the Common Market currency bloc. In November 1973 the Norwegian krone (NOK) was revalued by 5 per cent, in order to fend off part of the inflationary impulses from abroad.

When Sweden devalued twice in 1977, Norway, as well as Denmark, followed suit half-way, and the Norwegian krone lost 8 per cent in value relative to the other 'Snake' currencies. In February of the following year Norway undertook a depreciation of 8 per cent, with the consent of the other 'Snake' countries.

A comprehensive wage and price freeze was introduced in September 1978, to last through 1979.

With the transformation of the 'Snake' into the European Monetary System (EMS), Norway decided to follow the Swedish example of August 1977, and on 12 December 1978 the krone was pegged to a suitable basket of currencies.[1] At this point, about one-third of Norway's trade was with the 'Snake' countries.

In October 1979 foreigners' access to the Norwegian stock market was liberalized, as the investment quota in stocks per foreigner was increased from 50 000 to 1 million NOK[2] (as of 2 March 1981, US$1 was priced at NOK 5.52).

Stabilization policy of 1974–77

The economic problems of the mid-1970s were met by a very active countercyclical policy in Norway (see table 1). Through expansionary fiscal and monetary policies aggregate demand was kept at a high level, the growth rate of GNP was reasonable, and unemployment was kept between 1.5 and 2.3 per cent. However, the expansionary measures resulted in rapid inflation and deteriorated competitiveness. The current account was in the red every single year during the 1970s. Owing to expectations of increased earnings of foreign exchange from the oil sector, the policy of foreign borrowing was deemed appropriate, to avoid internal employment problems. Borrowing was undertaken in various national financial markets as well as in the Eurocurrency markets. About one-third of a total borrowing of about 100 billion NOK in the 1970s was undertaken by the government, whereas the remaining two-thirds was private borrowing, strictly controlled by the authorities. In 1976 and 1977 the deficit on current account reached alarming proportions – in 1977 Norway noted a record deficit of 14 per cent of GNP.

Table 1 Some economic indicators

	GNP growth	*Un-employment*	*Current account (per cent of GNP)*	*Inflation (CPI) (per cent annual average)*	*Growth of M2*	*Index of relative unit labour cost, adjusted for changes in exchange rates*
	%	%	%	%	%	
1970	2.0	1.6	−2.1	10.4	12.9	83.3
1971	4.6	1.5	−4.1	6.4	11.7	84.6
1972	5.2	1.8	−0.4	7.0	11.7	85.1
1973	4.1	1.6	−1.8	7.6	11.8	89.2
1974	5.2	1.5	−4.7	9.4	10.4	92.5
1975	4.2	2.3	−8.5	11.6	15.3	100.0
1976	6.8	1.8	−11.9	9.2	17.1	107.5
1977	3.6	1.5	−14.0	9.2	16.0	113.1
1978	4.5	1.9	−5.1	8.0	11.0	106.1
1979	4.5	2.0	−2.5	4.9	14.0	101.0
1980*	3.6	1.7	1.6	10.9	12.1	101.1

* Preliminary figures

In the industrial sector the growth of productivity slowed down from an annual average rate of about 4 per cent prior to 1973 to an average annual rate of 0.9 per cent for the remaining years of the decade.

In part, the expansionary fiscal policy can be attributed to government subsidies to ailing firms and industries, with the short-run effect of avoiding unemployment. This policy, however, led to a postponement of the adjustment of the structure of production to changing demand conditions, and also contributed to the slow-down of productivity growth.

Reduced competitiveness and lack of proper adjustment in production resulted in considerable losses in market shares, both domestically and in international markets.

To counter the negative effects on competitiveness, the government experimented with various forms of incomes policy. In order to moderate nominal wage claims, the government agreed to reduce taxes so as to have disposable real income growth materialize through lower taxes rather than through sharper increase in nominal pay. However, the incomes policy was not sufficient to stem the inflationary impulses originating from expansionary monetary and fiscal policies.[3]

Another factor that contributed to the weakening of fiscal policy was the emphasis put on reducing income differentials. In 1975 the Storting decided that the average earnings of farmers should be brought on par with those of industrial workers within six years. This decision gave the well-organized farmers the upper hand in bargaining for farm price increases and farm support programmes in the latter half of the 1970s. As the state negotiates with the farmers' organizations, it seems somewhat awkward that the Storting should rid itself of bargaining power by announcing in advance a very ambitious goal on behalf of the farmers.

A period of attempted restraint, 1978–80

In the autumn of 1977 it became increasingly obvious that Norway was living beyond its means (see table 2). The oil revenues were discounted at an inflated rate. At the same time, the prospects for oil were bleaker, owing, on the one hand, to a fall in the real price of oil of more than 25 per cent since 1974 and on the other hand to gross miscalculations of costs of oil production in the North Sea. Under these circumstances the government decided that the external balance needed more attention and embarked upon a programme of

Table 2 Development of external debt
(billion kroner)

	Private sector		*Public sector*	*Reserves of the Bank of Norway*	*Net debt*	
	Oil	*Other*				*(per cent of GNP)*
1973	5.2	13.9	4.0	8.9	14.2	12.7
1974	10.0	15.5	4.0	9.7	19.8	15.3
1975	14.4	24.1	9.3	12.4	35.2	23.7
1976	20.5	30.7	14.7	11.5	54.4	31.9
1977	27.8	39.6	25.7	8.7	84.4	44.1
1978	29.5	41.8	42.3	14.6	99.0	46.6
1979	28.1	44.6	51.7	20.9	103.5	44.2
1980*	80.5		49.9	31.6	98.8	34.9

* Preliminary figures

restraint. In addition to tighter monetary and fiscal policies, the krone was devalued by 8 per cent in February 1978. This devaluation was very successful, the main reason being that, in the nation-wide wage negotiations that already were taking place, the nominal claims were not increased to counter the inflationary impact that an 8 per cent devaluation is bound to have in an economy where the import-GNP ratio is close to 0.5.

In September 1978 a comprehensive wage and price freeze was introduced. This measure also won acceptance, and during the 15 months-long freeze period wages and prices were remarkably stable. The CPI inflation of 4.9 per cent in 1979 was as expected, and was due mainly to price increases emanating from abroad, which to some extent were allowed to sift through to the domestic economy.

In addition to the contractionary measures of 1978 and 1979, the development of the price of oil contributed to improving the external balance. From the second quarter of 1978 to the second quarter of 1980, the dollar price of oil more than doubled,[4] and the problems with the external balance eased. The net debt-to-GNP ratio declined from 47 per cent in 1978 to 35 per cent in 1980, and the current account swung into surplus.

In retrospect, it seems hard to escape the conclusion that the reasonably successful economic performance of Norway in the latter half of the 1970s must be ascribed as much to luck as to well implemented policies. Without the second oil price shock the external balance would have required more drastic domestic measures.

Although a programme of restraint was implemented in 1978 and 1979, it is clear that the effect on overall demand was quite modest. Through the comprehensive wage and price freeze, the rate of inflation was reduced from 9.2 per cent in 1977 to 4.9 per cent in 1979. However, the rate of growth of the money stock remained high, at 14.0 per cent in 1979 (see table 1). Thus, the freeze did not receive much support from the general policy of demand management, and inflationary pressure was built up during this period. The result was a marked increase in the rate of inflation in 1980.[5]

This pressure has not abated, and at the time of writing inflation is emerging as the most dominant economic problem in Norway, especially since the rate of inflation has peaked in most OECD countries, whereas no slow-down in the rate of price increase is evident in Norway.

Capital movements in the 1970s

In an open economy with a fixed exchange rate, it is well known that the growth rate of the money stock is difficult to control. Contractionary monetary policies will to some extent be countered by an inflow of funds from abroad. Also, changes in the rate of return abroad may induce capital flows. In spite of strict control of pure portfolio investments there will always be room for leakages – for example, through varying lines of credit in connection with commercial transactions.

In addition to the development of the domestic component of the stock of money and the foreign rate of interest, the growth rate of GNP as well as the result on the current account are expected to have an impact upon capital flows.[6]

A preliminary estimate[7] of a capital flow equation for the private sector is reported in connection with figure 1, where the observed and estimated capital flows are compared. The estimated equation gives quite reasonable results. It is worth noting that a contractionary monetary policy is countered by an inflow of capital of 0.42 per cent of the contraction. Such a leakage is comparable to that of Germany (see Neumann, 1978), and gives the authorities some autonomy in monetary policy. On the other hand, a 1 percentage point increase in the rate of interest in the Eurodollar market leads to a capital outflow of about 200 million NOK. The trend of the last couple of years towards higher and more market-determined interest rates in Norway may have had the effect of reducing the coefficient on Δi^*.

Fig. 1 Capital flows, observed and estimated

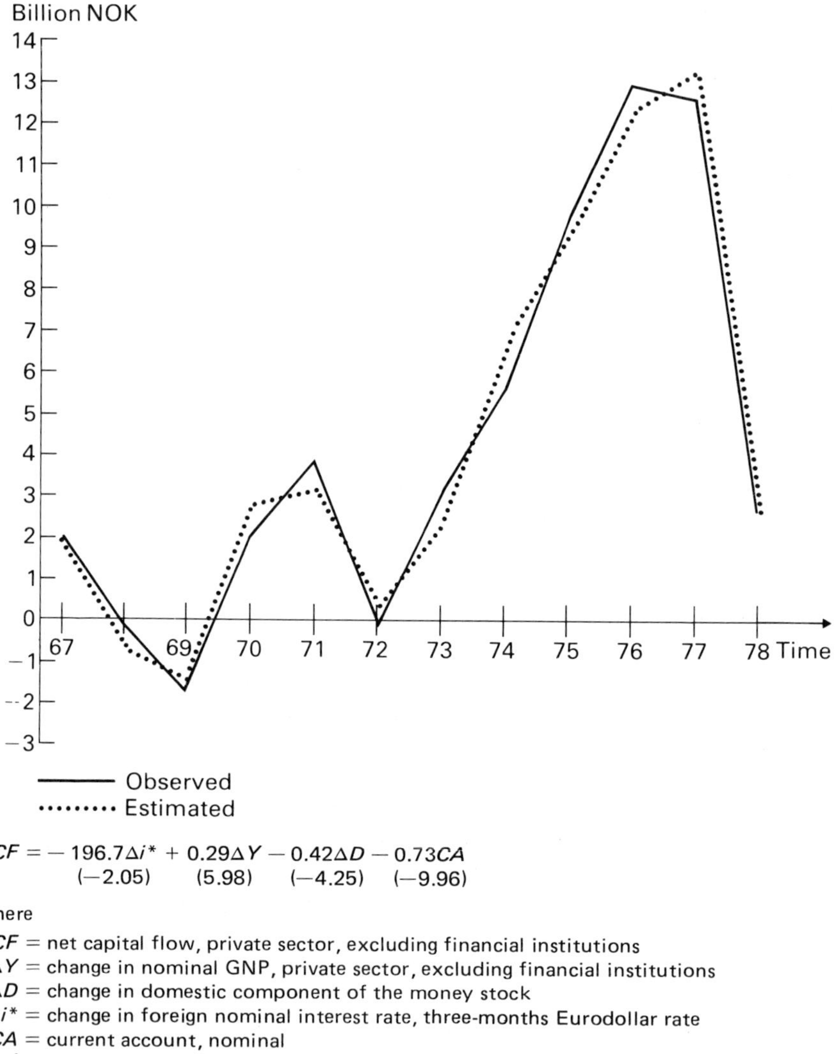

$$CF = -\underset{(-2.05)}{196.7\Delta i^*} + \underset{(5.98)}{0.29\Delta Y} - \underset{(-4.25)}{0.42\Delta D} - \underset{(-9.96)}{0.73CA}$$

where

CF = net capital flow, private sector, excluding financial institutions
ΔY = change in nominal GNP, private sector, excluding financial institutions
ΔD = change in domestic component of the money stock
Δi^* = change in foreign nominal interest rate, three-months Eurodollar rate
CA = current account, nominal
$R^2 = 0.974$
$DW = 3.19$
(t-values in parentheses)

Reflections on the policy of changing the exchange rate

The conventional view

The conventional theory is that a revaluation will dampen inflationary expectations and lead to more modest wage claims. A devaluation, on the other hand, will make the labour unions revise their wage demands upwards. The underlying rationale for such behaviour is that unions are no longer subject to any 'money illusion' and consequently bargain for a certain increase in real pay.[8]

The Norwegian experience in the 1970s

Considering the Norwegian experience of the 1970s, this view hardly fits reality. In November 1973 the Norwegian krone was revalued by 5 per cent, to be followed by an all-time postwar high in nominal wage increases. From 1974(I) to 1975(I) the increase in hourly wage rate for men in industry exceeded 25 per cent, compared with an annual average over the previous years six years of 10.8 per cent. The CPI increased by about 11 per cent through 1974, resulting in an unusual growth in purchasing power in the private sector.

The devaluation of February 1978 of 8 per cent was followed by an annual increase in the hourly wage rate of only 5.3 per cent. The annual rate of inflation was of about the same magnitude, and real wages stayed constant.

This seemingly odd behaviour can be explained by alluding to special factors in both instances. In 1974 the unions rightly maintained that labour had not received its share of the economic boom of 1972–73. The outlook for the exposed industries was considered quite good, as the wage negotiations took place in the spring of 1974 – it is well known that the international business cycles are felt in Norway with a six- to twelve-months lag – and competition for labour was strong. The impact of the revaluation of November 1973 was overshadowed by the feeling of general prosperity, and the wage increases were accordingly large.

In 1978 the wage and price freeze of September hindered the market forces so that increases in wages and prices were not allowed completely to work themselves out, following the devaluation in February.

An alternative view

Rather than emphasizing special circumstances, I would like to suggest a somewhat more general explanation of the wage and price effects of a change in the exchange rate in a modern economy. The main argument is that a change in the exchange rate has a signalling effect in the labour market. When the government decides to revalue, labour unions take this to imply that the profitability of the exposed industries is very good. With a strong competitive position in international markets, the labour unions feel entitled to press for considerable increases in pay. The dampening effect on inflationary expectations of a revaluation is not strong enough to counter the stronger wage claims that follow from the unions' realization of surprisingly good profit prospects, signalled to them by the decision of the government to let the currency appreciate.

When a devaluation occurs, the signalling effect to the unions is that the economy is in heavier water than previously conceived. To maintain reasonably full employment the government has undertaken the drastic measure of depreciating the currency. To restore competitiveness in industry the unions have to contribute in terms of moderating their wage claims. The inflationary effect of a devaluation is not reflected in the nominal wage claims, as the devaluation makes it quite clear that modesty is the order of the day, to avoid increased lay-offs.

In this alternative view of the effects of a change in the exchange rate, a reaction function of the labour market is explicitly introduced. Assuming that a change in the exchange rate, in addition to its well-known effects on prices, carries information on the government's evaluation of the general economic situation, the response in the labour market to a revaluation or a devaluation may be different from what the textbook tells us. In a highly organized economy with nation-wide wage negotiations, it may well be that the signalling effect of a change in the exchange rate outweighs the price effect. This seems to have been the case in Norway in the 1970s.

The alternative view of the effects of a change in the exchange rate suggested here can be applied successfully to Belgium and Finland.[9] In Belgium in the period 1974–79 there was almost a simultaneous occurrence of a wage explosion and an effective appreciation of the currency. In Finland the devaluation of 1967 was followed by modest wage claims, and competitiveness was restored. Again, in 1977–78 three devaluations of the krona of a total of 18 per cent did not result in wage compensation claims, and the economy recovered rapidly. In 1979 and 1980, on the other hand, the Finnish mark was revalued by 5 per cent in small steps. As nominal wage claims were not moderated, the result was accelerated inflation.

From the government's point of view, the effects of a change in the exchange rate put forward here indicate that a devaluation is more likely to have the desired effects. The 'devaluation-bias' of the Bretton Woods system, which usually is attributed to the asymmetry in pressure for adjustment in surplus and deficit countries, may be explained in terms of the signalling effect going in the desired direction when devaluing and in the undesired direction when revaluing.

A final point relating to the effects of a devaluation should be mentioned. When competitiveness has deteriorated owing to rapid increases in domestic wages and prices, it may be difficult for workers in an industry to accept a modest nominal wage increase, because there is no guarantee that other groups will show similar moderation. However, it may be more acceptable to all groups to have a devaluation restore competitiveness because the inflationary impact of a devaluation will be the same across all groups of wage-earners, and one's *relative income position* is not much affected.

Summing up

In addition to the effects on prices, a change in the exchange rate may have a signalling effect in the labour market. This signalling effect explains why the revaluation of the Norwegian krone of 1973 was unsuccessful whereas the devaluation of 1978 had the desired effects.

In a more general analysis I think it is necessary to incorporate a labour market reaction function of a change in the exchange rate. In this section I have elaborated on one alternative. The problem with modelling such a function is that as the size of the 'market sector' in the modern economy shrinks relative to the 'bargaining sector', it becomes increasingly difficult for an economist to model behaviour properly.

The impact of the oil sector on the Norwegian economy

Brief overview

To give a snapshot of the development of the oil sector, table 3 was constructed. The anticipated economic rent from the discovery of oil in the North Sea has meant a relaxation of the foreign exchange constraint that facilitated heavy borrowing abroad in the period 1974–78. With considerable tax revenues from the oil sector in the

Table 3 Some figures from the oil sector

	Taxes paid (million kroner)	*Oil sector as percent of GNP*	*Investment (million kroner)*	*Employment (no. of persons)*
1970	0	0	313	–
1971	0	0	704	–
1972	42	0.2	1 237	200
1973	69	0.2	3 108	300
1974	121	0.5	5 615	1 100
1975	209	2.4	7 713	2 400
1976	1 958	3.8	10 850	2 600
1977	3 122	4.1	13 383	4 200
1978	3 819	6.5	9 756	5 500
1979	6 552	9.2	6 961	6 900
1980	18 582	14.8	7 019	7 800

years to come, the government should be able to service its foreign debt without the need of rolling it over. It should be noted, however, that the level of oil production over the next five years will only increase in volume by 30 per cent, so that a continued acceleration of tax revenue is not likely. Note also that, although the income generated in the oil sector is considerable, the direct impact on employment is quite modest. As of 1980, less than 8000 persons were working in this very capital intensive sector.[10]

Norway is a fortunate country in a world beset with economic problems such as energy shortages, unemployment and slow economic growth. However, as Midas experienced, there are certain problems connected with becoming rich all too sudden. To these problems we now turn.

Some problems

To make room for domestic use of the oil revenue, traditional industries should be allowed to decline. As the foreign exchange earned in the oil sector can pay for an increased share of imports, factors of production should move from the tradeable sector, into the non-tradeable one. However, in Norway there is an unusual strong political preference for limiting geographical mobility, and job mobility is also resisted. The feeling is that with the oil revenue one can afford less mobility. To avoid unemployment in the short run, the government has stepped in to support many firms. The adjustments that are necessary from efficiency considerations are slowed down, and the rate of growth in productivity has been reduced.

In the period 1975–80 employment in the manufacturing sector decreased by 22 000 persons, or by 5.4 per cent, to 389 000 persons. In the same period employment in the service sector grew at an unprecedented rate; e.g., education, health and social services employed 384 000 persons in 1980 compared with 280 000 five years earlier, and employment in bank, insurance, real estate, consulting, etc., increased from 79 000 to 110 000 persons. Thus, the share of total employment in the public sector has increased considerably, especially in subsectors publicly financed. When the public sector continuously increases its share of employment, the concept of GNP becomes less meaningful. The reason is that most of the production of public services is measured by wages paid. Increased real wage in the public sector shows up as increased productivity, and growth in GNP. Whether the real services to the customers are improving or deteriorating is hard to tell. The health sector is a case in point. In spite of its continuous growth in terms of investment, employment and transfers, the queues are becoming longer, and satisfaction with performance is sliding.

Analytically, the new income provided by the oil discoveries can be conceived of as a transfer, which makes it possible for Norway to increase its use of tradables. In figure 2 it is assumed that the current account is continuously kept in balance, so that each year's oil revenue is used up. However, as the discussion above should have made clear, the oil wealth, or the discounted income stream from the oil sector, most likely influences present behaviour. There are two sorts of influences I would like to mention. First, the oil wealth

Fig. 2 Oil revenue considered as a transfer

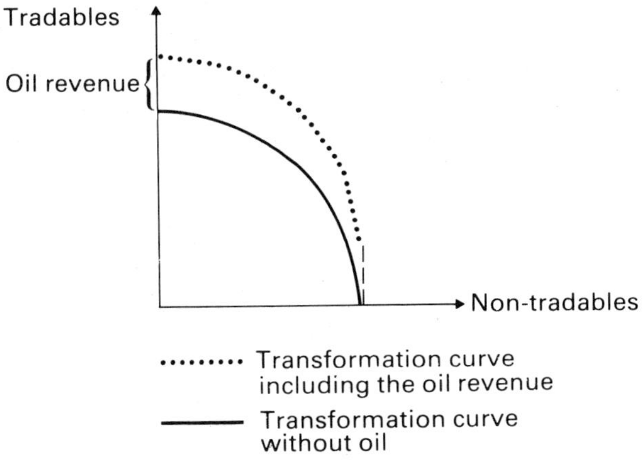

makes economic adjustments more difficult. Being richer, it is harder to win acceptance for labour mobility necessitated by efficiency considerations. Second, as the lion's share of the oil revenue accrues to the government, it becomes very difficult to limit public expenditure. The textbook analysis, in which public expenditure, G, is considered autonomous and tax revenues, T, are a function of GNP, seems less relevant in the mature welfare state. With well organized pressure groups it becomes difficult for the government to follow a policy of fiscal restraint when tax revenues are ample, although overall macroeconomic stability would require that. Although the oil revenue *as such* means increased resources and an extension of the consumption possibility frontier, the argument here is that the *decision-making* process in society becomes less effective. Increased pressure from various groups makes it difficult to realize the possible gains. The result is an expansionary budget with inflationary consequences.

In terms of figure 2, these two effects can be illustrated by changing the transformation curve, including the oil revenues, in two ways:

1 to account for less mobility, make the curve more square;
2 to account for an overall loss in efficiency, owing to an increase in the relative size of non-market activities paid for by the government, make the curve intersect both axes closer to the origin.

The outcome is illustrated in figure 3. In a long-term pessimistic scenario, one may venture that the oil wealth has such a detrimental impact upon economic performance in the non-oil part of the economy that Norway, with the passage of a couple of decades, may find itself worse off with the oil than it would have without the oil. As an historical example, the experience of Spain and the gold inflow during the sixteenth century easily comes to mind. Whether Norway with its 'black gold' will become a counter-example remains to be seen.

Handling the foreign exchange market

Short-run adjustments

In the short run, foreign exchange operations are now dominated by the oil companies' payments of taxes. In April and October these taxes, which are payable in Norwegian kroner, are due. In the period preceding the payment, the oil companies build up krone balances

Fig. 3 Oil wealth reduces efficiency and makes adjustment more difficult

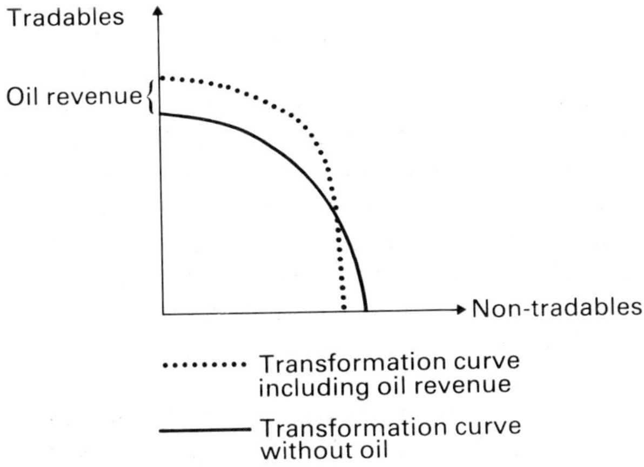

by selling dollars for kroner to the Norwegian banks and by buying kroner forward. To avoid an open position in dollars, the banks, when receiving an inflow of dollars, buy kroner in the forward market, sell dollars for kroner to the Bank of Norway or engage in swap operations. Over the last few years the Bank of Norway has become more sophisticated in combining the use of the forward market with swaps in foreign exchange with commercial banks, to stabilize the exchange rate as well as to control domestic credit creation. Lacking an active market in bonds, swaps in foreign exchange is an alternative way of conducting open market operations, to control domestic liquidity in the short run.

Some longer-run considerations

Even if Norway never becomes a net exporter of capital, certain sectors in the economy will most likely want and be able to increase savings and investments abroad. If the pessimistic scenario of the preceding section does not materialize and Norway emerges as a net supplier of capital in international markets, the question of how to organize an outflow of funds becomes even more important.

There are three ways in which to channel funds abroad:

1 portfolio investments;
2 direct investments;
3 increased foreign aid, i.e., one-way transfers.

If capital exports of some size materialize, it is likely that such exports mainly will take the form of portfolio investments. In addition to obtaining a reasonable return with minimum risk, portfolio investments abroad should be organized so as to maintain whatever autonomy there is in domestic monetary policy. On this background I would like to make two observations. First, one should not stimulate international demand for krone-denominated assets. Foreign speculation in such assets may lead to more frequent interventions by the central bank in the foreign exchange market in order to stabilize the value of the krone. The experience of Great Britain in abolishing controls on capital movements has led to a strong increase in the value of the pound and a sharp deterioration in British competitiveness.

Also, independence in domestic interest rate policy may be reduced once capital flows are liberalized and the krone goes international. The German experience seems to indicate that, with increased foreign holdings of the currency, nominal interest rates are hard to keep down, even though the expected rate of inflation is modest so that the expected real return on German assets in the long run compares favourably with that on dollar-denominated assets.

The second observation is that a future accumulation on private hands of claims in foreign exchange may be channelled through the so-called 'switch market'. This market consists of a pool of assets denominated in foreign exchange, and owned by Norwegians. At present the market value of these assets is about 1 billion NOK. The Norwegian switch market is a parallel to the British one, which was abolished in 1979. There are two outstanding features of this market. First, the exchange rate is freely floating. Second, only Norwegians are allowed to operate here. If the need to channel additional private funds abroad arises, one may consider enlarging the switch market, i.e., channelling more dollars into it. Volatile exchange rate changes arising from sudden shifts in portfolio preferences will then be felt mainly in the switch market and need not create problems with maintaining a stable exchange rate in the market for commercial transactions.

So far, the problem of controlling the switch market to avoid an unintended arbitrage between the switch market and the market for commercial exchange has not been overwhelming. As shown in figure 4, in periods the premium on dollars in the switch market has been close to 40 per cent. The reduction in this premium as of late 1977 is related to improved return on financial savings in Norway. This has led to less demand for foreign assets, which means that the premium on dollars in the switch market has been reduced.

Fig. 4 The switch market and the regular market: the NOK–US$ exchange rate

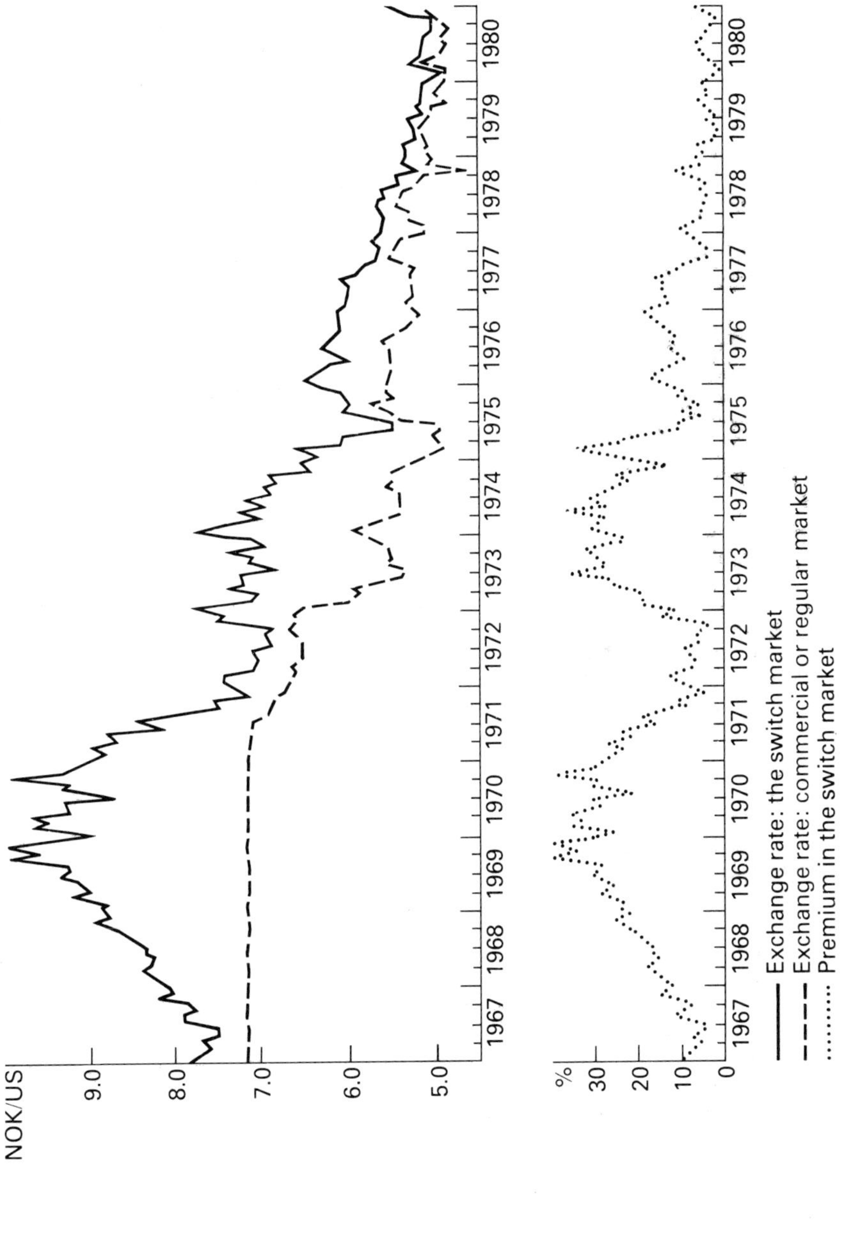

Notes

1 The currency basket established for the Norwegian krone consists of 12 currencies, with the following weights: US$ 25%, £ 13%, Dkr 7%, Skr 18%, Fmk 3%, Ffr 4%, Bfr 2%, Sfr 2%, Fl. 4%, DM 14%, lira 2%, yen 6%.

2 The index of the stock market averaging over the 12 months prior to October 1979 was 84.1, whereas the average monthly index of the ensuing 12 months was 107.1. This rise on the Norwegian stock market obviously was related to foreigners' increased demand.

3 The incomes policy in Norway is discussed in Isachsen (1978).

4 To calculate royalties and taxes payable to the Norwegian authorities, a 'norm price' of oil is estimated. This norm price was US$13.94 in 1978(II), US$20.05 in 1979(II), and US$36 in 1980(II).

5 In Isachsen and Klovland (1980) it is estimated that by the end of 1979(II) the stock of money exceeded the equilibrium level by more than 7 per cent. Thus a similar one-shot price increase was forecasted once the controls were lifted. Note that the CPI inflation from December 1979 to December 1980 was 13.7 per cent; the figure of 10.9 per cent in table 1 refers to *average* price increase.

6 For a theoretical treatment, see Kouri and Porter (1974), and the debate generated by this paper, e.g., Neumann (1978) and Fratianni (1977).

7 See Ytterhus (1981) for more details.

8 With bargaining for real after-tax wage, a progressive tax system will strengthen the effects of a change in the exchange rate alluded to in the text.

9 For more details, see Paul de Grauwe's paper on Belgium, and Halttunen and Korkman's on Finland, in the present volume.

10 Taking into account the fact that the oil activities have linkage effects to other sectors of the economy, such as transport, catering, building and maintenance of platforms and the petro-chemical industry, total employment in oil and oil-related activities was 38 000 persons at the beginning of 1981, compared with 12 000 in 1974.

The views presented are my own and not necessarily those of the Bank of Norway.

References

Fratianni, M. (1977), 'A note on the theory of offsetting capital flows'. *Journal of Monetary Economics*, vol. 3, 133–8.

Isachsen, A. J. (1978), 'Inntektspolitikk og inflasjon i Norge'. *Ekonomisk Debatt*, vol. 6, 26–33.

Isachsen, A. J. and Klovland, J. T. (1980), 'Pengemengde og inflasjon', *Sosialøkonomen*, vol. 2, 13–23.

Kouri, P. J. K. and Porter, M. (1974), 'International capital flows and portfolio equilibrium', *Journal of Political Economy*, vol. 82, 443–67.

Neumann, J. M. (1978), 'Offsetting capital flows: a re-examination of the German case'. *Journal of Monetary Economics*, vol. 4, 131–42.

Ytterhus, B. E. (1981), 'Kapitalbevegelser mellom Norge og utlandet. Estimering av kapitalbevegelser på grunnlag av årsdata' (Norsk utenrikspolitisk institutt, Oslo), mimeo.

International Adjustment, the EMS and Small European Countries: The Danish Experience

JØRN H. KJAER
Denmark National Bank, Copenhagen

Introduction

The principal changes in Denmark's international economic environment during the 1970s were the breakdown of the Bretton Woods system, the entry into the EEC and the associated monetary regimes ('Snake' and EMS), and the oil shocks.

Among these external factors the oil shock has by far been the most important as far as the need for internal and external adjustment is concerned.

The oil shock

Until recent years no domestic energy resources were exploited in Denmark.[1] When energy was in abundant supply in world markets in the 1960s this was probably an advantage, as energy-users were free to 'shop around' for the best prices available while other countries felt obliged to support domestic energy production in one form or another.

On the other hand, this also meant that the new demand–supply relationship in oil markets had a stronger impact in Denmark than in countries where some indigenous energy resources were available. This goes for the balance of payments effect as well as the price effect, since consumer prices were allowed to adjust fully and immediately to the movements in import prices. Following the second oil price increase the price effect was even reinforced by a tax on heating oil and a fairly sharp increase in the petrol tax.

Table 1 Economic indicators, 1970–80

	Current account*					
		of which:				
	Total	*Energy*	*Interest payments*	*Other items*	*Growth*†	*Unemploy-ment*‡
	%	%	%	%	%	%
1970–73 ave.	−2.1	−2.7	−0.5	1.1	3.9	1.2
1974	−3.4	−5.7	−0.9	3.2	0.4	2.1
1975	−1.7	−4.9	−1.0	4.2	−1.5	5.1
1976	−5.4	−4.6	−1.0	0.2	7.5	5.3
1977	−4.4	−4.7	−1.3	1.6	2.3	6.4
1978	−3.1	−4.1	−1.8	2.8	1.8	7.3
1979	−5.2	−5.3	−2.3	2.4	3.4	6.1
1980	−4.4	−6.6	−3.2	5.4	0.8	6.9
1974–80 ave.	−3.9	−5.1	−1.6	2.8	2.1	5.4

* Percentage of GDP at factor cost
† GDP at constant prices
‡ Percentage of total labour force

The balance of payments effect of the oil price increase is illustrated in table 1, where the second column indicates that net imports of energy as a percentage of GDP rose by no less than 3 per cent in 1974 compared with the 1970–73 average. As also indicated in table 1, the Danish economy was not in external equilibrium before the oil shock, as witnessed by an average current account deficit of 2.1 per cent of GDP in 1970–73. In fact, the current account had been in deficit for most of the preceding decade as well.

As in other countries, the real income loss resulting from the oil price increase had a strongly depressive effect on the economy, and as unemployment rose to a level unseen in the preceding 15 years, a precautionary increase in household saving reinforced the contractionary effects. Thus the spontaneous reaction of the economy resulted in an improvement in the non-energy trade balance in 1974 and 1975 offsetting the larger oil bill.

Against this background it was felt that some fiscal and monetary stimulus to the economy could be afforded all the more since such a strategy was recommended internationally.

One interesting element of the fiscal stimulus applied was a temporary reduction of the VAT of 5¾ percentage points from October 1975 to March 1976. This measure proved to be very effective in stimulating household demand in that period, particularly for household durables.[2] A large part of the additional demand was however satisfied by foreign suppliers, who could increase their previous substantial market share. The incentive to Danish producers to step up production was limited by the temporary nature of the tax reduction.

As the fiscal stimulus was almost fully financed by government borrowing from the banking system, private sector liquidity increased and interest rates fell.

With the benefit of hindsight, it is fairly clear that this policy was overdone and caused a delay in the more fundamental adjustment to the oil price increase as the current account deteriorated sharply in 1976. It appears that some of the decline in domestic demand in 1975 had been due to a temporary 'scare' effect, which gradually wore off. Furthermore, some other industrialized countries seemed to be less faithful in following the recommendation to expand demand, and this of course reinforced the adverse effects on the Danish balance of payments. Finally, as discussed below in greater detail, the competitive position of Danish industry deteriorated somewhat as a result of both exchange rate and wage movements.

The expansionary economic policy had to be given up in the autumn of 1976 when fiscal as well as monetary policy was tightened. In the following years monetary policy was kept fairly tight and indirect taxation was raised several times. The effect on the budget balance was partly offset, however, by increased outlays for unemployment benefits, etc.

These policies, together with the moderate decline in relative oil prices, resulted in a 40 per cent reduction of the current account deficit (measured against GDP) from 1976 to 1978, despite an increase in net interest payments on accumulated foreign borrowing (table 1).

When the second oil price increase hit the industrialized countries in 1979–80, the stance of fiscal and monetary policy was basically unchanged, in marked contrast to the reaction in 1975, although the general decline in economic activity has led to a sharp increase in the budget deficit through the 'built-in stabilizers'.

Given the size of the current account deficit and the temporary nature of the spontaneous improvement in 1975, high priority had to be given to a sustained improvement even at the risk of a further increase in unemployment. In fact, the initial spontaneous improvement of the non-oil trade balance was very similar to the reaction in 1975 (table 1).[3]

It remains to be seen what part of this spontaneous improvement can be maintained if any discretionary easing of fiscal and monetary policy is avoided. The other uncertainty facing economic policy-makers is the trend in economic activity among our principal trading partners. These two factors will determine whether a sustained improvement of the balance of payments is compatible with a gradual reduction in unemployment.

Exchange rate policies

Since the breakdown of the gold/dollar-centred exchange rate regime in 1971–73, stability of exchange rates in terms of the currencies of our principal trading partners has been a main objective.

The principal advantages expected from this policy are a favourable environment for mutual trade and a contribution to domestic price stability; and, after joining the EEC, an important consideration has been the need for reasonably stable exchange rates under the Common Agricultural Policy (CAP).

Denmark was therefore in the first group of non-EEC members that joined the 'Snake' arrangement in May 1972 and was one of the small group of countries remaining when that arrangement was replaced by the EMS on 13 March 1979.[4]

In fact, the krone–Deutschmark rate was unchanged for three years following the abolition of intervention limits in terms of the dollar in March 1973 (the 'Snake' leaving the 'tunnel') and the revaluation of the Deutschmark in terms of the other 'Snake' currencies in September.

This stability in terms of the Deutschmark did however imply a rise in the effective exchange rate of the krone (table 2, last column), as the (remaining) 'Snake' currencies moved up against other currencies, in particular US dollars and sterling. This led to some loss of competitiveness and may have contributed to the delay in effective adjustment to the first oil price increase referred to in the previous section.

During 1976 the krone came under pressure as the current account moved into substantial deficit, given a large overhang of liquidity in the private sector. This was reinforced by some general tension within the 'Snake' as the market expected a revaluation of the Deutschmark. Following rather heavy intervention over some months, a realignment was undertaken in October on German initiative. The adjustment involved a 6 per cent rise in intervention limits for the

Table 2 Balance of payments and effective exchange rate (billion kroner)

		External net borrowing				*Effective exchange rate index, end of year*
	Current account	*Public sector*	*Private sector**	*Total*	*Increase in reserves*	*(end 1971 = 100†)*
1970	−4.1	0.6	3.5	4.1	0.0	–
1971	−3.2	2.1	1.9	4.0	0.8	100
1972	−0.5	1.5	0.2	1.7	1.2	103
1973	−2.9	0.4	4.5	4.9	2.0	105
1974	−5.8	0.6	4.4	5.0	−0.8	108
1975	−3.2	0.3	0.9	1.2	−2.0	108
1976	−12.0	10.1	2.2	12.3	0.3	115
1977	−10.7	8.6	7.9	16.5	5.8	111
1978	−8.3	7.4	6.4	13.8	5.5	115
1979	−15.4	4.9	11.0	15.9	0.5	106
1980	−13.8	9.5	2.3	11.8	−2.0	99

* Including direct investment and errors and omissions
† Calculated by Danmarks Nationalbank

Deutschmark in terms of the krone. Smaller adjustments were made with respect to the other 'Snake' currencies.

This adjustment was followed by similar realignments in following years. The result in terms of the effective exchange rate of the krone was sometimes reinforced and sometimes weakened by the movements of the 'Snake' against the dollar, but there was no further systematic increase in the effective rate.

This policy was taken a step further in the autumn of 1979 when two adjustments were undertaken lowering the effective exchange rate by about 8 per cent. This decline was reinforced by the rise of the dollar, yen and sterling against the EMS currencies participating in the narrow margins arrangement.

Although single adjustments of 'Snake'/EMS intervention limits never exceeded 6 per cent, their cumulative effect has been quite substantial, as illustrated by a 25 per cent depreciation of the krone in terms of the Deutschmark from 1976 to 1979.

The effect on competitive positions is brought out quite dramatically by a comparison of exchange rate-adjusted wage increases in two periods (table 3). It must be emphasized, of course, that comparisons with other EMS currencies would give much less dramatic results, as changes in the Deutschmark–krone rate reflect the combined effect of revaluations of the strongest currency and depreciation

Table 3 Danish and German wage increases, 1973–76 and 1976–80 (exchange rate-adjusted)

	Increase in Danish industrial earnings	*Increase in Danish industrial earnings (expressed in DM at current rates)*	*Increase in German industrial earnings*
	%	%	%
1973–76	59	51	26
1976–80	50	16	26
1973–80	138	75	60

of one of the weaker currencies in terms of a common denominator such as the ECU.

Throughout the period considered here, a large unilateral (strategic) adjustment of the krone has been rejected by the authorities as an element of balance of payments adjustment on the grounds that any competitive advantage would be quite temporary and would quickly be offset by an acceleration in domestic prices and costs. The widespread indexation of wages on the cost of living is an important factor in this mechanism. The two adjustments within a fairly short time in September and December 1979 do not represent a departure from this policy, and it is significant that the 5 per cent unilateral devaluation in December was accompanied by a cancellation of the devaluation effect on the wage escalator together with a removal of energy prices from the wage escalator index. For this and other reasons, the devaluation in the autumn of 1979 does seem to have permitted a more lasting improvement of the competitive position of Danish industry. However, such a combined effort can be successfully pursued only when a certain number of political–psychological conditions are met.

One important aspect of making necessary adjustments in small steps at infrequent intervals is the limitation of profits that can be made by anticipating such changes. In fact, a change in intervention limits will often be offset in the short run by movements within the limits. This was particularly true of the adjustment in October 1976, when the krone was at the bottom of the 'Snake' just before the adjustment but moved to the top just after because of a reflow of foreign exchange. Although the adjustment of intervention limits in terms of the Deutschmark was fairly substantial (6 per cent), the market rates for the Deutschmark were practically unchanged. In addition to the satisfaction of limiting speculative profits, this technique should reduce future speculative movements as market participants realize that even correctly anticipated parity changes do not guarantee short-term exchange rate gains of any importance.

In addition to exchange rate movements within the 'Snake'/EMS, fluctuations of this group of currencies *vis à vis* the dollar have also occasionally affected short-term capital movements. In particular, a low exchange rate for the dollar has induced companies to accelerate payment of their dollar liabilities, thus exerting some pressure on the krone. This inconvenience of the exchange rate linkage is however to a large extent offset by access to the associated short-term credit arrangements, as the outflows – mainly representing swings in leads and lags – have often been reversed prior to the settlement of drawings under the credit arrangements.

Financing of current deficits

Abstracting from the above-mentioned drawings on the short-term credit arrangements, Denmark has relied entirely on borrowing in private capital markets to finance the current account deficit. Borrowing abroad has been undertaken both by companies and the public sector, primarily the central government (table 4).

There are several reasons for this combination of private and public sector borrowing. In the 1960s and early 1970s access to foreign borrowing was considered a privilege for industry when high credit demands from the housing sector (which could not borrow abroad) exerted upward pressure on domestic interest rates. On the

Table 4 External debt of central government by currency and instrument

	Total debt (billion kroner)	*Denomination*					*of which: Variable rate loans*
		$	*DM*	*S.fr.*	*Other*	*Total*	
		%	%	%	%	%	%
end							
March 1975	7.2	46	27	5	22	100	27
March 1976	10.4	41	32	9	18	100	29
March 1977	19.0	50	30	8	12	100	41
March 1978	27.0	43	36	9	12	100	41
Dec. 1978	29.1	40	36	11	13	100	42
Dec. 1979	35.7	36	40	11	13	100	39
Dec. 1980	45.7	44	28	12	16	100	39

other hand, private net borrowing could be quite volatile and some public sector borrowing was necessary to compensate for this.

More recently, some industrial circles have argued that borrowing abroad is a burden on industry given the fairly high domestic interest rates necessary to encourage such borrowing and the exchange risk involved. Borrowing for balance of payments purposes should be undertaken by the government alone, as this would permit greater autonomy in domestic credit and interest rate policies. In this connection it should be kept in mind that even quite small companies have availed themselves of the possibility of borrowing abroad often against the guarantee of a Danish bank but with the borrower carrying the exchange risk.

Although some lowering of interest rates would be desirable, the room for manoeuvre in this respect is quite limited even if it were accepted to cover all of the current deficit by public sector borrowing. There must be an incentive to renew the outstanding private debt, which - given its size - cannot be taken over by the central government or other public sector borrowers.

The balance of payments purpose of government borrowing abroad is underlined by an arrangement with the central bank to deposit the proceeds of such borrowing in a special 'Consolidation Account' with the bank. Foreign borrowing therefore does not represent 'monetary financing' of the government's domestic expenditure.

Practically all of the borrowing abroad, public as well as private, is denominated in foreign currency. A precise breakdown of external borrowing by currency and instruments is available only for central government borrowing (table 4). Loans with a variable rate of interest (about 40 per cent) probably represent Eurocurrency borrowing in a narrow sense.

Concluding remarks

In a formal sense, the question of whether borrowing in Euromarkets has allowed Denmark to be less severely affected by the world recession can be answered in the affirmative. If this opportunity had not been available a more restrictive domestic policy would have been required. Nevertheless, domestic economic policies have in fact been quite restrictive, particularly since 1976–77, and a considerable amount of real adjustment has been achieved at the price of a sharp increase in unemployment. The explanation of this apparent paradox is the lack of external balance *before* the oil shock.

It could therefore be argued that the facilities offered by international capital markets have been a mixed blessing, in the sense that they permitted Denmark to run fairly persistent current account deficits in the period before the oil crises when more energetic domestic demand management would have been appropriate. The further deterioration caused by the two oil price increases could therefore be offset by additional borrowing for a short period only, and had instead to be compensated by a fairly prompt improvement of the non-oil trade balance.

In retrospect, it also appears that, even after the first oil price increase, fiscal and monetary as well as exchange rate policies were too ambitious and were geared mainly to the stabilization of domestic economic activity and prices at the cost of delaying the necessary external adjustment.

Notes

1 In 1980 North Sea oil production was equivalent to about 2% of total energy requirements, but this is expected to be 20–25% in 1985 (oil *and* gas production).

2 The reduction did not apply to purchases of private cars.

3 In 1975 the maximum effect on growth and non-oil trade probably coincided with the calendar year, whereas the effects of the second oil price hike are likely to culminate in the 12-month period from mid-1980 to mid-1981 and will therefore not be fully reflected in the calendar year figures in table 1.

4 The intervention *obligation* was suspended for a few months in the summer of 1972 but margins were in *fact* observed also in that period.

The Netherlands: Financial-Economic Adjustment Policies in the 1970s

GODERT POSTHUMUS
Ministry of Finance, The Hague

Introduction

This paper attempts to provide an analysis of financial–economic policy in the Netherlands during the period between the two oil shocks (1973–74 and 1979–80) with particular attention to adjustment and exchange rate policies.

In order to understand this policy, a few particular factors and developments have to be taken into consideration. In the first place, at the end of the 1960s and during the greater part of the 1970s, labour income grew faster than labour productivity. For this reason, the profits and competitive position of Dutch trade and industry gradually weakened. After 1978, however, there was a gradual change for the better in this position owing to limited wage increases, which were partly enforced by legal measures.

Second, particularly during the 1970s, the public sector grew very rapidly owing to the strong increase of income transfers (expansion and improvement of the social security system, increase of the number of people eligible for social security benefits). This development, coupled with the lower wage increases, led to a continuing increase in the share of consumption, and a continuing decrease in the share of investments, in national expenditure. As a percentage of national income, national savings decreased from 20 per cent at the beginning of the 1970s to 13 per cent at the end of the decade.

Third, the discovery of considerable natural gas reserves and their use for domestic consumption and production as well as for export have proved to be of great importance. An increase of the oil price itself, for the Netherlands as well as for other countries, means a decrease in the terms of trade and, consequently, in income: this loss becomes apparent in the 'non-gas sector'. The natural gas sector, however, profits very much from the increase of the oil prices, since gas prices are linked to oil prices. And it is mainly the public sector that profits from the increase in the terms of trade caused by increasing gas export prices.

The Netherlands entered the period of the first oil shock (1973–74) with a considerable surplus on the current account of the balance of payments. Gas price increases together with rising natural gas exports contributed to maintaining this surplus position. Nevertheless, the shock of the oil price increase was quite severe for the Dutch non-gas sector, and unemployment rates soared. The room for manoeuvre at the outset offered by the balance of payments surplus and the small budget deficit was used for a stimulating policy.

Since 1976, however, the current account of the balance of payments has been deteriorating rapidly. The structural problems of the non-gas sector, mentioned above, started to show more distinctly. A policy, focused on reducing collective expenditure and making room for the private sector (and within that sector for profits), began to take shape.

In the following sections a short analysis is given of the structural weaknesses of the economy, especially of the profit and competitive position, after which the importance of natural gas is illustrated. Then, with 1977 as a turning point between two periods (in that year the balance of payments turned negative), an insight is given into the fiscal, monetary and balance of payments policies conducted during these respective periods.

Many aspects of the development of the Dutch economy in the 1970s are not covered below. Table 1 gives an overview of this development. The most striking figures relate to unemployment, which shows strong increases after both oil price shocks and which is perhaps the clearest indication of the structural adjustment problems that the Netherlands faced and has not yet solved.

Structural developments in the Dutch economy

In the 1970s the Dutch economy was subject to considerable changes which highly determined and influenced the adjustment policy necessary to absorb the increase of the oil price in 1974–75 and 1979–80.

The following sections describe developments in the non-gas and gas sectors of the economy. It will become apparent that the distinction between the sectors is more a theoretical construction than an

Table 1 The Dutch economy, 1970–80: macroeconomic data

	1970	*1971*	*1972*	*1973*	*1974*	*1975*	*1976*	*1977*	*1978*	*1979*	*1980*
Percentage changes (annual)											
Volume of private consumption	7.7	3.0	3.2	3.9	2.7	3.4	5.7	4.9	3.7	2.2	−0.5
Volume of private investments	15.7	0.8	−8.9	10.7	−0.3	−7.5	−6.2	18.2	6.2	3.8	−2.0
Volume of exports	14.4	11.0	12.8	14.0	2.9	−4.6	11.4	−1.7	3.0	10	0
Labour productivity	6.2	4.2	5.0	6.5	4.0	0.6	6.3	3.1	2.6	1.5	0.5
Terms of trade	−2.8	−1.9	1.5	−1.0	−4.9	0.6	−0.1	0.2	0.3	−2.0	−1.5
Real private income (average)	8.5	2.0	2.9	0.9	2.7	3.8	1.3	2.6	2.9	2.0	−1.0
Real national income	6.0	3.3	4.7	5.9	0	−2.1	5.9	2.9	2.2	0.5	0
Absolute figures											
Unemployment ('000)	44	62	108	110	135	195	211	207	206	210	247
Absolute figures as % of national income											
Savings	19.9	19.7	20.2	21.9	20.5	15.1	15.9	14.6	13.4	12.2	12.1
Taxes	28.4	29.5	30.4	29.8	30.4	30.8	30.8	31.4	31.9	32.9	33.2
Social premiums	15.9	16.8	16.9	18.3	19.4	20.4	19.7	19.8	20.1	20.8	21.2

economic subdivision that can be quantified. In the present study the distinction is made primarily to assist the reader in getting an insight into the Dutch economy. It should also be remembered that the Dutch economy is strongly interwoven with the international economy: more than half of the national income is earned in export production.

Development of the non-natural gas sector

The process of gradual deterioration in the profitability of industry had already started in the middle of the 1960s, and concerned especially those firms that could be described as belonging to the non-gas sector of the economy.

The fact that the real increase in wages per labourer almost continuously exceeded the increase in productivity particularly contributed to this phenomenon. The wage increases, in turn, were caused mainly by the fact that the increase of taxes and social security contributions on individuals had become unacceptable, and as much as possible had to be compensated by even higher wage increases. In this way a large share of the collective tax burden was shifted on to trade and industry, where the profit position gradually deteriorated. This situation was seriously aggravated in 1974–75, when the considerable loss in terms of trade of 1974, owing to the first oil crisis, was also shifted on to trade and industry via wage indexation. Consequently, in the middle of the 1970s the profit position of the non-gas sector had shrunk to a dangerous minimum.

As illustration it may be pointed out that, between 1965 and 1973, the cumulated real increase of labour costs was 7½ per cent higher than the increase in labour productivity in the non-gas sector. In 1974 and 1975 the cumulated increase in real labour costs per worker was once again 7½ per cent more than labour productivity. As a result, the earned income ratio[1] in the non-gas sector increased from 77.3 per cent in 1965 to 85.0 per cent in 1973 and 93.9 per cent in 1975. In the following years this ratio hardly decreased. Influenced by the second oil shock and the recession that followed, it increased again (to an estimated 95.5 per cent) in 1980.

An indication of the weakening of the competitive position of the Dutch economy caused by this development is given by the development of labour cost per unit of product in the processing industry compared with that abroad, taking exchange rate changes into account (table 2). The competitive position thus calculated deteriorated during the years 1972–74 by approximately 10 per cent on

Table 2 Competitive position, 1970–80
(labour cost per unit of product)

	Nominal effective exchange rate	*Real effective exchange rate*
1970	100	100
1971	100.15	99.53
1972	101.65	101.47
1973	104.6	106.55
1974	109.4	108.49
1975	111.65	107.39
1976	114.2	105.26
1977	119.0	109.03
1978	121.3	107.97
1979	122.4	104.84
1980	122.5	100.44

aggregate. The years 1975 and 1976 showed a slight improvement, of approximately 2 per cent, but 1977 showed a deterioration of 3–4 per cent again. In particular, the shifting on to trade and industry of both the increase in the collective burden and the considerable loss in terms of trade that took place in 1974 contributed to this development – so unfavourable for the Dutch economy – in relative labour costs.

During the first half of the 1970s Dutch industry could still compete internationally, by not passing on the excessive increase in labour costs to export prices, but instead charging them to profit margins. The continued increase in export prices, however, caused such a serious profit erosion in 1974–75 that this was no longer possible. Dutch export prices in 1976 and especially 1977 increased by 3–4 per cent more than competitors' export prices (measured in guldens) and corrected for the specific composition of the export package). Consequently, export markets were lost during 1977 and 1978.

The natural gas sector: the Netherlands as a semi-OPEC country

In the course of the 1960s, when the exploitation of natural gas in the Netherlands started, no worldwide energy shortage was envisaged, and the world energy price in real terms showed a decline. Furthermore, the development of nuclear energy as a source of power in the near future was being taken into account. Under these circumstances the energy policy of the Netherlands aimed at a rapid exploitation of the natural gas reserves for domestic use as well as exports.

The quadrupling of the oil prices in 1973, and the realization both that the era of cheap oil had come to an end and that the development of nuclear energy was costly and controversial, led to a radical change in the energy policy. It was decided that after 1976 exports of natural gas would not be increased, and that they would be reduced during the 1980s. The internal as well as the export price of natural gas was brought into line with the increased oil price, although not entirely and with a time lag. Smaller discoveries of natural gas were exploited and imports of natural gas (especially from Norway) increased. The amount of natural gas used to generate electricity was gradually replaced by oil or coal. These and other measures to preserve the national natural gas reserves as much as possible were aimed at continuing their exploitation in the coming decades for specific purposes such as domestic heating.

Before 1970 the effect of the natural gas exploitation on the balance of payments was unimportant. This changed in the 1970s, when both export volume of natural gas and its price increased. The direct contribution of natural gas to the current account of the balance of payments (i.e., exports of natural gas and substitution of energy imports) increased from 1½ per cent of national income in 1970 to approximately 7¾ per cent (over 22 billion guldens) in 1980. The net contribution, however, is considerably less, since the exploitation of natural gas has led to a higher level of domestic expenditure and consequently to higher imports.

All this means that the underlying unfavourable trend in the balance of trade transactions during the second half of the 1970s was partly disguised by the exploitation of natural gas – a phenomenon that must continuously be taken into consideration when looking at the Dutch balance of payments.

The energy account of the balance of payments, which in 1977 and 1978 was by and large in equilibrium, subsequently showed increasing deficits owing to increased domestic consumption of oil, oil products and imported natural gas as well as to the further increase in oil prices. For the medium and longer term it is expected that the deficit will increase further (1985: −10 billion guldens; 1990: −30 billion guldens), especially because of the policy directed at preserving the domestic natural gas reserves. It is expected that the import of energy will increase, and the volumes of natural gas exports will decrease.

Before 1970, the direct effect of the exploitation of natural gas on government income – as for the balance of payments – was rather small. In 1970 the share of the receipts – on natural gas – (in the form of company tax, royalties, etc.) out of both domestic and foreign sales amounted to only about 2 per cent of total budget receipts. The increase in sales volume of natural gas and the linking of the natural gas price to the increased oil price since 1973 considerably increased this share: i.e., to an estimated 14½ per cent in 1981. This proportion will possibly increase further in the near future, owing to the favourable results of the recent negotiations on the revision of (gas) export contracts. Over a longer period, however, these receipts will diminish in accordance with the expected reduction of natural gas sales.

The increase in government income in the 1970s from gas exploitation facilitated the financing of the public sector. To this may be added the effects of a fiscal policy that was expansive up to 1976. All this led to an accelerated increase in the share of the public sector in national income. This share increased from 48.2 per cent in 1970 to 65.4 per cent in 1980. During this period the proportion of the transfers of income via the public sector rose from 21.3 per cent of national income to 35.6 per cent.

The current account of the balance of payments in the 1970s

During the years 1972–76 the current account of the balance of payments registered large surpluses averaging 3½ per cent of national income. However, in 1978 the current account registered a deficit that, according to the latest data in 1980, increased to 1½–2 per cent of national income.

In this section we shall analyse the account of trade and invisibles with foreign countries. As will be apparent from table 3, both have contributed to the deterioration of the current account of the balance of payments. The analysis shows a structural deterioration, which continued throughout the 1970s. In 1977–78 this deterioration, which of course must be seen in relationship with the structural developments described above, got the upper hand over the positive effects of the gas export proceeds. This had important consequences: the turning point in 1977 can be seen as a watershed between financial–economic policies followed before and after that year. It is for this reason that the development of the current account over the whole period is analysed here in some detail.

Table 3 Balance of the current account of the balance of payments (percentage of net national income at market prices)

	Balance of trade (f.o.b.)	*Balance of in-visibles*	*of which:* *Trans-port*	*Travel*	*Invest-ment income*	*Other*	*Balance current account*	Pro memoria *direct contribution of natural gas* *
	%	%	%	%	%	%	%	%
Average								
1960-64	−3.5	4.6	2.6	0.2	1.2	0.6	1.1	—
1965-69	−2.6	2.5	2.0	−0.4	1.0	−0.1	−0.1	0.6
1970-74	−0.2	2.0	1.9	−0.5	0.6	0.0	1.8	2.6
1975-79	0.0	0.9	2.0	−1.4	0.0	0.3	0.9	5.8
1972	1.0	2.2	1.9	−0.3	0.5	0.1	3.2	2
1973	1.8	2.5	1.7	−0.4	0.8	0.4	4.3	$2\frac{1}{2}$
1974	0.9	2.5	2.3	−0.5	0.8	−0.1	3.4	5
1975	1.2	1.5	2.4	−0.7	−0.1	−0.1	2.7	$5\frac{1}{2}$
1976	1.6	1.9	2.2	−1.1	0.3	0.5	3.5	6
1977	−0.2	1.1	2.0	−1.4	0.2	0.3	0.9	6
1978	−1.2	0.3	1.6	−1.8	−0.1	0.6	−0.9	$5\frac{1}{4}$
1979	−1.1	−0.3	1.6	−1.9	−0.2	0.2	−1.4	$6\frac{1}{4}$
1979(IV)-1980(III)	−1.2	−0.8	1.7	−2.1	−0.2	−0.2	−2.0	$7\frac{3}{4}$†

* The direct contribution of natural gas comprises the total effect of natural gas exports and the import substitution of raw materials for energy products.
† Estimate.
Source: The Netherlands Bank (data on natural gas: Central Planning Bureau)

Balance of trade

During the second half of the 1970s the Netherlands were, by volume, a net exporter of energy. Up to now, therefore, the direct adverse effect of the oil price increases on the balance of the current account has been rather modest, even though adjustment of the export prices of natural gas to increases in the oil prices has been incomplete and has taken place with a time lag. However, increases of the oil prices also influenced the trade balance in an indirect way. As shown in table 4, the composition of the Dutch export package is relatively energy-intensive. In 1979 exports of energy and chemical products (SITC sections 3 and 5) accounted for $35\frac{1}{2}$ per cent of Dutch exports (exclusive of natural gas: $29\frac{1}{2}$ per cent), while for the four major EEC countries this share amounted to 17 per cent. After the first oil crisis, worldwide demand for energy-intensive products had been lagging behind average demand development. This also had a relatively unfavourable effect on the Netherlands' export performance, and gives at least a partial explanation for the fact that during the years 1974–78 the development of Dutch exports was over 13 per cent lower than the growth of world trade reweighted geographically for the Netherlands.

From table 4 it is clear that, besides energy-intensive products, agricultural and food products are also relatively well represented in the Dutch export package. The share of industrial products, especially machines and transport equipment, is on the other hand relatively unimportant.

If world trade is reweighted not only geographically but also for the specific composition of the Dutch export package, there still results a considerable loss on foreign markets that cannot be explained by the composition of the export package. During the years 1974–78 growth of Dutch exports lagged about 7 per cent behind the growth of world trade (weighted both geographically and for the composition

Table 4 Composition of Dutch exports in 1979, classified by sections of the Standard International Trade Classification (SITC)

SITC section	*Netherlands*	*Four major EEC countries*	*Germany*	*France*	*UK*	*Italy*
0 Food and live animals chiefly for food	18.0	6.0	4.0	11.4	4.1	5.6
1 Beverages and tobacco	1.5	1.8	0.5	2.9	2.8	1.8
2 Crude materials (inedible) except fuels	5.4	2.6	2.1	3.9	2.8	1.6
3 Mineral fuels, lubricants and related materials (34 – natural and manufactured gas)	19.1 (6.1)	5.4 (0.2)	3.4 (0.1)	3.7 (0.7)	10.1 (0.2)	6.5 (0.1)
4 Animal and vegetable oils, fats and waxes	1.1	0.4	0.5	0.4	0.2	0.2
5 Chemicals and related products	16.3	11.6	13.1	11.9	11.5	7.9
6 Manufactured goods classified chiefly by material	14.5	21.3	20.4	20.7	22.2	23.2
7 Machinery and transport equipment	17.6	38.2	44.9	35.8	34.7	30.0
8 Miscellaneous manufactured articles	6.1	11.4	9.3	8.9	9.3	22.1
9 Commodities and transactions not classified elsewhere	0.4	1.3	1.8	0.4	2.3	1.1
Total	100	100	100	100	100	100

Source: OECD, *Statistics of Foreign Trade*

of the Dutch exports). The loss of ground became entirely manifest during the years 1977 and 1978, the same years in which the deficit on the trade balance seriously deteriorated. This development cannot be separated from the weakening of the competitive position of Dutch trade and industry that took place during the 1970s. It is for this reason that the development of the deficit on the trade balance is actually less favourable than appears from table 3. For, as already pointed out above, the underlying trend is being disguised by the contribution of natural gas, which greatly increased in the course of the 1970s.

Balance of invisible transactions

Table 3 shows that the deterioration of the current account of the balance of payments after 1976 resulted not only from an unfavourable turn of the trade balance, but also from a decline in invisible transactions. The latter decline is part of a deteriorating trend in the invisible transactions balance that has been apparent since the early part of the 1950s. Apart from the transport surplus that declined in the second part of the last decade, two developments strike the eye: the rising deficit on the travel balance, and the unfavourable development in the balance on investment income.

As to the travel balance, receipts have been stable in nominal terms since 1973, and consequently declined in real terms (in 1980, for the first time since 1973, a nominal and even a slight real increase of these receipts could be detected). This stagnation of receipts probably results partly from too strong a wage and price increase in the tourist sector. In the same period travel expenditures continued to grow steadily. The declining surplus of the balance on investment income is a result of a number of factors. Direct foreign investment in the Netherlands has been lagging behind Dutch investment abroad since 1973. If the total corresponding investment income would have been repatriated, one would have expected a positive development in the balance of investment income, but the opposite has been the case. First, and most important, this stems from the fact that repatriation of this income has been minimal. Second, substantial foreign interest in Dutch securities arose during the years 1968–71 and after 1976, while Dutch interest in foreign securities declined in the second half of the 1970s. A third negative element for the balance on investment income has been the strong decline after 1976 of the net external position of the banking system. This resulted from the fact that current account deficits in these years were totally financed at the expense of the net external assets of the banking system, even turning it into a net external liability position in 1979.

It goes without saying that the developments mentioned in this section greatly influenced the policies of adjustment to the oil shocks in the 1970s. These policies will be described in the following two sections, in which we discuss first the period with large surpluses on the current account of the balance of payments, and then the period with large deficits.

The period 1973–76

Fiscal and income policy

The period of persistent excess expenditure during 1964–71 came to an end in 1972, mainly as a result of a sharp decrease in the volume of private investment.

The current account of the balance of payments developed a surplus in 1972, which it maintained through 1977. Under these circumstances it was possible for policy to be directed towards stimulating expenditure and fighting unemployment in order partly to compensate for the recessive consequences of the 1973 oil price rise.

The first stimulation measures date back to 1974. They were followed rather quickly by a series of programmes to stimulate business activities and employment. The composition of the programmes differed but in all cases they included an employment programme, involving the stimulation of the construction industry, reorganization of threatened branches of industry and support to individual companies. Other elements were a tax reduction for families (especially to maintain the purchasing power of lower-income groups) and for companies (among others in the form of an increase of fiscal investment facilities) and government contributions to the social funds in order to limit the increase of social security premiums (necessary to cover these social funds' costs).

The effects of these policy measures were increased by endogenous factors. Wages in the public and semi-public sector increased owing to their being linked to contractual wages in the private sector, which strongly increased during these years. Moreover, other factors played a role, including increasing unemployment payments and payments on account of other social facilities. Because fiscal policy was directed at compensating for the deflationary consequences of the higher oil prices, the share of expenditure of the public sector in national income increased from over 51 per cent in 1972 to nearly 60 per cent in 1976. The major part of this increase (nearly $6\frac{1}{2}$ percentage points) was accounted for by income transfers. The expansion of expenditure was financed partly out of extra natural gas proceeds; however, it also resulted in an increase in the net borrowing requirement of the total government (on cash basis), which increased from 2 to over 5 per cent of national income during the period 1972–76.

After 1972 the growth of national expenditure lagged behind that of the real national product for a number of years. But this was not accompanied by a reduction of the high rate of inflation. The fight against the autonomous process of price and cost inflation was hampered by external inflationary impulses and also, since 1974, by private consumption. Therefore in 1974 policy was directed at keeping the increase in nominal incomes as limited as possible. After the social partners had failed to come to an agreement in 1974, the government took legal measures to fix an increase of wages with an equal amount for every worker.

Although these measures allowed for some improvement for the lower-income groups, there was almost no room for an increase of real wages. As a result, a large part of the loss in terms of trade caused by the increase of oil prices was shifted on to the higher-income groups and especially to company profits.

After the social partners failed to reach a mutual agreement for 1975, wage discussions were held in 1975 at the branch levels of industry and companies. These negotiations resulted in an improvement of the real purchasing power of the average worker of 2.5 per cent, which was accepted owing to the weak economic situation.

After the negotiations between the government and the social partners for a mutual agreement for 1976 failed as well, the government decided to freeze the existing wages for six months. The restriction of wage growth was intended to improve the profitability of trade and industry and consequently to stimulate employment. Owing to the uncertainty about whether this objective would be achieved, the government also intervened in the formation of wages later in 1976.

Notwithstanding all these efforts to slow down the increase of the total wage sum, the wage policy conducted during the years following the first oil crisis resulted in an increase of real net disposable income per worker in the industry of 7.5 per cent (1973–76), compared with an increase of real national income of 3.9 per cent. This was one of the reasons why the earned income ratio in the non-gas sector increased from 85 per cent in 1973 to almost 94 per cent in 1976.

This development gives an indication of the decrease in the relative size of profit income during this period and illustrates that an important part of the loss in terms of trade during the years after the first oil crisis was borne by trade and industry.

Monetary and exchange rate policy

During 1973–76 the exchange rate policy was determined primarily by the participation in the European 'Snake', and the influence of the exploitation of natural gas on the Netherlands external position.

The Netherlands are an advocate of a system of stable exchange rates. Uncertainties and costs caused by fluctuating exchange rates are considered to impede the development of world trade, while a stabilization of the exchange rate level promotes a certain discipline in general economic policy. The aim of stabilizing the nominal effective exchange rate is also based on the fact that in a highly indexed open economy the exchange rate as an instrument of real adjustment is ineffective, because it produces, with a certain time lag, only nominal results. After termination of the Bretton Woods system, the European 'Snake' constituted for the Netherlands the best approach to the exchange rate objective.

During the period under review the Benelux countries, the Federal Republic of Germany, Denmark, Norway and Sweden participated in the 'Snake' arrangement. France withdrew in January 1974 and joined again in July 1975. Its participation this time lasted until March 1976. Because of this low-profile participation of France – after earlier withdrawal by the United Kingdom and Italy, the only large economy besides the Federal Republic of Germany – the 'Snake' during this period must be regarded as a D-mark bloc. Long-term developments of the 'Snake' were dominated by the Deutschmark in its role as currency of the largest and strongest economy.

For the Netherlands, the termination of the Bretton Woods system did not mean a transition to a floating exchange rate. The exchange rate policy of the gulden was now tuned to the development in the exchange of the Deutschmark, not to the US dollar any more. Thus, the Netherlands continued to have stable exchange rates with a group of countries to which about 55 per cent of Dutch exports is directed.

Because of the strength of the Deutschmark the 'Snake' appreciated *vis à vis* the US dollar by about 15 per cent from early 1974 to late 1976. The gulden followed this development without structural problems. The strong external position caused by the fact that oil price increases coincided with the maximum exploitation of natural gas reserves, and by an at first weak development of domestic expenditure, made this possible. Current account surpluses in 1974 and 1975 amounted to 4.5 and 5.2 billion guldens respectively. In 1976 the current account surplus even increased to a record high of 6.3 billion guldens. Domestic monetary development experienced the consequences of the strong external position. The large surpluses on current account led to a very large liquidity inflow from abroad, which was further increased by a very large surplus in the balance of direct investments.

In order to limit the liquidity creation from abroad and at the same time reduce the upward pressure of the gulden, the promotion of the export of long-term capital became an objective of financial policy. The aim was to bring the non-monetary sectors account – the combined account of current and long-term capital transactions – into balance (see table 5).

Except in 1975 – when an absolute low in the recession caused by the oil crisis was recorded – money creation by the banking sector after 1972 remained at a high level. Relatively low money market interest rates, required to limit the appreciation of the gulden, stimulated this money creation. Furthermore, the expansionary fiscal policies led, in 1975, to a considerable increase in the net borrowing requirement of the government. To an important extent this was financed from monetary sources, in order not to endanger the objective of promoting the export of long-term capital. However, the result was that the objective of capital export – to limit liquidity creation – was thwarted. Notwithstanding the fact that liquidity

Table 5 Some relevant monetary quantities, 1971–76

	1971	*1972*	*1973*	*1974*	*1975*	*1976*
(1) Domestic liquidity creation (% of M2)	1.5	10.1	10.3	9.8	3.6	19.7
of which: government	−1.0	−8.1	−2.9	−1.9	3.3	3.7
private sector	2.5	18.2	13.2	11.7	0.3	16.0
(2) Liquidity supply from abroad (% of M2)	6.9	7.7	4.7	5.8	5.9	0.8
Growth domestic liquidity (1) + (2) (%)	8.4	17.8	15.0	15.6	9.5	20.5
Nominal growth net national income (%)	12.0	13.3	15.1	12.8	8.5	15.5
Real growth net national income (%)	3.6	4.7	5.9	0	−2.1	5.9
Increase in price index private consumption (%)	8.3	8.8	9.3	10.1	10.7	8.8
Balance on current account (billion guldens)	−0.2	4.8	5.8	4.5	5.2	6.3
Short-term interest rate (yearly average)	5.3	3.0	7.3	10.5	5.3	7.1

Source: The Netherlands Bank (DNB); Central Planning Bureau (CPB)

growth continuously outstripped the growth of national income, the central bank hesitated to intervene in view of the weak business cycle. This attitude changed in 1976: in that year a boom in the housing market took place, caused by mounting inflation and still-unimpaired expectations of continuing real income increases, and fuelled by an excessive expansion of mortgage grants. Liquidity growth in 1976 surpassed the growth of nominal national income by more than 5 per cent. This prompted the central bank to re-introduce the direct credit ceiling which it had abolished in 1972.

In spite of the rather expansive monetary developments during the period 1974–76 as a whole, and in spite of the policy to promote the export of long-term capital, the balance of the non-monetary sectors in 1974 and 1975 showed surpluses of 2 billion guldens, surpluses that led to an increase in national reserves. Here we have come to exchange rate policy proper: by manipulation of the money market interest rate, it is possible in principle to determine whether a balance on account of the non-monetary sector leads to a mutation in the official reserves or in the net foreign asset position of the banking system.

In 1974 the surplus of the non-monetary sectors was fully reflected in the foreign reserve position. This was caused mainly by the fact that in this period of unrest large, expansionary currency market interventions had to be conducted, which could not be prevented by a decrease of the money market interest rate. On the other hand, in 1975, when the conditions on the foreign exchange market were more stable, an on-average lower short-term interest rate *vis à vis* other countries caused an important part of the surplus of non-monetary sectors to reinforce the net foreign asset position of the banking sector.

As regards the Netherlands interference with the Eurocurrency markets, it can be mentioned that during the period under review this country, on balance, constituted a source of short-term funds.

The period 1977–80

Fiscal and income policy

In the mid-1970s it became more and more apparent that the profit and competitive position of trade and industry had been badly affected, that the continuous increase of the collective burden had been shifted on by income earners to companies, and that full wage indexation caused the loss in terms of trade to be passed on to companies as well.

In 1976 the first attempts were being made to limit the expansive growth of government expenditure as well as to slow down the increase in labour costs. For this reason, the cabinet introduced a policy aimed at restricting the yearly growth of the collective sector to about 1 percentage point of national income. The idea behind this was to slow down the increase in real income, in order to prevent a further increase of unemployment and inflation. In order to continue to realize a certain improvement of real income of employees, it would be necessary to restrict growth of government expenditure and thus of taxes and social premiums. According to calculations made at that time, which were based on a growth of 3¾ per cent per annum, a reduction of the growth rate of the collective burden to 1 per cent per annum would require a reduction of the increase in expenditure in 1980 of a total of 7½ billion guldens. Moreover, a limitation of income growth in the private sector was considered to be inevitable, in the interest of a recovery of the profitability of industry.

In the meantime economic prospects, especially for the long term (and in connection with the slack development of the world business trend), had deteriorated. Against this background doubts began to arise about whether a restriction of the annual growth of the collective burden to 1 per cent would still be sufficient.

In view of the decrease in the growth of the economy, which was still estimated at 3 per cent per annum, the cabinet subsequently set itself the task of stabilizing the collective burden and thus bringing about a responsible division of growth between the collective sector and the private sector and, within the latter, between wage income and profits.

The objective of both policy programmes since 1976 was to create more employment, to combat inflation, and to safeguard the social security system. Efforts to limit the growth of the collective burden and, later, to stabilize it proved on balance, however, insufficient. Medium-term budgetary expenditure estimates were based on economic growth rates which proved to be too high. This hampered efforts to limit the growth of these expenditures. To nevertheless limit the growth of the collective burden, an increase in the net borrowing requirement of the public sector was initially accepted.

At the time of the execution of the 1979 budget, however, it turned out that without further provisions the estimated maximum net borrowing requirement still considered acceptable would be significantly exceeded. In order to counter this development, measures were taken in the spring of 1979 consisting of accelerated collection of taxes and a deferment of cash expenditure.

The new wave of increases in the oil price in 1979 and 1980 demonstrated the structural weaknesses of the economy even more clearly and complicated the policy aimed at structural adjustment. The starting points of the 1980 budget were to maintain the purchasing power of both lower incomes and social benefits as much as possible and to limit the development of the net public borrowing requirement. Since, quite soon after that, the economic and budgetary prospects deteriorated badly, a considerable policy adjustment had to be carried out in March 1980. The major elements of the adjustment consisted of a reduction of the 1980 budget by 3 billion guldens, and legal measures to limit the growth of wages.

This course was continued in the 1981 budget, in which the central objectives were both the reduction of the net borrowing requirement and a considerable moderation of individual income claims. In order to realize this, further budgetary cuts were carried through, among others in the sphere of social security and the remuneration of government employees, while some increase of the collective burden, especially in the form of an increase in social security contributions, was considered unavoidable.

From 1979, therefore, the size of the net borrowing requirement had become such a constraint that the objective of stabilizing the collective burden had to be subordinated to the control of the net borrowing requirement.

Like budgetary policy, income policy also was directed more and more towards limited growth after 1977. Initially (1978 and 1979) the policy objective was to maintain the purchasing power of the average employee and the lower-income groups. During the discussions on wage increases for 1980, however, the government took the line that the purchasing power of only the lower-income groups could be maintained. The deterioration of economic prospects, resulting mainly from oil price increases and leading to a further slowing down of economic growth and to large deficits on the balance of payments and government finance, urged a tighter grip on wage developments.

After a three-month wage freeze in early 1980, the government took legal measures in April of that year. With some exceptions, it contained a freeze of wages and labour conditions. Furthermore, the index-linked half yearly wage adjustment due on 1 July was replaced by a temporary monthly allowance of a fixed amount. To maintain the purchasing power of incomes at the minimum level, a differentiated tax relief was given as from 1 July. This wage measure, which lasted until the end of 1980, aimed at limiting the wage increase per employee to between $1\frac{1}{2}$ and $6–6\frac{1}{2}$ per cent.

The large increase of unemployment in 1980 and the threat of a further deterioration of the economy necessitated an even more substantial wage limitation for 1981. In the autumn of 1980 the government stressed the desirability of limiting the endogenous wage increase – forecast to be 8 per cent over 1981 – to about 6 per cent. Though the social partners agreed to this endeavour in principle, no consensus could be reached about the size and modalities of a wage limitation. Consequently, at the end of 1980 the government announced a wage measure intended to reduce the increase of the wage sum per employee from the estimated 8 to about 5 per cent in 1981. In order to limit the decrease in purchasing power, tax relief measures came in force as from 1 January 1981.

Thus, in the period 1977–81, fiscal policies were increasingly directed towards a limitation of the net borrowing requirement of the public sector. Incomes policies were aimed at controlling the increase of wage costs; the relatively slow increase of these costs compared with those of competitor countries has started gradually to improve the competitive position of Dutch trade and industry.

Monetary and exchange rate policy in 1977

As of 1977, monetary policy was determined to a large extent by the decision to introduce a system of direct credit control after the previous years of excessive growth of liquidity and balance of payments deficits.

In order to maintain a stable gulden and avoid a more or less permanent decrease in international reserves – i.e., the aggregate of official reserves and the net foreign asset position of the banking sector – the objective of the financial balance of payments policy was to ensure a balance on the account of the non-monetary sectors. With the aim of restoring this balance, the deficit on current account should lead to a contraction in domestic liquidity, which would imply the avoidance of compensating domestic liquidity creation. Both objectives are complementary: the desired level of capital import also depends on the realization of an adequate level of monetary contraction.

In 1977 the Nederlandsche Bank decided to impose a credit ceiling, under which a yearly growth norm for the so called 'net-monetary creation' was set. This implies an increase of M2, which equals the difference between the increase of long-term liabilities of the banks on the one hand and domestic credit on short and long term of the banks on the other.

Under this system of direct credit control, monetary expansion is not determined by means of money market instruments (although the situation on the money market does influence the expansion of credit). Money market instruments such as discount policy, open market policy, swap transactions, etc., can thus be used to safeguard the external value of the gulden. Because extension of credit to the private sector above a certain level is possible only on the basis of long-term funding, the burden of this direct system is passed primarily on to the capital market.

The practical execution of this policy was thwarted by a number of factors. First, by the end of 1976 liquidity in the economy was too high. The liquidity ratio was 39.5 per cent; in the early 1970s this ratio oscillated around 33. Consequently, even a considerable decrease of the ratio would not lead to an effective monetary contraction. Also, it appeared that as of 1979 the actual growth of national income was lower than the growth rate that had formed the base for calculating the acceptable level of domestic liquidity creation (see table 6). Finally, it should be mentioned that actual domestic liquidity creation in the years 1978–80 turned out to be considerably higher than was acceptable. This was caused by high public borrowing requirements, which had to be financed by monetary liquidity

Table 6 Domestic liquidity creation as percentage of national income growth, 1977–80

	1977	*1978*	*1979*	*1980*
	%	%	%	%
Domestic liquidity creation				
Planned	7	7	8	8
Actual	8.4	10.0	10.7	7.6
of which: government				
Planned	2.0*	2.0*	3.1	3.0
Actual	1.8	3.6	5.3	3.7
Actual growth net national income	8.9	7.2	5.6	5.8

* In 1977 and 1978 a target of liquidity creation of 1.9 billion guldens was set for government and the foreign sector together. While for 1977 some liquidity inflow from abroad was expected, for 1978 some drain was forecast

Source: Central Planning Bureau

creation (see table 6). This development was facilitated by the fact that government monetary financing is not covered by credit restriction. The banks were able to finance Treasury bills placed with them with short-term funds drawn from abroad (see table 7).

Thus, the intended monetary contraction did not materialize, and the balance of capital transactions of the non-monetary sectors did not contribute to the financing of the rising deficits on the current account (see table 8) until 1980. In fact, the balance on the non-monetary sectors' account of the balance of payments continued to deteriorate. The pressure on the exchange rate of the gulden, which itself stems from a deficit on current account, was then enlarged in 1978 and 1979 by deficits on the capital account. Consequently, the burden of maintaining the exchange rate of the gulden had to be carried by the money and exchange market policy.

Table 7 Some relevant monetary quantities, 1977-80

	1977	*1978*	*1979*	*1980*
(1) Domestic liquidity creation (% of M2)	8.4	10.0	10.7	7.7*
by: (a) government	1.8	3.6	5.1	3.7
(b) private sector	6.6	6.4	5.6	3.9*
(2) Liquidity inflow from abroad (% of M2)	−1.2	−4.7	−3.9	−4.9*
Increase in M2 (1b) + (2)	7.2	5.3	6.8	2.7
Nominal growth net national income (%)	8.9	7.2	5.6	5.8
Real growth net national income (%)	2.5	2.2	0.3	0.5
Increase in price index family consumption (%)	6.4	4.1	4.2	6.5
Balance on current account (billion guldens)	1.0	−2.7	−4.8	−6.5*
Short-term interest rate (yearly average)	4.9	6.7	9.5	10.5

* Provisional
Source: The Netherlands Bank (DNB); Central Planning Bureau (CPB)

Table 8 Non-monetary sector account, 1977-80 (cash basis, billion guldens)

	1977	*1978*	*1979*	*1980*
Current account	1.4	−2.5	−4.4	−6.0
Capital account non-monetary sector	−2.9	−2.1	−0.7	0.0
Total account non-monetary sector	−1.5	−4.6	−5.1	−6.0

Source: The Netherlands Bank (DNB)

As mentioned above, this policy in principle faced the choice of drawing down either the official reserves or the net foreign position of the banking sector with the deficit of the account of the non-monetary sectors. A decision was made in favour of the latter, because continuing and extensive supporting interventions directly undermine the confidence in maintaining the exchange rate in the framework of the EMS. It goes without saying that this consideration is more important the larger and the more persistent the balance of payments deficit is. After another substantial decrease of 2 billion guldens in the official reserve position in 1978, the policy was focused even more on financing the balance of payments deficit by the banking sector (table 9). The inverse interest rate structure that prevailed from the end of 1978 to mid-1980 can be ascribed to this policy.

Table 9 Balance of non-monetary sector of finance, 1977–80 (billion guldens)

	1977	*1978*	*1979*	*1980**
Balance non-monetary sectors	−1.5	−4.6	−5.1	−6.0
Mutation foreign position banking sector	−2.3	−2.6	−4.1	−7.5
Mutation official reserves	+0.7	−2.0	−0.8	+1.5

* Estimates
Source: The Netherlands Bank (DNB)

This development changed the net foreign asset position of the banking sector into a net liability position by the end of 1979. By the end of the third quarter of 1980 the position had almost reached the 6 billion gulden mark. Because foreign transactions of the banking sector are carried out mainly on the Eurocurrency market, this means that the Netherlands, after having played the role of net supplier to these markets until 1977, since that year has been a net user of funds from these markets.

Summary and concluding remarks.

Before the oil crisis of 1973–74 the Dutch economy could be characterized by three particular developments: the gradual weakening of the profit and competitive position of the non-gas sector; the rapid growth of the government sector; and the increasing influence of the exploitation of the natural gas reserves. On the basis of the preceding analysis, one can conclude that the first round of oil price increases had a catalytic impact on these three developments. The 'boom' of natural gas reserves, and especially the way in which they have been spent, seems to be of major importance for both other developments. At the same time, the gas revenues were very much responsible for developments in the external position of the Netherlands and consequently for the monetary and exchange rate policy.

When in 1974 the oil price shock caused a large decrease in national expenditure, the simultaneously increasing gas revenues enabled the Dutch government to opt for an expansive budget policy. The strength of the gas sector provided the means to meet the consequences of the oil price shock for the non-gas sector. This policy was further enhanced by endogenous factors, in particular by the enlarged use of the already extensive social security system, which had been built up and expanded during the 1960s and the early 1970s.

The gas revenues also contributed to a permanently high surplus on the current account of the balance of payments, which enlarged the scope for expansion. The use of gas revenues for collective and consumption purposes implied that the industries in the non-gas sector, whose position had gradually been deteriorating, had to put up with the full impact of the oil price increases without receiving sufficient compensation from profits resulting from higher gas prices. Higher energy prices turned out to be discounted in the wages through the existing indexation mechanisms. Also, real disposable income per capita increased considerably, in spite of the measures being taken in order to stop the upward trend in the wage–price spiral. Owing to this development, the loss in terms of trade was almost completely shifted on to the private business sector, and in a rather short time critical limits of the competitive position were reached. Thus, the substantial proceeds of the gas sector disguised to a large extent the deterioration of the position of the non-gas sector. The deterioration of the competitive position of the private sector is reflected in a considerable loss of ground on foreign markets and a strong worsening of the trade deficit.

A monetary development, which could be considered expansive too, ran parallel to the expansive budget policy after the first oil crisis. Initially, in view of the state of the business cycle, this was not considered incompatible with domestic economic development. By 1976 De Nederlandsche Bank decided to reduce the monetary expansion. In that year M2 soared, primarily as a result of the strong demand for mortgage credits. This demand was stimulated by increasing inflation and the prevailing expectations of a continuing rise in real income, expectations that were supported by the actual developments in income. At the same time, the government also contributed to the monetary expansion by partially monetary financing of the enlarged budget deficit. The appreciation of the gulden in the period 1974–76 could thus be limited to that of the European 'Snake' as a whole, in spite of a rather favourable external position during that time.

By the time that the consistency in the objectives of monetary and exchange rate policy threatened to be endangered, and De Nederlandsche Bank, late in 1976, decided to follow a more restrictive monetary policy, the current account moved into deficit and the upward pressure on the gulden came to an end.

The exchange rate policy conducted in this period led to a nominal effective appreciation in the years up to 1978. The question of whether the effective appreciation of the gulden in the 1970s has contributed to the weakening of the Dutch competitive position has quite often been the subject of discussion during the last few years. Over all, the appreciation of the gulden *vis-à-vis* foreign competitors over the last decade corresponded to the appreciation *vis-à-vis* foreign suppliers. In other words, at macroeconomic level at least, the appreciation loss on the export side was more or less compensated on the import side by an appreciation gain. The complete absorption of the appreciation gain at the import side takes some time, however. Apart from the direct benefit as a result of the mitigating effect of the appreciation on import prices, there is, though with a time lag, an absorption effect on domestic prices and wages. After a while lower import prices as well as domestic price and wage levels roughly offset the appreciation loss at the export side. However, one can conclude that the appreciation of the gulden has not played a significant role in the weakening of the Dutch competitive position in the 1970s. It is in fact more likely that the appreciation has contributed to a reasonable reduction of nominal developments that compared increasingly favourably with average inflation rates abroad.

The year 1977, when the current account surplus diminished strikingly and a period of deficits began, illustrates the fact that the adjustment process following the oil shock of 1973–74 did not work satisfactorily in every respect. On the contrary, the rate of growth of public sector expenditure had become very high, leading to an alarming development of the net borrowing requirement. Partial monetary financing of the budget deficit in a situation of a current account surplus, as in 1975 and 1976, was justified from the point of view of the exchange rate. In later years the external deficit made the situation completely different.

In these circumstances budget and income policy became increasingly directed towards a restriction of public sector expenditures and to a substantial moderation of individual income claims. Of course, monetary policy underwent a clear change too. Nevertheless, it is evident that in 1979 and 1980, when the room for manoeuvre had been narrowed, the current account of the balance of payments showed a large deficit and the public sector net borrowing requirement was too high. It proved very difficult to control domestic liquidity creation because disappointing budget deficits gave rise to substantial monetary financing.

Consequently, monetary policy contributed insufficiently to the redress of the current account. This was because of the system of credit restriction and the way in which the balance of payments deficit was financed. In the framework of the exchange rate policy, of which participation in the EMS arrangement is the nucleus, the authorities have chosen to finance the deficit of non-monetary sectors mainly via a build-up of liabilities in the external position of commercial banks. Thus the banks were able to finance their purchases of Treasury paper, with which the government financed a large part of its budget deficits, with short-term credit acquired abroad.

Reviewing the 1970s, one can conclude that the approach to structural problems came too late and was not fundamental enough. One of the main causes of this development was that structural problems were too long considered as being of a conjunctural nature. Consequently demand stimulating measures were taken, an increase in deficit financing was allowed, and a relaxed monetary policy could be justified. Moreover, the approach to the structural problems was delayed, and these problems were even aggravated because the current account showed substantial surpluses and the natural gas revenues increased rapidly. On top of that, in 1974 and 1975 there was still some room for reducing profit margins of the private sector.

Shortly after the time when fiscal and monetary policy definitely took another course, the second oil crisis occurred. The negative effects of this crisis outweighed the positive impulses of the policy changes of the years just before it. In this situation the structural weakness of the Dutch economy became fully manifest.

The current economic situation in the Netherlands is one of structural weakness. Investments, both private and government, are decreasing. The net borrowing requirement of the government shows a strong upward movement. Unemployment is increasing very fast. A possible bright element is the relatively moderate rise of wages and prices, which may be the beginning of gradually improving profit margins, and competitive position. Moreover, the still abundantly flowing natural gas revenues are a potential source for strengthening the economy. But it remains necessary to decrease the share of consumption and thus to make room for an increasing share of investment in national income, and for this purpose both to stabilize or perhaps even decrease the share of collective expenditures and to change the composition of these expenditures as well.

Notes

I thank my colleagues in the Treasury for their contributions to this paper, which remains however my personal responsibility.

1 The earned income ratio represents the proportion of wage income, including earned income imputed to self-employed persons (which is supposed to be equal to the medium wage income), in the total income formed in industry. The adjusted earned income ratio is based on the total income formed in industry excluding mineral extraction, public utilities and housing operations.

Symptoms of an Overvalued Currency: the Case of the Belgian Franc

PAUL de GRAUWE
Universities of Leuven and Michigan, Ann Arbor

Introduction

Like most other industrialized nations, the Belgian economy has been subjected to a number of considerable shocks during the 1970s. The consecutive oil price increases, the world recession of 1975 and the upsurge of a group of developing countries starting to compete in traditional industrial sectors are well-known phenomena and help to explain the economic problems of Belgium and other countries.

Some of the shocks that have affected the Belgian economy during the 1970s have a domestic origin or are the results of policy decisions. The nature and the effects of these shocks are analysed in this paper. One issue that will be addressed in some detail is how the exchange rate policy of the Belgian authorities has affected the adjustment of the economy to these exogenous shocks.

The nature of the disturbances

Since the middle of the 1970s two major disturbances affecting the Belgian economy stand out.

First, during the period 1974–75 substantial wage increases occurred. During both years nominal wages increased by 20 per cent per year. As a result, *real* wages increased by 16 per cent during this two-year period. Unit labour costs likewise increased as the productivity increases were relatively low. In 1975 alone unit labour costs increased by 21 per cent.[1] Following this two-year period the *growth rates* of wages and unit labour costs declined substantially. Unit labour costs, however, continued to increase at a yearly rate of 2 to

3 per cent, despite the fact that the 1974–75 wage explosion had substantially raised the Belgian *level* of unit labour costs.

Second, as a result of the pegging of the Belgian franc to the Deutschmark (as part of the 'Snake' agreement), the Belgian franc appreciated substantially on an effective basis after 1974–75; during the period 1975–79 it appreciated effectively by 15 per cent. The evolution of several measures of effective exchange rates is shown in figure 1. Note that since the beginning of 1980 this effective appreciation has been halted; in fact, at the start of 1981 the Belgian franc had depreciated by more than 5 per cent relative to one year earlier.

The immediate result of these two shocks was that the wage share in value added of the manufacturing sector increased substantially in Belgium. This is illustrated in figure 2, which compares the labour share in industrial value of the EEC countries. It can be seen that Belgium, which had the lowest labour share in 1970 except for France, had reached the highest level of labour share at the end of

Fig. 1 Effective exchange rates and special drawing rights (SDR) rates of the Belgian franc

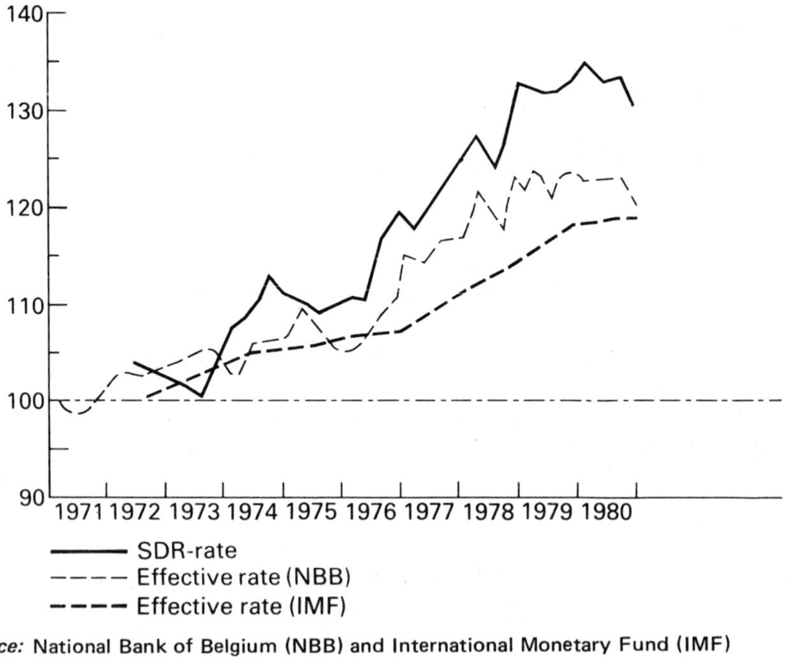

Source: National Bank of Belgium (NBB) and International Monetary Fund (IMF)

Fig. 2 Wages share in manufacturing in OECD countries, 1970–78

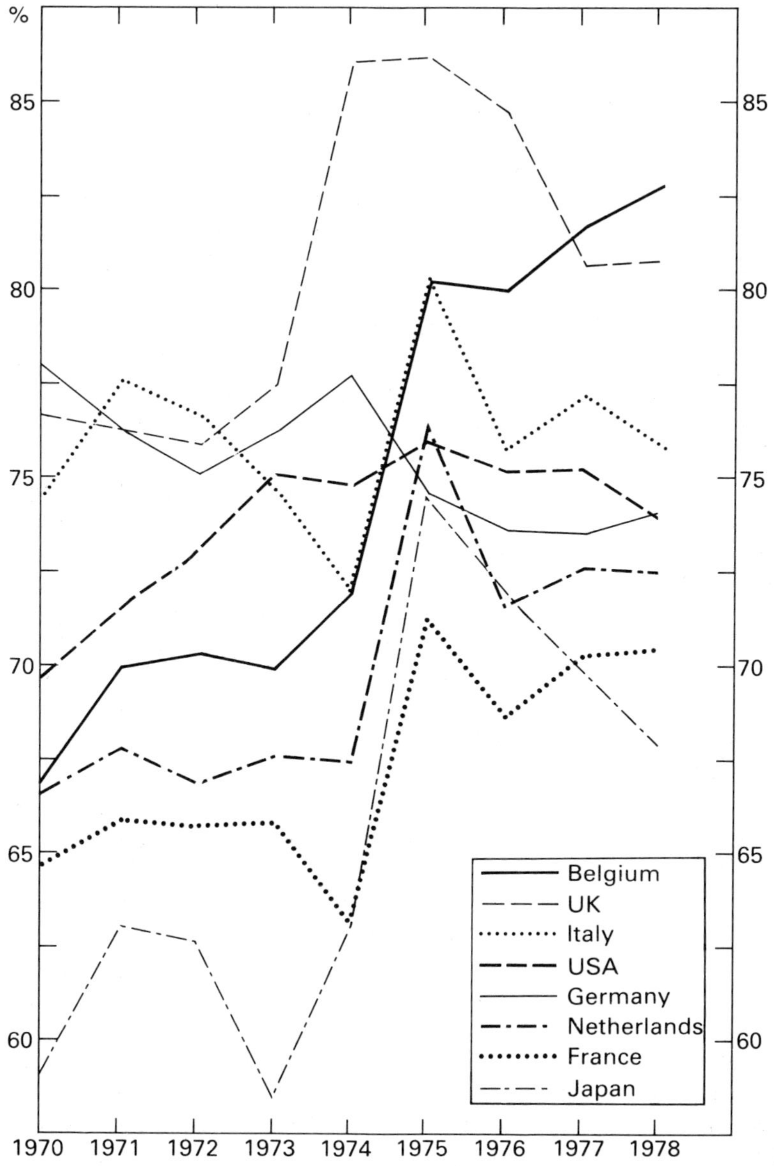

Source: IRES, Louvain-la-Neuve

the 1970s. Thus Belgium started the 1970s as a country with a relatively low wage cost in manufacturing and ended the decade as a country with the highest wage cost in manufacturing in the EEC.

Effects of the disturbance: the theory

The almost simultaneous occurrence of a wage explosion and an effective appreciation of the currency has affected (and still affects) the Belgian economy. Before examining the empirical evidence it is useful to present a brief theoretical analysis of the probable effects of these disturbances.

It is convenient to distinguish two sectors in the economy, a tradable goods (open) sector and a non-tradable goods (closed) sector. Being a small economy, Belgium approximates the case of price-takership in the open sector; i.e., the foreign currency prices for its exports and import substitutes are given.

The effects of a domestic wage increase can now be analysed as follows. In the closed sector wage increases can be translated into higher output prices. The degree to which this can be done depends on the state of domestic aggregate demand. The latter will be determined mainly by monetary and fiscal policies. In the open sector, where domestic firms are price-takers on the world markets, cost increases can be translated into higher prices (in domestic currency) only if the world prices increase and/or if the domestic currency depreciates. If the domestic currency appreciates, the possibility for price-taking firms to transmit domestic cost increases into higher output prices will be reduced. Every 1 per cent appreciation of the currency implies a 1 per cent decline of the domestic currency price of the traded goods.

The simultaneous occurrence of wage increases and an appreciating currency leads to a situation whereby firms in the open sector will experience a decline in profit margins. A continuing appreciation of the currency reduces the rate of price increases in the open sector to below the world price increase. If the domestic cost increases are likewise below the world average no problem will occur. If, however, domestic cost increases are similar or even higher than the cost increases in the rest of the world, profits are squeezed in the open sector. In the closed sector, generally speaking, these cost increases will be translated into higher output prices, if domestic demand is sufficiently strong.

As a result of these phenomena the relative price of tradables versus non-tradables will tend to decline. If this relative price change is maintained, a reallocation of factors of production will occur from the open to the closed sector.

The preceding describes the typical and well-known phenomena inherent in a situation of an overvalued currency. When the currency is too expensive, the tradable goods sector is penalized relative to the non-tradable sector, so that investment in the open sector will be discouraged in favour of investment in the closed sector.

An overvalued currency must also lead to effects on the pattern of aggregate demand. In particular, the decline of the relative price of tradables versus non-tradables leads to an increased demand for tradables (for any given level of the government budget and the money supply). The result will be a deterioration of the current account, and an increased need to support the currency in the exchange market by selling foreign exchange.

Another symptom of an overvalued currency relates to the effects on productivity increases in the tradable goods sector. The pressure on the profit margins of the open sector leads to enhanced pressures towards rationalization. These can take two forms. First, firms in the open sector will be forced to reduce the labour force in order to remain competitive in world markets. Second, domestic firms will disappear from the market. In general, the least efficient firm will drop out first. The result of these two effects is an increase in the average labour productivity in the open sector. To the extent that the second effect dominates, the increased productivity is a statistical phenomenon: the elimination of the less efficient firms drives up the statistical average of labour productivity.

To conclude this theoretical discussion it is important to point out that there exists an automatic mechanism of correction tending to eliminate a situation of overvaluation of the currency. First, on the demand side the current account deficit will have deflationary effects. The money supply will tend to decline, interest rates to increase, and aggregate demand to decline. This will reduce the growth rate of prices (in the closed sector) and wages. On the supply side, the productivity growth will tend to reduce the growth rate of unit labour costs. During the adjustment process employment will be negatively affected.

This adjustment mechanism can be retarded or even made impossible. An expansionary fiscal policy, for example, may prevent aggregate demand to decline, thereby preventing the current account deficit from disappearing.

Empirical evidence: the relative price of tradable goods

In the previous section it was argued that an appreciation of the currency and/or a domestic wage increase leads, *ceteris paribus*, to a decline in the price of tradables relative to the price of non-tradables. In this section proxies for the tradable goods prices are compared with proxies for the non-tradable goods prices.

In figure 3 the export prices and wholesale price indices (as proxies for tradable goods prices) are compared with the nominal wage index (as a proxy for non-tradable goods prices) in a number of industrialized countries. It can be seen, for example, that the Belgian wage increases were substantially larger than the German and Dutch ones, whereas the export and wholesale price indices increased at almost the same rate in these three countries. The result is a decline of the export price relative to wage costs of 30 per cent from 1972 to 1978, and a similar relative decline of wholesale prices. This relative decline of the price of tradables is also illustrated in figure 4, which shows the ratio of export prices to wages in different European countries.

It is also surprising to find (see figure 3) that the nominal wage increases were stronger in Belgium than in a number of countries with higher inflation and depreciating currencies (Sweden and the United States). It is evident that this strong deterioration of the relative price of tradables relative to wage cost has put the Belgian tradable goods sector under severe pressure, leading to profit squeezes and rationalization. These phenomena will be documented in the next section.

A similar exercise of comparison of tradable and non-tradable goods prices is performed in figure 5. As a proxy of the tradable goods prices the wholesale price index was selected again, whereas the price index of services was chosen as a proxy for the non-tradable goods prices. The evolution of these two price indices shows that Belgium appears to have experienced an extreme relative price change: the price of tradables relative to non-tradables has declined more than in any other country of the EEC. Between 1974 and 1978 the price of services increased by more than 50 per cent whereas the wholesale price index increased by 9 per cent only.

Again, it is interesting to find that during 1974–78 the price index of services in Belgium increased at approximately the same rate as in a number of countries with high inflation rates (France, Sweden, Italy). This means that the inflationary impulses in the Belgian non-tradable goods sector were comparable to the inflationary impulses in other high-inflation countries. (In the following section the causes of these domestic inflationary pressures are analysed.) The difference between Belgium and these other countries is that during 1974–78 the Belgian monetary authorities followed an anti-inflationary policy concentrated on letting the currency appreciate. This had the effect of preventing significant increases in the prices of traded goods and kept the consumer price index (CPI) increases at a relatively low level. The domestically generated inflationary impulses as measured by the increases of wages and service prices, however, were not eliminated, so that a significant decline in the relative price of tradables resulted.

It should be mentioned that, since the start of the European Monetary System (EMS) (beginning of 1979), the Belgian franc has depreciated by more than 5 per cent. Together with the acceleration of world prices, this explains the recent strong increase of the Belgian export price index (13 per cent during 1979). During the same period hourly wages increased on the average by 7 per cent. As a result, some correction took place in the movement of the relative price of tradables versus wages (see figure 4). It is doubtful, however, whether this recent turnaround will be sufficient to correct for the substantial deterioration that occurred prior to 1979.

Further effects of the overvaluation of the Belgian franc

The relative price shock that occurred in Belgium during the second half of the 1970s had important implications for the Belgian economy.

First, the strong decline of the relative price of tradables contributed to the sharp decline of rates of return in the industrial sector during 1975–78. This is illustrated in table 1. One can see that the rate of return on equity in the industrial sector declined substantially during 1975–78 whereas the rate of return in the non-tradable goods sector (banking, utilities, distribution) stayed at a relatively high level. Note also that during 1979 the rate of return in industry recovered. This may be associated with the improvement of the relative price of tradables observed in 1979.

Second, employment in industry declined substantially. Here again, Belgium appears to be an extreme case. Manufacturing employment in Belgium declined by more than 20 per cent during 1973–79, more than in any other EEC country. This is shown in figure 6.

The counterpart of this employment effect is the productivity effect. An overvalued currency will accelerate trends towards rationalization and plant closures in the industrial sector. This increases the average labour productivity. During the period 1974–78 the Belgian

Fig. 3 Tradable goods, prices and wages, 1970–78

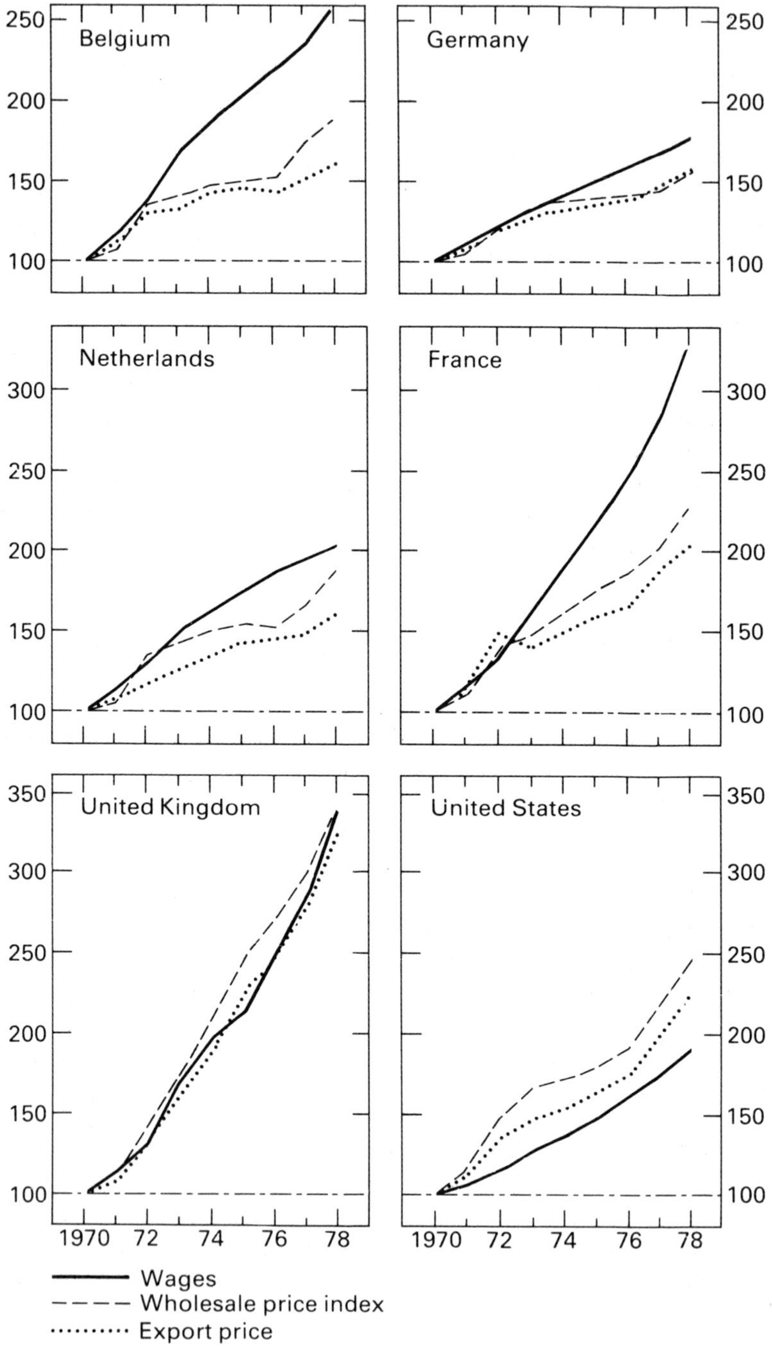

Fig. 3 – *continued*

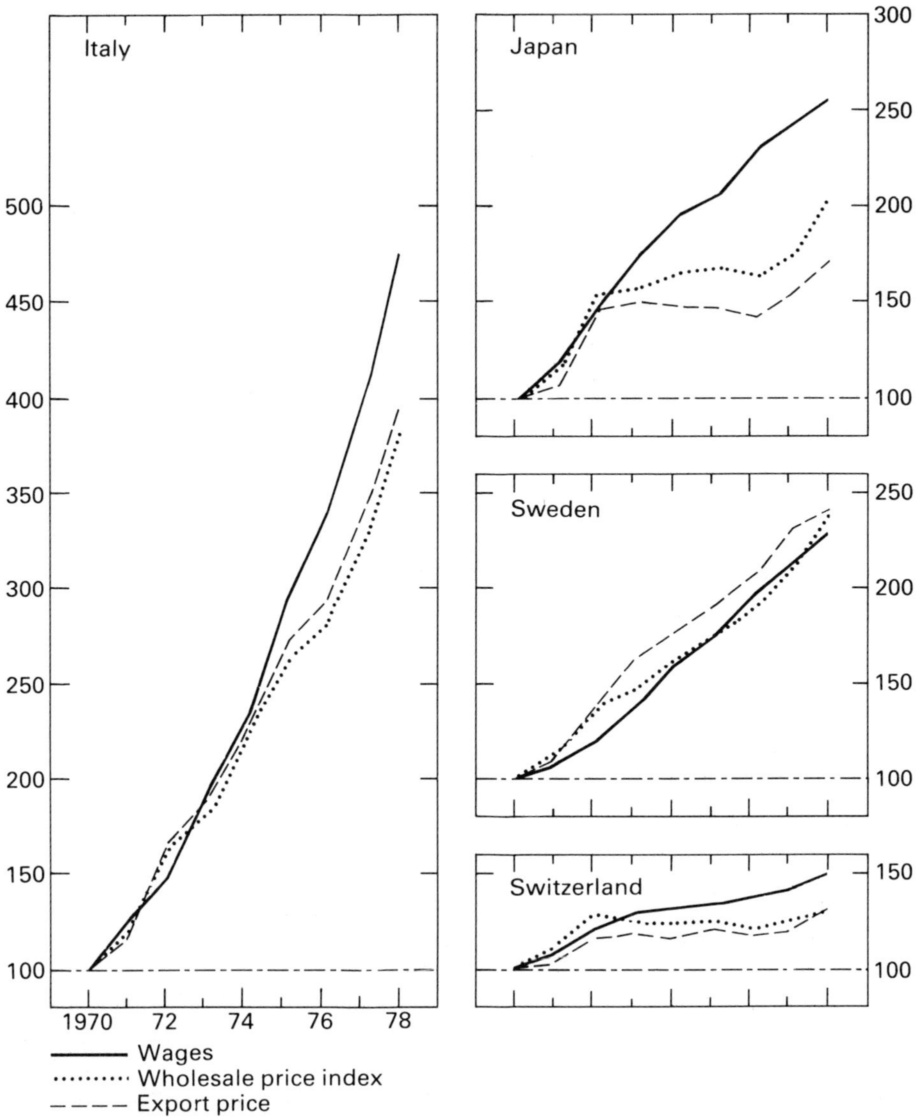

Source: IMF *International Financial Statistics*

Fig. 4 Ratio of export prices to nominal wages in eight countries, 1972–80

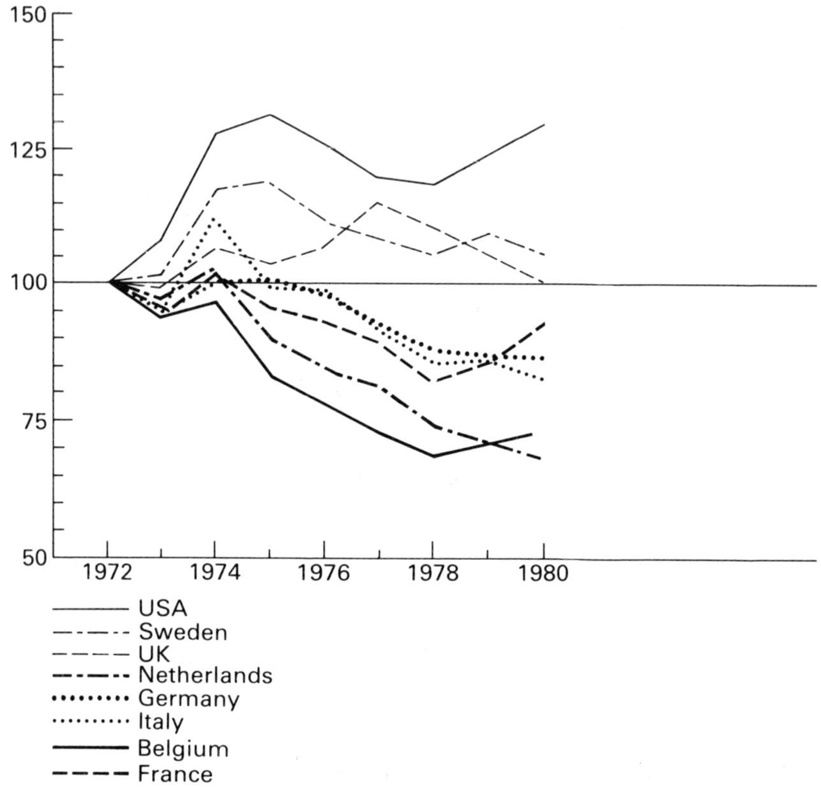

Source: IMF *International Financial Statistics*

industry has experienced the highest productivity growth rate of the EEC countries (see also figure 6).

Third, the overvaluation of the Belgian franc has contributed to the continuing deterioration of the current account. This deterioration is illustrated in table 2, which compares the current account situation of Belgium and the EEC countries. It can be seen that Belgium had the largest current account surplus (as a percentage of GNP) in 1972; whereas by 1980 Belgium had become the country with the largest deficit in its current account. The mechanism that produced this result was explained earlier: the decline of the relative price of tradables discouraged the production of tradables (exports plus import substitutes) and encouraged the demand for imports. Obviously, the exchange rate is not the only variable determining the

Fig. 5 Wholesale and service price indices for six countries, 1970–80

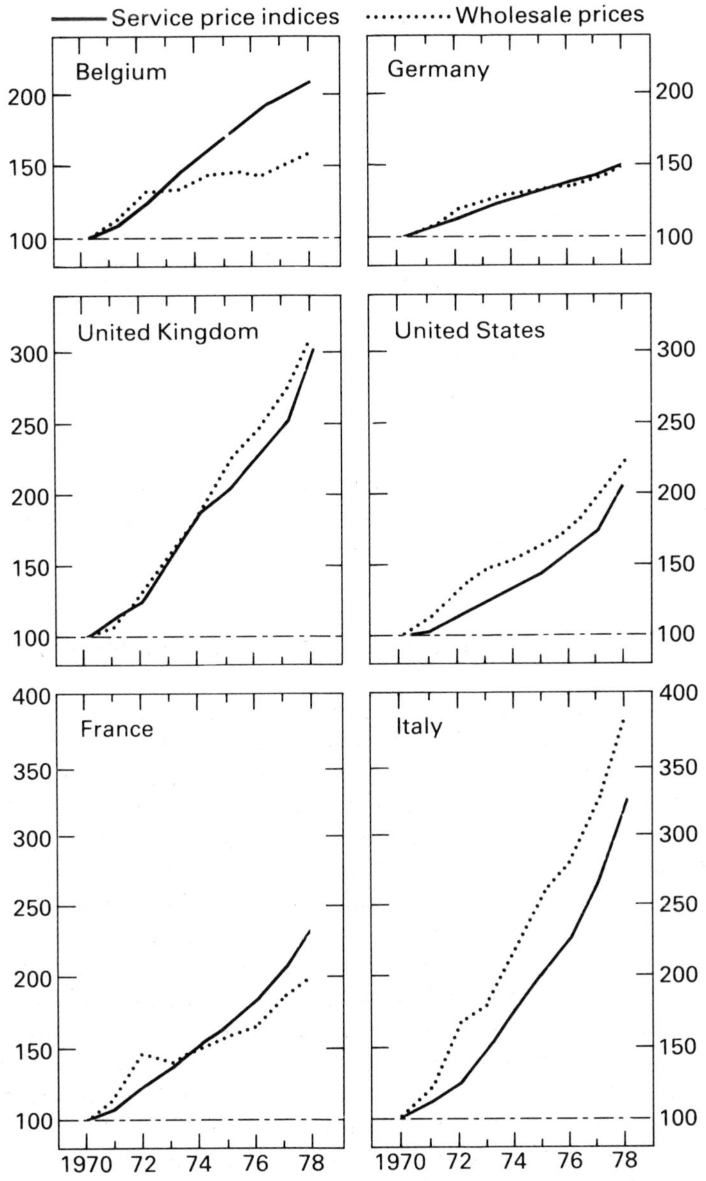

Source: IMF *International Financial Statistics*, and OECD *Main Economic Indicators*

Table 1 Rates of return in the Belgian industrial sector after taxes, 1970–79

	Industry	*Banking and finance*	*Utilities*	*Distribution*	*Average of Belgian firms*
	%	%	%	%	%
1970	7.6				8.1
1971	5.9				6.8
1972	6.6				7.3
1973	9.1				9.3
1974	8.7				8.1
1975	−0.3				3.7
1976	3.0	8.9	12.8	14.7	5.5
1977	−2.4	10.2	12.1	12.2	3.0
1978	0.1	10.2	11.7	16.8	4.8
1979	6.1	9.1	11.6	17.8	8.1

Source: Kredietbank; Weekberichten

current account; in addition to the exchange rate, there is the role played by monetary and budgetary policies. The role of budgetary policies is taken up in the next section.

The government budget and external equilibrium

The important question that has not been answered yet is why the inflationary tendencies that occurred in the closed sector did not decline significantly despite the effective appreciation of the Belgian franc and the inflation-dampening effects that result from this. The answer has to do with the evolution of the government budget.

In table 3 the evolution of the government expenditures and revenues are shown for Belgium and for the EEC as a whole. During 1975–79 Belgium experienced the fastest increase of government expenditures of all EEC countries. Expenditures of the Belgian government sector increased from 45.5 per cent of GNP in 1975 to 52 per cent in 1979; in the EEC as a whole government expenditures remained practically constant as a percentage of GNP. Government revenues, however, increased substantially less in Belgium, so that the Belgian government deficit increased substantially during 1975–79 (from 5.2 to 7.2 per cent of GNP). In the EEC as a whole the government deficit declined during the same period. It should be stressed also that transfers constitute the major source of the rapid expansion of government expenditures in Belgium.

Fig. 6 Employment and productivity in manufacturing (1973 = 100)

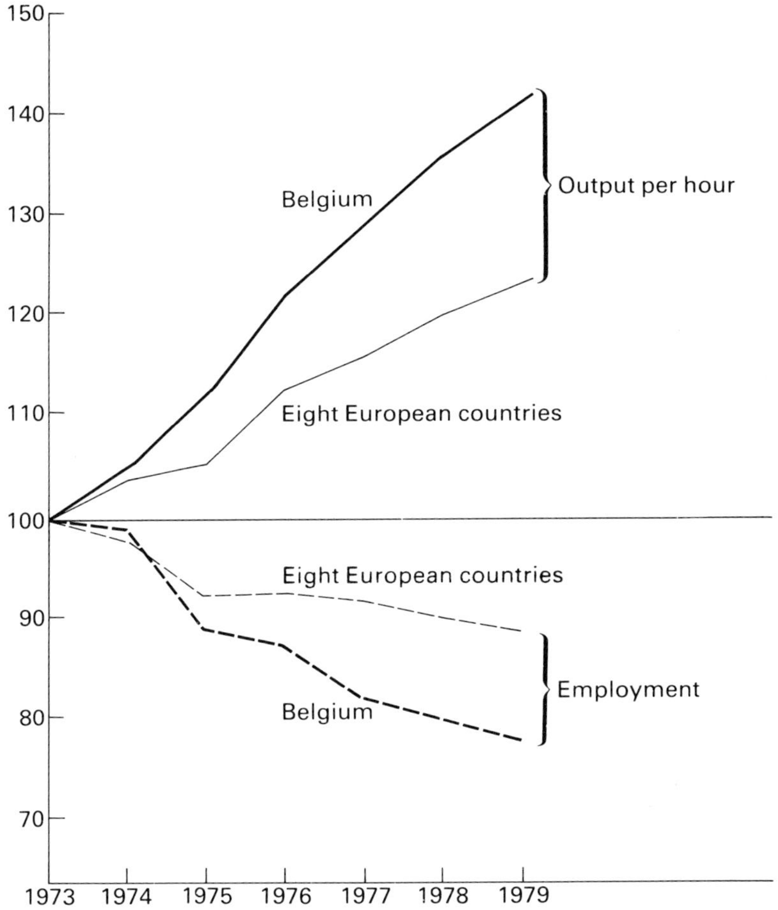

The eight countries are: Germany, France, UK, Italy, Netherlands, Sweden, Belgium and Denmark.

This expansionary budgetary policy had several important implications for the external equilibrium. The increased government expenditures (mainly transfers) financed by the issue of bonds or by monetary means led to a situation where private household disposable income increased faster than GNP.[2] This then increased the demand for imports and contributed to the deterioration of the current account. In addition, it led to a relatively strong demand for

Table 2 Current account of the Belgian–Luxembourg Economic Union and a number of EEC countries (percentage of GNP)

	1972	*1973*	*1974*	*1975*	*1976*	*1977*	*1978*	*1979*	*1980**
	%	%	%	%	%	%	%	%	%
Belgium	+3.7	+2.6	+1.2	+0.4	−0.1	−0.9	−1.0	−3.0	−4.7
Netherlands	+2.8	+4.0	+3.1	+2.4	+3.0	+0.6	−1.1	−1.6	−1.8
Germany	+0.3	+1.3	+2.7	+1.0	+0.9	+0.8	+1.4	−0.7	−2.1
France	+0.2	−0.3	−2.3	—	−1.7	−0.8	+0.8	+0.2	−1.2
Italy	+1.5	−1.8	−4.7	−0.4	−1.5	+1.2	+2.4	+1.6	−1.3
Denmark	−0.5	−1.7	−2.8	−1.3	−4.5	−3.6	−0.7	−4.6	−4.4
UK	+0.3	−1.9	−4.0	−1.6	−0.9	−0.2	−0.4	−1.0	+0.9

* 1980 is estimated
Source: National Bank of Belgium *Annual Report* (1980), p. 42

Table 3 The government budget as a percentage of GNP

	1960	*1975*	*1977*	*1978*	*1979*	*1980*
	%	%	%	%	%	%
Total expenditure						
Belgium	30.5	45.5	49.2	50.9	52.0	57.7*
EEC	32.7	46.6	45.9	46.7	46.9	
Total current receipts						
Belgium	27.6	42.6	43.6	44.6	44.8	45.9*
EEC	33.4	41.0	42.6	42.7	43.0	
Deficit surplus						
Belgium		−5.2	−6.4	−6.4	−7.2	−11.8*
EEC		−5.9	−3.2	−4.5	−4.6	

* Estimates made by the National Bank of Belgium
Source: Commission of the EEC

non-tradables and thereby contributed to maintaining inflationary impulses in the non-traded goods sector as documented in the previous sections. Thus the budgetary policy contributed directly to the deterioration of the current account, and indirectly in that it tended to maintain inflationary conditions in the closed sector at a time when the National Bank was allowing the currency to appreciate. As a result the budgetary policy contributed to the sharp decline of the price of tradables versus non-tradables.

One can conclude that the budgetary policies prevented the automatic adjustment mechanism triggered by an overvalued currency from operating. Indeed, the budgetary expansions probably reinforced the overvaluation of the Belgian franc as it contributed to the divergent trends in the prices of the open and the closed sector. The question arises here whether it made sense for a country to allow its currency to appreciate, and thereby effectively to prevent industrial prices from increasing, when at the same time the budgetary policies were highly expansionary.

An often-heard argument is that the effective appreciation of the Belgian franc led to greater 'discipline' on the wage and price front. The preceding evidence suggests that this 'discipline' exerted by the exchange rate policy was far from being exemplary. What is more, one can argue that the overvaluation of the currency set loose another type of indiscipline; i.e., it can be argued that the overvaluation of the Belgian franc itself contributed to the increased government transfers and the government deficits. The decline in industrial employment led to large increases of unemployment compensation. It induced the government to operate more and more as employer of last resort, and a great variety of public employment programs were set up. In fact, whereas after 1974 employment declined by 200 000 in industry, the government hired 120 000 new employees. All this strongly affected government expenditures.

What is particularly disturbing about this is that the overvaluation of the currency, which normally is a temporary phenomenon, leads to an automatic and permanent expansion of the government sector. This then makes further adjustment difficult, and as was argued earlier may transform a temporary overvaluation into a protracted one. 'Vicious circles' may also exist for overvalued currencies.

The traditional indicators of overvaluation of the currency

It is common to evaluate the degree of under- or overvaluation of a currency by computing 'real' exchange rates. The procedure usually consists of comparing a domestic price index with a similar foreign price index corrected for exchange rate changes. This allows us to determine whether during a particular period relative price changes between countries have mirrored exchange rate movements. Table 4 contains some examples of real exchange rate movements for Belgium. It is interesting to find that the real exchange rate of Belgium has moved relatively little during the period 1974–78 when large exchange rate and wage shocks occurred. The explanation is as follows. First, to the extent that Belgium is a price-taker in the tradable goods sector, the real exchange rate cannot move. Put differently, the Belgian export prices expressed in foreign currency

Table 4 Real exchange rates for Belgium, 1973–80 (1972 = 100)

Based on	*Relative export prices*	*Relative wholesale prices*	*Relative unit labour costs*
1973	100.1	105.4	97.9
1974	103.0	107.2	100.2
1975	102.0	101.1	100.3
1976	102.9	103.0	100.6
1977	104.1	103.5	103.6
1978	104.8	99.0	100.7
1979	105.2	98.0	96.4
1980(III)	106.8	91.3	98.0

Source: IMF *International Financial Statistics*

will not deviate from the world prices, even if the Belgian export firms are subjected to large domestic cost increases. As a result real exchange rate calculations based on export prices (or wholesale prices) usually tend to underestimate the overvaluation of the currency in small price-taking economies.

The idea that for small countries export or wholesale prices are imperfect indicators of over- or undervaluation is not new. It can be found in Triffin (1937–38). Triffin noted that when the pound sterling devalued in 1931 the Belgian wholesale price index declined substantially, whereas nominal wages decreased by a smaller amount. The mechanism involved was similar to the one described here. The effective appreciation of the Belgian franc reduced the BF price of the goods for which Belgian was a price-taker in the foreign market. This price decline, however, was not compensated by a proportional decline of nominal wages, so that real wages increased and the profit margins in industry declined. During the period 1931–35 industrial prices declined by 25 per cent more than wages.[3] During 1974–78 Belgian wages increased more than 30 per cent faster than industrial prices (wholesale and export prices).

A second, more satisfying, way to compute real exchange rate changes consists of comparing the evolution of unit labour costs domestically and in the rest of the world corrected for exchange rate movements. This procedure, however, also has drawbacks. As was indicated earlier, domestic cost increases tend to accelerate productivity growth through rationalization and reductions in industrial employment. These productivity increases may partially compensate the wage cost increases so that the domestic unit labour cost index increases in a limited amount only. This mechanism may explain why the Belgian unit labour cost index has changed relatively little in relation to the other countries.

Conclusion

During the second half of the 1970s Belgium has experienced large increases in wages and service prices. In fact, the inflationary pressures in the non-tradable goods sector were larger than in other 'Snake' countries (except Denmark) and were comparable to the inflationary pressure in a number of countries with depreciating currencies (Sweden, France, USA). The Belgian policy to combat inflation consisted of letting the currency appreciate (on an effective basis) despite the inflationary tendencies in the closed sector. As a result, Belgian industrial prices were effectively prevented from increasing (until 1979). This substantially reduced the industrial prices relative to domestic wages and domestic service prices, and contributed to the drastic reduction of the rates of return in the industrial sector and the phenomenon of 'de-industrialization' of the Belgian economy.

There can be no doubt that policies to combat inflation should receive a high priority. Belgium seems to have scored well in this area. The outside observer may then wonder, why make so much fuss? The question that is raised here, however, concerns the appropriate instrument of fighting inflation. By letting the Belgian franc appreciate, industrial prices were effectively controlled, without, however, doing much to limit domestic cost increases. In fact, the budgetary policies added fuel to these domestic cost increases. As a result, large current account deficits ensued.

Finally, since the introduction of the EMS the exchange rate trend has changed substantially. From an appreciating currency the Belgian franc has become since 1979 a depreciating currency (on an effective basis) together with the other EMS currencies. This turnaround has halted (and even reversed) the previously observed trend of declining relative prices of tradable goods. This reversal, however, has as yet been insufficient to improve substantially Belgium's competitive position. In addition, since this effective depreciation is due mainly to the appreciation of the dollar and the pound sterling, it has not changed the unfavourable competitive position of Belgium versus the other EMS countries.

Notes

This paper is an extended and updated version of a paper I presented at the Economic Outlook Conference, DRI International, Brussels. 13 May 1980. I am grateful to T. Vanoverbeke for his competent research assistance.

1 It has been argued that this wage explosion was to a certain degree the result of the undervaluation of the Belgian franc in the beginning of the 1970s. This undervaluation contributed to a strong expansion of the export sector and to domestic inflationary pressures.

2 During 1975–78 the proportion of private disposable income in GNP was 78%, compared with 76% during 1970–73. See *Annual Report of the National Bank* (1979), p. xxx. Private consumption increased from 59.9% of GNP during 1970–73 to 61.6% during 1975–78.

3 The Belgian franc was devalued by 28% in 1935. See Triffin (1937–38).

References

Triffin, R. (1937–38). 'La théorie de la surévaluation monétaire et la dévaluation belge'. *Bulletin de l'Institut de Recherches Economiques.*

Stabilization Policy in Austria, 1970-80

HELMUT FRISCH
University of Technology, Vienna

Scenario and targets

Austria is a small open economy which is connected with the world economy through its 'exposed' sector. This exposed sector (E-sector) comprises export industries and those firms that produce for the domestic market but are open to international competition. The greater part of manufacturing and large parts of the trade and service sector belong to the E-sector. On the other hand, construction, agriculture and public services, as well as smaller parts of manufacturing and general services, belong to the 'sheltered' sector (S-sector) of the economy. Roughly estimated, about one-third of the value-added is produced in Austria in the E-sector and two-thirds in the S-sector.

The Austrian economy is connected with the international business cycle and international price developments through its E-sector. The price index of the E-sector follows international price developments closely. This is no surprise, since Austrian firms are not able to influence world market prices with the quantities they buy and sell. They are above all price-takers. In the same manner, the Austrian economy receives strong impulses from the international business cycle. The graph in figure 1 shows that the cyclical phases of the Austrian economy were almost identical with those of the international business cycle during the period 1965–80. An exception was the Austrian boom of 1969–73, which was not interrupted by a recession in 1971 and 1972 as in other countries.

The Austrian cycle is above all export-induced. Every upswing starts with an increase in foreign demand for domestic exports which occurs regularly about the middle of the recessionary phase (figure 1). The next phase is a change in the stock of inventories in the same direction, which in turn strengthens the export stimulus. In the later phase of the business cycle, investment in equipment and private

Fig. 1 Real exports and total investments (% change from previous year) and changes in real inventories (as % of real GDP), 1965–80

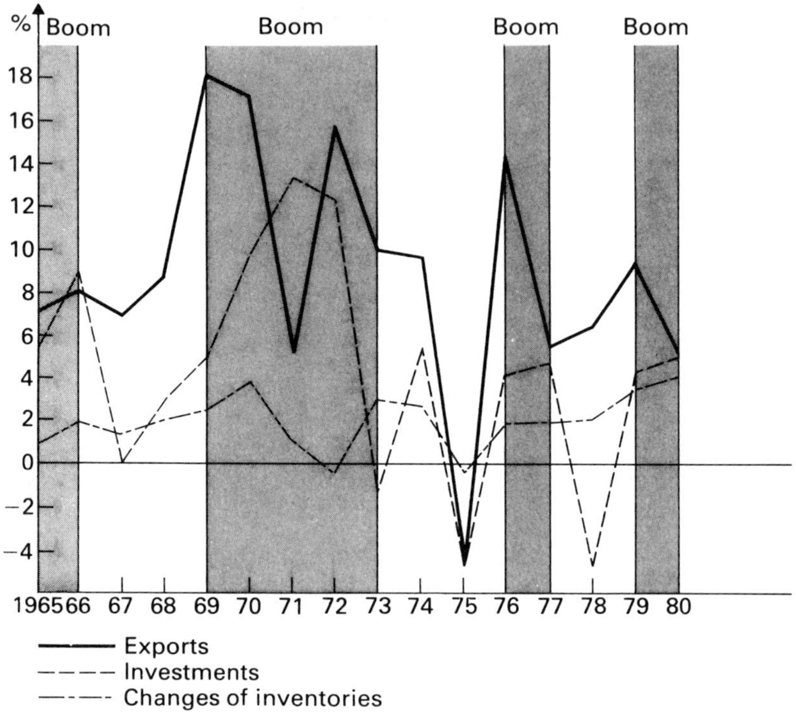

consumption increases. At the end of the boom and at the beginning of the recession the inflation rate as well as the rate of growth of money wages reach their highest values (figure 2).

The Austrian boom of 1969–73 was interrupted unexpectedly by the sharp world recession of 1975, after a phase of light release in tension during 1974. The abrupt ending of economic growth had not been anticipated. The Austrian Institute of Economic Research had forecast a positive real rate of growth of 3.5 per cent for 1975, whereas real GNP decreased in the end by 2 per cent. Austrian economic policy tried to dampen the shortfall in private domestic and foreign demand to a great extent by means of compensatory fiscal policy. While the net budget deficit was 1.4 per cent of the GDP in 1974, it increased to 4.4 per cent in 1975 and remained at about the same level in 1976 and 1977. The fact that caused the greatest concern to policy-makers, not only in Austria but in most

Fig. 2 Employees' per capita income and consumer price index (CPI), 1965–80 (% changes from previous year)

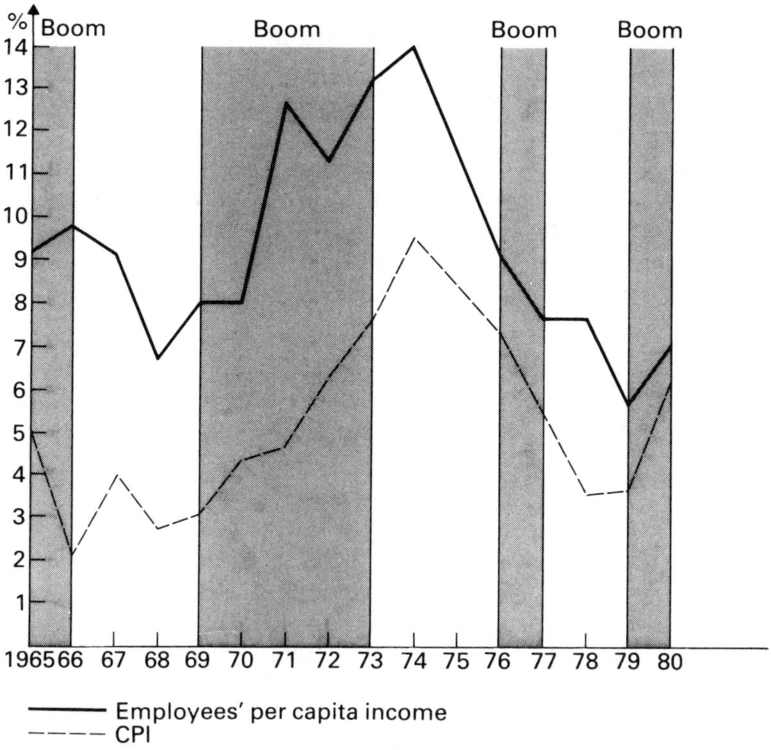

countries, was the persistent high rate of inflation in spite of the sharp economic downturn. The international boom of 1973–74 had been built upon an already high inflationary base, where world inflation was aggravated by the coincidence of various unfavourable factors (a food crisis, the 'oil shock' and international speculation in raw materials). The long and accelerating inflation brought about an almost complete loss of 'money illusion' and the development of considerable inflationary expectations. The stagflation episodes in the context of the world recession in 1975 can be explained mainly by the fact that inflation rates remained at a high level and decreased only slowly, in spite of a decline in production and employment, because of stable inflationary expectations. Economic activity recovered rapidly in the following years in Austria, and after a policy-induced dampening of total demand in 1978, output and aggregated demand increased again above their long-run trend rates, which had been relatively unaffected by the sharp rise in oil prices since the end of 1978.

Table 1 shows that the inflation rate in Austria was considerably below the OECD average during the 1970s and especially in the period of accelerating inflation (1972–75). This was a favourable result of the attempt of the Austrian policy-makers to dampen the direct international price dependencies that resulted from fixed exchange rates. This was done by linking the exchange rate of the schilling to the strong currencies of Austria's main trading partners, especially to the Deutschmark. With this trick Austria achieved, so to speak, a 'free ride' in (price) stabilization policy.

Table 1 Consumer price rises in Austria and all OECD countries, 1971–80

	1971	*1972*	*1973*	*1974*	*1975*	*1976*	*1977*	*1978*	*1979*	*1980*
	%	%	%	%	%	%	%	%	%	%
Austria	4.7	6.3	7.6	9.5	8.4	7.3	5.5	3.6	3.7	6.4
OECD Europe	6.6	6.5	8.6	13.4	13.1	10.8	10.9	9.1	10.8	13.0

In general, economic policy in an open economy is confronted with two problems: internal stability and external stability. The problem of internal stability is to control total aggregate demand through monetary and fiscal policy so that the unemployment and the rate of inflation stay within reasonable limits; the external problem results from the development of the balance of payments, the current external account. The policy mix used in Austria is fundamentally different from the one in Switzerland and differs partially from the policy mix in West Germany (see Androsch, 1978). In Austria the target of employment stability clearly dominated the price stability target. The unemployment rate hardly exceeded the 2 per cent mark in the period 1970–80. This was achieved mainly through an expansive fiscal policy which resulted in a strong increase in budget deficits. The Austrian monetary policy was 'accommodating' in the 1970s as a whole; in no case did it pose difficulties in financing the sizeable budget deficits.

The dynamics of inflationary expectations that caused the acceleration of inflation in many OECD countries were checked in Austria by an incomes policy that consisted of a system of voluntary agreements between the social partners and the government in order to prevent inflationary expectations from becoming part of the actual development of income (see Suppanz and Robinson, 1972). With this 'policy mix' it was possible for the Austrian economy to absorb the shocks of 1975 relatively smoothly within a major loss of employment.

The intention of the activist fiscal policy was to stabilize the level of nominal income. As a consequence, domestic absorption (i.e., consumption of domestic and foreign goods and services) increased faster than domestic production, which led to increasing deficits in the balance of payments. The deficit in the current external balance increased, and in 1977 amounted to 3.6 per cent of the GNP. The 'hard currency' policy reinforced these developments by making imports more price-attractive and by discriminating exports. At the end of 1977 tax policy measures were being taken (specifically, tax increases for durables). These measures, together with a more restrictive monetary policy, led to a decline in domestic demand and brought about a sharp reduction in the deficit in the following year. More recently, the oil-related terms of trade loss and the relative cyclical position of the Austrian economy have contributed again to a marked increase in the current account deficit.

We have described in the broadest terms the development of Austrian economic policy. Let us now turn to a closer analysis of the Austrian stabilization model.

An Austrian version of the Scandinavian model

The Scandinavian model provides an adequate basis from which to study the Austrian stabilization policy for the 1970s from a general point of view. Of fundamental importance is the division of the economy into a sector producing 'traded' goods, the 'exposed sector' (E-sector) and the 'sheltered sector' (S-sector), producing 'non-traded' goods (i.e., commodities that are not traded internationally). To explain the Austrian inflation a 'Phillips Curve-augmented' version of the Scandinavian model on the lines of Calmfors (1977), Frisch (1977) and Lindbeck (1979) can be used. The model differs from the original Scandinavian model (Aukrust, 1970) by introducing a Phillips relation into the E-sector of the economy. The following six equations make up a generalized version of the Scandinavian model.

Direct international price dependence of the E-sector

$$p_E = p_w. \tag{1}$$

The rate of inflation in the E-sector equals the world rate of inflation (prices measured in domestic currency).

Phillips Curve

$$w_E = A\lambda_E - B\left(\frac{U-V}{N}\right) + Cp_E^*. \tag{2}$$

The rate of increase of nominal wages w_E is explained by λ_E, the rate of increase of labour productivity in the E-sector, $(U-V)/N$, excess demand on the labour market (where V is the number of vacancies, U the number of persons unemployed and N the number of persons employed), and p_E^*, the rate of expected inflation in the E-sector.

Wage spill-over hypothesis

$$w_E = w_S. \tag{3}$$

The rate of wage increase in the exposed sector acts as a wage leader.

Mark-up pricing in the S-sector

$$p_S = w_S - \lambda_S. \tag{4}$$

The rate of inflation in the S-sector is the difference between the rate of increase in nominal wages and the rate of increase in labour productivity, λ_S.

Definition of the rate of inflation

$$p = \alpha_S p_S + \alpha_E p_E; \qquad \alpha_S + \alpha_E = 1. \tag{5}$$

As a solution of the system (1)–(5) we get the following reduced form equation:

$$p = (1-\alpha_S)p_w - \alpha_S B\left(\frac{U-V}{N}\right) + \alpha_S Cp_E^* + \alpha_S(A\lambda_E - \lambda_S). \tag{6}$$

This model is approximated by the following ordinary least squares (OLS) estimation; equations (7)–(11) are estimated; the resulting reduced-form equation (12) is computed.

Empirical results for Austria, 1966–79, OLS

(Numbers in brackets are standard deviations of the coefficients.)

$$p_E = \underset{(0.883)}{0.926} + \underset{(0.143)}{0.434} p_w + \underset{(0.142)}{0.310} p_{w-1} \tag{7}$$

$R^2 = 0.61 \qquad SE = 1.88 \qquad DW = 2.26$

$$w_E = \underset{(1.825)}{7.803} + \underset{(0.179)}{0.385} p_E + \underset{(0.179)}{0.379} p_{E-1} + \underset{(0.212)}{0.197} \lambda_{E-1} - \underset{(0.60)}{2.89} \left(\frac{U-V}{N}\right) \tag{8}$$

$R^2 = 0.83 \qquad SE = 1.62 \qquad DW = 1.57$

$$p_S = \underset{(1.051)}{1.242} + \underset{(0.105)}{0.558} (w_S - \lambda_S) + \underset{(0.112)}{0.116} (w_S - \lambda_S)_{-1} \tag{9}$$

$R^2 = 0.75 \qquad SE = 1.41 \qquad DW = 1.67$

$$p = \underset{(0.0014)}{0.350} p_E + \underset{(0.016)}{0.68} p_S - \underset{(0.102)}{0.149} \tag{10}$$

$R^2 = 0.99 \qquad SE = 0.15 \qquad DW = 2.31$

$$w_S = \underset{(1.241)}{2.731} + \underset{(0.124)}{0.465} w_E + \underset{(0.121)}{0.211} w_{E-1} \tag{11}$$

$R^2 = 0.75 \qquad SE = 1.24 \qquad DW = 2.71$

$$p = 4.91 + 0.437 p_w + 0.061 \lambda_E - 0.458 \lambda_S - 0.895 \left(\frac{U-N}{N}\right) \tag{12}$$

Equation (7) links the inflation in the E-sector and the international rate of inflation, p_w (a weighted average of the Austrian export and import price index) with a reasonably good fit. In the long run, with $p_w = p_{w-1}$, the rate of inflation in the E-sector is explained by approximately 75 per cent by the exogenous change in the world prices.

Equation (8) is an estimated Phillips Curve. According to the results, the rate of growth of money wages W_E can be explained in terms of two variables: the demand pressure on the labour market, and the expected rate of inflation. The demand pressure variable is highly significant: the coefficient is 2.9. It tells us that a difference of 1 per cent between the rate of unemployment and the rate of vacancies will change the rate of increase of money wages by about 3 per cent. Table 2 shows the actual values of the excess demand variable $(U-V)/N$. For example, in the boom phase 1973 excess demand contributed $2.9 \times 0.9 = 2.7$ per cent to the increase in nominal wages; in 1979 it dampened the wage increase by the same amount. The inconveniently large constant in the Phillips relation might be attributed to the construction of the excess demand variable $(U-V)/N$, which is scattered about zero.

Table 2 Values of the excess demand variable, 1971–79

	1971	*1972*	*1973*	*1974*	*1975*	*1976*	*1977*	*1978*	*1979*
$(U-V)/N$	−0.2	−0.5	−0.9	−0.6	0.8	0.9	0.7	1.1	0.9

The expected rate of inflation is presumed to be generated by an adaptive expectation formation mechanism. For a steady-state situation we can argue that the coefficient for the expected rate of inflation is 0.76, saying that in a steady state 0.76 of the expected rate of inflation is reflected in the actual wage increase in the E-sector. The contribution of labour productivity is small and statistically not significant.

Equation (9) shows that it would be a mistake to reject the hypothesis that unit labour costs in the S-sector explain the price development. The sum of coefficients is smaller than 1: namely, 0.68. This implies that the profit share drops when unit labour costs rise in the S-sector; the constant term is statistically insignificant.

The spill-over equation (11) shows that in the long run about 67 per cent of the growth of nominal wages in the S-sector can be explained in terms of the wage increase in the E-sector, but there also exists an autonomous component of about 2.7 per cent per annum.

Equation (12) is a reduced-form equation computed from the estimated system. Let us discuss this equation in the context of the tables 3 and 4. Table 3 shows the average annual rates of growth of

Table 3 Average annual values of exogenous variables, 1965–79

p_W	λ_E	λ_S	$(U-V)/N$	p
4.09	4.9	2.7	+0.56	5.2

Table 4 The contribution of the exogenous variables to the average annual rate of inflation (=consumer prices), 1965–79

Constant	p_W	λ_E	λ_S	$(U-V)/N$	$\hat{p}$	p
4.908	1.782	0.297	−1.236	−0.5	5.25	5.2

the exogenous variables for the period 1965–79. Table 4 shows the contribution of the exogenous variables to explain the average rate of change in consumer prices.

In accordance with table 4, we suggest the following explanation for the rate of inflation in Austria.

1 The direct influence of the international rate of inflation is expressed by the coefficient of transmission in equation (12) with 0.437. It can be seen that, for the period 1965–79, on average 1.7 per cent of the rate of inflation of 5.2 per cent is explained by 'imported' inflation.

2 The rate of growth of labour productivity in the E-sector, λ_E, influences the rate of inflation positively, whereas that of the S-sector has a considerable dampening influence (namely, −1.23 per cent) on the domestic rate of inflation. The development of labour productivity in both sectors is consistent with the *a priori* expected effect.

3 The overall demand component is approximated by the demand pressure on the labour market $(U-V)/N$. Figure 3 portrays the time path of the excess demand variable and shows that it coincides with the business cycle. The variable is scattered between 1.7 per cent (max.) and 0.9 per cent (min.). Thus it contributes to explaining fluctuations of the domestic rate of inflation between −1.5 and 0.8 per cent around a trend value determined by labour productivity and the world rate of inflation.

4 The Austrian situation is presented graphically in figure 4 for the two regimes, the period 1966–74 and the period 1975–79. The line *AU* determines the 'inflation margin' according to the Aukrust

Fig. 3. The time path of the excess demand variable

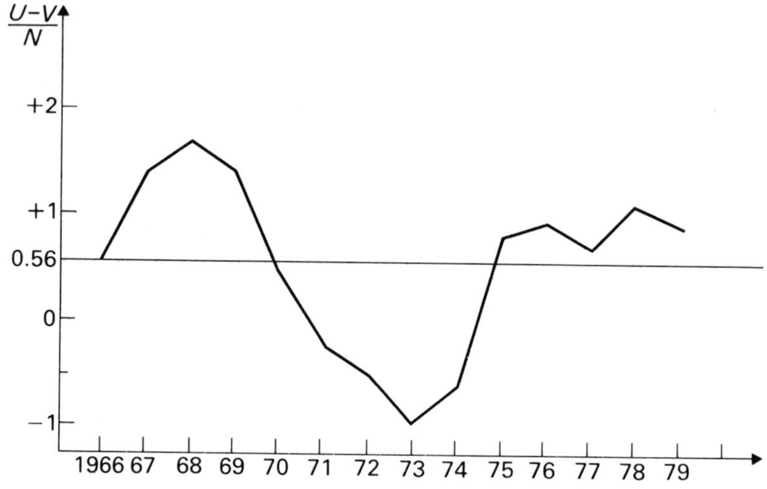

equation: $p = p_w + \alpha_S(\lambda_E - \lambda_S)$. For Austria for the periods under observation this gives:

$$1966\text{–}74 \quad p = 4.53 + \tfrac{2}{3}(5.21 - 3.39) = 5.74$$

$$1975\text{–}79 \quad p = 3.30 + \tfrac{2}{3}(4.28 - 1.41) = 5.21$$

A point on the Aukrust line (*AU* line) implies that prices and unit labour costs in the E-sector increase at the same constant rate and that the relationship between the profit share and the wage share remains constant. Furthermore, the international competitiveness does not change.

(a) Combining the Aukrust equation *AU* and the Phillips relation *R* enables us to make the following interpretation of the intersection of both curves: the rate of inflation of a small open economy ('the inflation margin') is determined exogenously. The Phillips Curve, on the other hand, shows the level of excess demand (= rate of unemployment) that generates the required rate of an adjustment inflation.

(b) We can now consider the performance of the Austrian economy in the context of the Scandinavian model for the periods 1966–74 and 1975–79. In 1975–79 the rate of domestic inflation lies above but 'near' the 'inflation margin' defined by the Aukrust line. Therefore the profit share in the E-sector had a tendency to

Fig. 4 Inflation in Austria: (a) 1966–74; (b) 1975–79

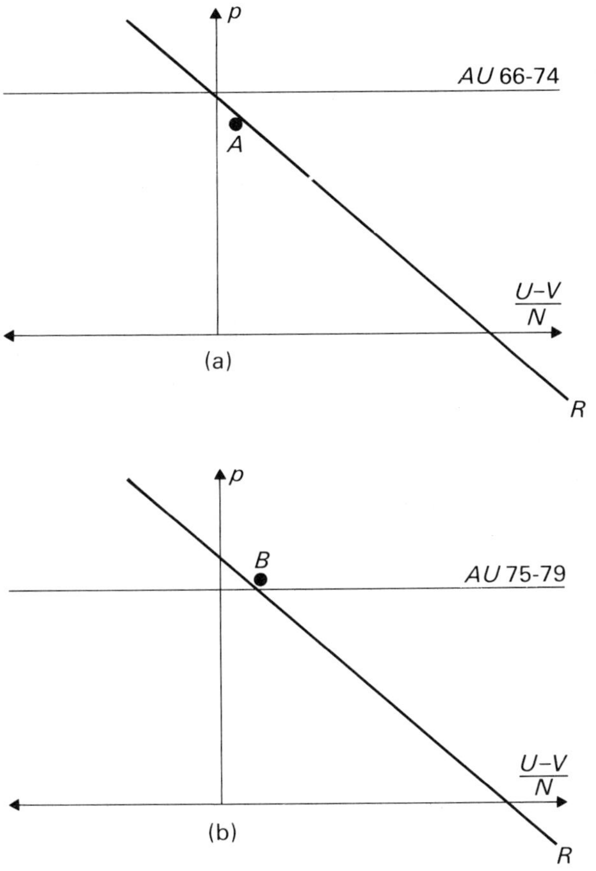

decrease in this period, and in addition under fixed exchange rates the international competitiveness of the E-sector deteriorated. The rate of growth of money wages has overtaken the rate $\lambda_E + p_E$.

In the period 1966–74 the domestic rate of inflation lay, on average, below the 'inflation margin' and was 'near' the Phillips Curve. Thus in this period the share of profit per unit of output and the international competitiveness of the Austrian economy increased.

(c) The real sector of the Austrian economy benefited from the acceleration of international inflation during 1970–74, as it was possible to reduce the rate of unemployment under the level of the previous period. The average value of $(U-V)/N$ was:

1966–70	1.12
1961–75	−0.28
1976–79	0.9

An acceleration in the world inflation p_w shifted both the Aukrust equation (the 'inflation margin') and the Phillips Curve upward. Since the 'coefficient of transmission' (0.437 in equation (12)) is less than 1, the upward shift of the Phillips Curve was smaller than that of the Aukrust line and the new intersection implies a decrease on the rate of unemployment. The situation is portrayed in figure 5. The starting point is A, the crossing point of p_0 and R_0. After an acceleration of the international inflation the economy will be at position B, with more (imported) inflation but less unemployment.

(d) The inflationary transmission process in Austria in the period under discussion can be interpreted as follows. An acceleration of international inflation first raises the profit share in the E-sector and thus induces an increase in production and employment. On the labour market excess demand develops ($(U-V)/N < 0$), whereby (through the Phillips relation) the rate of unemployment falls and money wages rise. A greater rise in prices in the E-sector than in the unit labour costs will result in an improve-

Fig. 5 The acceleration of inflation

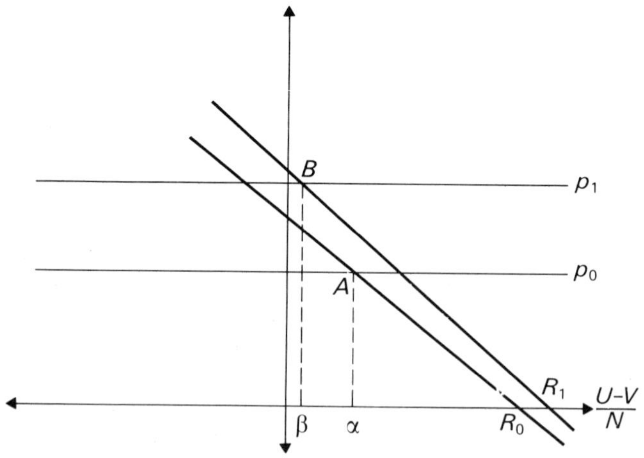

ment in the current external account. A surplus in the balance of payments will lead to an increase in the monetary base, thereby increasing the rate of money supply. On the other hand, if the rise in unit labour costs overtakes the price rise in the E-sector, the current external account will deteriorate. Under the condition of a 'neutral' monetary policy, aggregate demand will shrink and unemployment will develop on the labour market.

Fiscal policy

The Austrian policy-makers tried to conduct an activist countercyclical fiscal policy. According to it, the public sector should withdraw purchasing power from the economy in the boom period through budgetary surpluses. Can the Austrian fiscal policy be labelled 'anticyclical'? This is a rather important question, since budget surpluses and deficits will, to a certain extent, be generated automatically through the fluctuations of economic activity, and these automatic or induced changes should be distinguished from discretionary changes in fiscal policy. The actual budget does not reveal to what extent the balance arose because of discretionary measures by the government or as an induced result of economic fluctuations. For the judgement upon expansive or restrictive effects of the budget, we use the concept of the full employment budget (FEB). The actual expenditures are thereby compared with (fictitious) tax revenues at the level of full capacity utilization ('full employment'; see Guger, 1978). In figure 6 we plot on the abscissa the GDP gap (the difference between the potential output (PO) and the actual output as a percentage of the PO); on the ordinate, the FEB as a percentage of the PO. It seems that the points scattered in this diagram can be explained through two regression lines, one indicating a more restrictive regime of fiscal policy (line *A*, period 1965–72), the other, a more expansive regime (line *B*, 1973–79).

In the sub-period 1970–72, when the GDP gap was less than 1 per cent, the government generated surpluses in the FEB. The policy was clearly countercyclical in the sense of dampening aggregate demand.

Consider the sub-period 1973–75. In 1973 and 1974 the economy remained in a strong expansionary position (the points lie exactly on the PO line); however, the fiscal stimulus was procyclical because the FEBs are negative. In the recession year 1975 and the following years (1976, 1977, 1978), with underutilization of capacity, the budget deficits exhibit unambiguously expansive effects although they could

Fig. 6 Full employment budget, 1960–80: line *A*, 1960–72; line *B*, 1973–81 (PO = potential output)

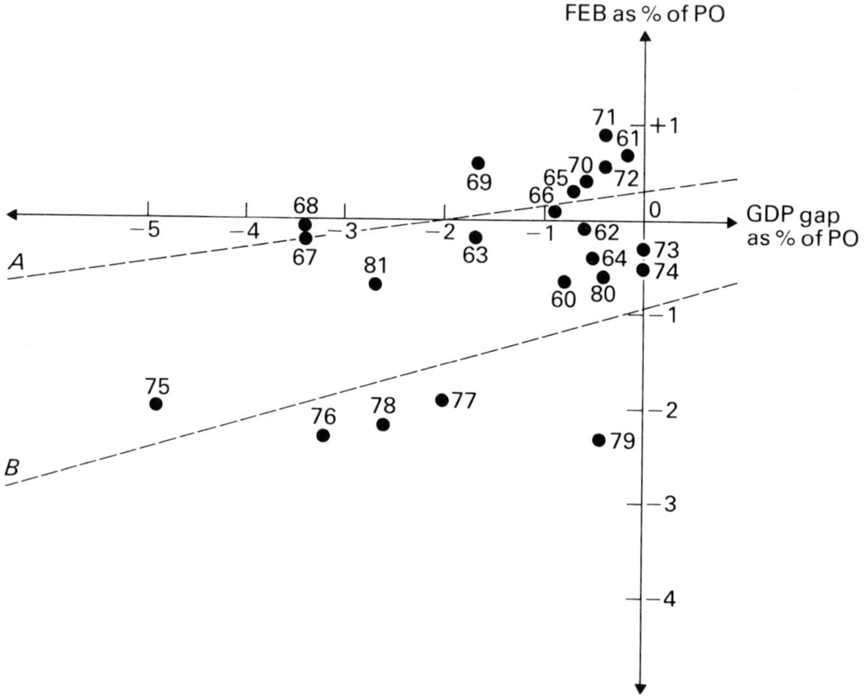

not entirely compensate for the strong economic downturn. In 1978 and 1980 economic activity recovered rapidly and the actual output again approached PO. In these two years the federal budget was clearly 'procyclical'. If we consider the last decade the fiscal policy was anticyclical seven times – in 1970, 1971, 1972, 1975, 1976, 1977 and 1978 – and procyclical four times – in 1973, 1974, 1979 and 1980.

The 'expansive' effect of the budget deficit is based upon the operation of the 'multipliers'. The multiplier effect of an open economy is essentially characterized by two parameters: the marginal rate to consume, c, and the marginal rate to import, h. The multiplier has been estimated for 1975 (in normal terms) under the assumption:

$$c = 0.88$$

$$h = 0.3$$

$$t = 0.2$$

The quantity t can be called the marginal tax rate in macro. The multiplier was:

$$\frac{1}{1-c(1-t)+h} = 1.67.$$

Since the marginal propensity to import has greatly increased ever since 1975, to about $h = 0.6$, the multiplier has declined to about 1.1 in 1980. An additional schilling spent and financed through a budget deficit creates only 1.1 schilling additional domestic income. The rise in imports represents a leakage from the domestic spending stream and implies that a growing part of public expenditure flows abroad. Furthermore, the multiplier is a 'real' rather than a nominal concept. Because of the high inflation rate of 1975 and 1976, the 'real' effect of the multiplier was further dampened. One can say, therefore, that the multiplier has lost its effectiveness with the transition of the 1975 recession to a period of recovery in 1976 and 1977. The reduction of the multiplier effect, as far as it can be explained by the increased propensity to import, was favoured by the Austrian 'hard currency' policy as well as by the fact that in this period the most important trading partners of Austria developed a less activist countercyclical policy (like West Germany) or even aggravated the recession, as for instance Switzerland.

The other side of the coin of the activist countercyclical fiscal policy is the growth of national debt. The financial debt of the Austrian state (federal government) per capita corresponds to the average of the OECD countries; it has, however, increased rapidly in recent years in the wake of deficit spending. Total national debt was about 10 per cent of the GDP in 1971–72 and rose until 1980 to about 25 per cent of the GDP. Through the work of E. Domar (1944) it has been known for a long time that the public debt in relation to the national income, the debt–income ratio, approaches a certain limit if the rate of growth of real income, g, is constant and the government borrows a certain fraction α of the national income. Under these conditions the debt–income ratio will converge to α/g and the 'interest burden' (the interest payment–income ratio) to $r/(r/\alpha+r)$. Domar's conclusion was that the 'burden of debt' defined as one (or both) of these ratios will not exceed a certain limit in the context of a growing economy. If the budget deficit remains at 4 per cent of the GDP ($=0.04$) – as was the case in Austria in the last three years – and if the nominal rate of growth amounts to 7.5 per cent[1] on average ($g = 0.075$), then the debt–income ratio would tend towards $\alpha/g = 0.53$ and would remain at this value. The public debt would then make up about one-half of one year's gross domestic product.

Under the further assumption that the rate of interest r for government debt is 10 per cent, the ratio of interest payments to private income will approach to 0.05, which means that a tax of 5 per cent on private income would be necessary in order to meet the costs of interest payments. These results are valid only when the economy grows at a constant relative rate. However, if real income grows in absolute rates, and if the government again borrows each year a constant fraction of the GDP, then a less pleasing situation develops: the 'burden of interest' (the interest payment–income ratio) approaches 1 – although relatively slowly – and public debt increases practically beyond limits (see Blaas and Matzner, 1976).

Although it is theoretically impossible to formulate exact limits for the national debt, it is not feasible in economic practice to go on to make household deficit beyond control. The actual practice of the Austrian national debt policy consists of financing about one-quarter of the budget deficit by foreign credit and three-quarters on the domestic capital market. To resort to foreign capital markets means that Austria is continuously exposed to international credit rating in foreign currency; on the other hand it supports the Austrian policy of 'hard currency' since it balances out the losses in international reserves resulting from the frequent external account deficits. In the long run, a high national debt has the unfortunate effect of reducing the possibilities for stabilization policy, although it was the stabilization policy that created the national debt in the first place.

Monetary policy

For good Keynesians, as the Austrian policy-makers are, it appears obvious that money supply by itself cannot be considered the objective of monetary policy. In contrast to the (quasi-) monetarist practice in West Germany or Switzerland, the Austrian National Bank did not pursue a quantitative money target. The principal objective of monetary policy was to maintain a fixed exchange rate against the Deutschmark. In effect, the exchange rate is then fixed for a major part of foreign transactions, thus implying interventions in the exchange market and fluctuations in the monetary base (see table 5). The stable exchange rate relation to the strong currencies of

Table 5 Effect of Austria's monetary policy on some variables

Year	*M1*	*MB**	*m†*	*x+p‡*
	%	%	%	%
1971	11.1	8.8	2.3	10.0
1972	15.6	16.0	−0.4	12.6
1973	11.4	10.0	1.4	12.9
1974	5.9	3.5	2.4	13.8
1975	10.9	12.9	2.0	6.7
1976	11.6	6.3	5.3	13.1
1977	5.9	6.8	−0.9	9.9
1978	4.3	9.3	−5.0	4.6
1979	−0.8	7.1	−7.9	8.8

* Monetary base † Multipler ‡ Nominal income

the Austrian trading partners means that money supply is to a large extent endogenous and strongly influenced by changes in the balance of payments. This is the reason why the Austrian monetary authorities consider money supply as an inappropriate objective for a small open economy (OECD, 1981, p. 45). As a consequence, within the limits set by exchange rate policy, monetary policy was directed towards a control and stabilization of the interest rates. The Bank's board of directors, for instance, stated that the Bank aimed at 'interest rates which will ensure that not every influence coming from the market will have a direct effect on the interest level' (Kernbauer, 1976, p. 29). Recently this monetary policy was characterized as 'an active policy for nominal interest constancy' (Winckler, 1979, p. 62).

In the first half of the 1970s Austria's level of the interest rates was below the German level, but in the second half a positive interest rate differential against West Germany developed. Domestic interest rates cannot be kept below foreign rates by domestic money creation, since capital outflows would tend to depreciate the Austrian schilling against the Deutschmark and thus interfere with the exchange rate target (see Handler, 1980a).

Owing to the dominating role of the exchange rate policy, it was unavoidable to make monetary policy – at least as a medium-term objective – compatible with the exchange rate target. Under the impression of an extraordinary influx of international reserves in 1972 (the monetary base increased by 16 per cent – see table 5), which built up a considerable monetary inflationary potential, the

Austrian National Bank began to devote direct attention to the development of money supply.

As a consequence, a system of credit rationing (the so-called 'limes') for commercial banks was implemented according to which the rate of credit expansion (for non-bank credits) was not allowed to exceed a certain announced percentage rate per month.

Changes in the rate of growth of money supply affect price and income developments in Austria but only indirectly, and with a rather long lag, because of the existing prices and incomes policy. Direct effects upon real aggregated demand, however, can be found under certain conditions. The monetary expansion in 1975 and 1976 (table 5) clearly stimulated the domestic absorption of domestic and foreign goods and led to a deterioration of the current account in the following years. On the other hand, a stabilization programme consisting of a more restrictive monetary policy and a tax increase for durables generated a decline in domestic demand and brought about a significant reduction in the deficit of the current external account in 1978.

Let us have a closer look at the figures. Table 5 shows a decomposition of the growth of money supply M1 into two components: the monetary base, MB, and the multiplier, m. (Both components are represented in percentage rates of growth.)

The last column shows the rate of growth of nominal income $(x+p)$. It will be observed that the development of M1 is largely explained by the development of the monetary base. The contribution of the multiplier is relatively modest, except in 1976, where the mutliplier explains a significant portion of the money supply increase, and in 1978 and 1979, where the negative multiplier effect accounts for the retardation in the rate of growth or in the contraction of the level of M1. The negative contribution of the multiplier was caused by a reallocation of the private sector's portfolio from demand deposits to time and savings deposits owing to a rise in the interest rate for deposits. Table 5 also shows that a restrictive monetary policy in Austria was effective in the years 1974 and 1977. In these two years the rate of growth of nominal income (= rate of increase of demand for money) exceeded considerably the rate of money supply measured by M1. In 1974 the Austrian National Bank followed the restrictive monetary policy of the OECD countries with the delay of one year; in 1977 a restrictive monetary policy was pursued to reduce the external account deficit.

In the 1960s and the first half of the 1970s the long-run expansion of the monetary base was ensured by the accumulation of international reserves. Fluctuations have been offset by compensatory operations of the Austrian National Bank (discounts and advances to commercial banks). The repeated appearance of deficits in the current external account (in the second half of the 1970s) led to an important change in the sources of the monetary base. The net domestic assets became increasingly important for the permanent provision of the monetary base. The share of the domestic component of the monetary base increased from 10 per cent at the beginning of the 1970s to 36 per cent in 1979.

In summary, one can say that the Austrian National Bank did not define a money supply target. The monetary policy was directed towards a stabilization of the entire structure rather than the money supply. From 1973 onwards it tried to slow down the growth of money supply through the instrument of credit rationing. The objective of this moderate restrictive monetary policy was to avoid an increasing inflation differential between Austria and Germany, and to support the 'hard currency policy'.

Exchange rate policy

The exchange rate policy has played a central role in the Austrian stabilization policy. After the breakdown of the Bretton Woods system the Austrian National Bank decided to pursue an 'index-oriented' exchange rate policy. An export-weighted average of the 'Snake' currencies and the Swiss franc were used as a yardstick for exchange market interventions. This approach implied that most of the time the Italian lira, the pound sterling and the French franc were excluded from the currency basket. From the middle of 1976 onwards the schilling was *de facto* linked solely to the Deutschmark (see Kienzl, 1978). This linkage of the exchange rate to the Deutschmark has had considerable consequences. Since the Deutschmark floated continually upwards during the period 1970–77, this specific construction of a 'hard currency policy' meant an effective appreciation of the schilling of about 26 per cent in this period. Table 6 shows the development of the effective exchange rate of the Austrian schilling.

If the exchange rate appreciates exactly to the extent of the differential between the international rate of inflation, p^*, and the domestic rate of inflation, p, there are no 'real' effects. In percentage rates we have $\hat{w} = p^* - p$; where $\hat{w}$ is the change in the exchange rate. If the rise in the effective (=nominal) exchange rate exceeds

Table 6 Development of the effective exchange rate of the Austrian schilling

		% change
1970	100	
1975	115.1	2.9
1976	119.5	3.8
1977	126.1	5.5
1978	127.2	0.9
1979	128.9	1.3
1980	132.7	2.9

Table 7 Development of the real exchange rate of the Austrian schilling

		% change
1970	100	
1975	109.6	1.0
1976	113.1	3.1
1977	116.7	3.1
1978	115.5	−1.1
1979	113.1	−2.1
1980	112.5	−0.5

the inflation differential ($\hat{w} > p^* - p$), a 'real' revaluation takes place. If, on the other hand, the effective exchange rate increases, but increases less than the domestic rate of inflation falls short of the international rate ($w < p^* - p$), one can speak of a 'real' devaluation (see Seidel, 1978, and Dorn, 1979).

Although the index of the effective exchange rate moved up during the period 1970–79, there was a devaluation in real terms in 1978 and 1979. The appreciation of the effective exchange rate was smaller than the difference between the foreign rate of inflation and the domestic rate of inflation (table 8).

The concrete form of the Austrian hard currency policy, namely to keep the schilling in a relative stable relation to the strong currencies of its main trading partners, especially the Deutschmark, seems to fit the stabilization policy in the framework of the Scandinavian model. H. Handler (1980b) collected the following arguments in favour of the hard currency policy that might reflect the concept of the Austrian policy-makers (see also Kienzl, 1978).

Table 8 Appreciation of the effective exchange rate compared with the difference between foreign and domestic rates of inflation

	$\hat{w}$ *(change in the effective exchange rate)*	$p^* - p$ *(difference in the rates of inflation)*
	%	%
1978	0.9	2.0
1979	1.3	3.4
1980	2.9	3.4

1. Pegging the schilling to the currency of an important trading partner that has a higher degree of price stability than Austria will result in 'importing' stability.
2. A small open economy is a price-taker in the world market. Prices in foreign currency are therefore assumed to be given. The 'hard currency' policy therefore will squeeze profits in the E-sector and motivate the firms to resist excessive wage claims of the trade unions. This will reduce inflationary pressure in the whole economy.
3. The hard currency policy is likely to create a climate of monetary stability, thus breaking inflationary expectations and facilitating income policy.
4. The profit squeeze in the E-sector as a result of the appreciating schilling will change the production structure and induce entrepreneurs to raise productivity. This in turn will improve the long-run competitive position of the E-sector.
5. Empirical experience in other countries (UK, Italy) shows that a 'weak currency policy', i.e., a purposely downward-floating of the exchange rate, very easily becomes a vicious circle. Devaluation produces greater inflation, which in turn induces offsetting movements in money wages; the higher wage costs leads to further devaluations; etc.
6. From econometric estimations about price elasticities it can not be expected that a devaluation of the schilling would significantly reduce the share of imports or increase exports.

The dominant argument in this selection for hard currency seems to be based on the vicious circle argument. Following an exogenous depreciation, the vicious economy will suffer a consecutive process of self-reinforcing inflation and depreciation, ending with a new equilibrium position where prices and exchange rates are higher than in a non-vicious economy with flexible prices and a controlled money supply. The avoidance of this vicious circle seems to be a prerequisite to carrying out 'incomes policy', one of the basic concepts of Austrian economic policy.

Incomes policy

A speciality of the Austrian economic policy is incomes policy, the so-called 'social partnership' between the unions and the employers. While monetary and fiscal policy are used to influence aggregate demand and the level of employment, incomes policy is implemented to control 'cost-push' developments. These are inflationary developments resulting from wage-push and/or profit-push impulses. The Austrian variant of incomes policy can be characterized by three factors:

1. it is a long-run concept;
2. it is based upon voluntary co-operation between the 'social partners' and the government;
3. it does not formulate any quantitative, binding wage and price guide lines.

Contrary to wage and price controls and wage and price stops introduced for a while in the early 1970s by Great Britain and the United States, incomes policy in Austria represents a continuous economic policy activity. It is based upon the co-operation of representatives of employers, trade unions and the government in the so-called 'parity commission', where questions pertaining to wage agreements ('wage-rounds'), as well as demands for price settlements by particular firms or even industries, are subjected to a voluntary procedure of approval. The objective of the parity commission is to accept price increases only as a consequence of cost increases, and to keep wage agreements within a framework given by labour productivity increases as well as accepted inflationary expectations. It is quite easily possible to interpret the objective of the Austrian incomes policy in terms of the 'Scandinavian' model of inflation (see Frisch, 1977). It is important to align the development of money wages to changes in the productivity of labour in the exposed sector as well as to the international inflation rate in order to guarantee the long-term competitive position of the Austrian economy. The acceptance procedure of the parity commission could admittedly not prevent inflation as well as corresponding increases in money wages during the period 1971–76; it could, however, considerably dampen the transmission of the rapidly growing international inflation in 1973 and 1974 upon the Austrian price development. Above all, incomes policy prevented excessive inflationary anticipations from becoming an element in wage and price determination and thus further enhancing the dynamics of the inflationary development. This incomes policy, which is directed towards price stability and a dampening of inflationary expectations, has been supported decisively by the policy of a hard currency through its 'import of stability'.

In recent years the need for wages moderation has been accepted by the social partners, and the inevitable terms of trade loss caused by the oil price rise was not offset by higher nominal wage agreements. The incomes policy reflected in wage moderation has been an important factor in enabling the domestic eonomy to absorb relatively smoothly the second oil shock without a major loss of employment.

In summary, it can be said that the Austrian variant of incomes policy (the 'social partnership') has had a general effect of retardation. In inflationary periods it has dampened the increase in income and prices; in periods of recession it has prevented a rapid reduction of excessive nominal income levels corresponding to a reduced rate of real growth and inflation.

Notes

1 This assumption is made by the Council of Economic and Social Affairs (1978), p. 30.

2 Kernbauer quotes the president of the Austrian National Bank, H. Kloss: 'Every change in the interest structure poses problems as it can have unforeseen and undesirable consequences.' See also 'Mitteilungen des Direktoriums der Osterreichischen Nationalbank' (1976), p. 734.

References

Androsch, H. (1978), 'Stabilisierungsprobleme einer offenen Volkswirtschaft – Das Österreichische Beispiel'. *Quartalshefte der Girozentrale*, vol. 13, nos. 2/3.

Aukrust, O. (1970). 'Prim. I: A model of the price and income distribution mechanism of an open economy'. *Artikler fra Statistik Sentralbyra*, vol. 35.

Blaas, W. and Matzner, E. (1976), 'Budgetdefizite bei langsamen Wirtschaftswachstum – Möglichkeiten und Grenzen', *Quartalshefte der Girozentrale*, vol. 21, no. 4.

Calmfors, L. (1977), 'Inflation in Sweden'. In L. B. Klein and W. S. Salants (eds), *Worldwide Inflation, Theory and Recent Experience* (Brookings Institution, Washington DC).

Council of Economic and Social Affairs (1978), *Budgetvorschau 1978–1982* (CESA, Vienna).

Domar, E. 'The "burden" of the debt and the national income'. *American Economic Review*, vol. 34.

Dorn, H. (1979), 'Wechselkurspolitik ohne feste Spielregeln: Österreichs Hartwährungspolitik 1971–1979'. *Wirtschaftspolitische Blätter*, vol. 26, no. 6.

Frisch, H. (1977). 'The Scandinavian model of inflation: a generalization and empirical evidence'. *Atlantic Economic Journal*, vol. 5.

Guger, A. (1978), 'Der Vollbeschäftigungssaldo als Instrument zur Beurteilung der konjunkturellen Wirkungen der Budgetpolitik des Bundes'. *Wirtschaft und Gesellschaft*, vol. 4, no. 4.

Handler, H. (1980a), 'Internationale und nationale Rahmenbedingungen für die monetäre Entwicklung in den achtziger Jahren'. In, H. Seidel and H. Kramer (eds), *Die österreichische Wirtschaft in den achtziger Jahren* (G. Fischer, Stuttgart).

Handler, H. (1980b), 'The exchange rate as an intermediate target of stabilization policy in Austria'. Supplement to *Kredit und Kapital*, no. 6, reprinted in H. Frisch und G. Schwödiauer, 'The Economics of Flexible Exchange Rates', p. 383.

Kernbauer, H. (1976), 'Die zinspolitischen Möglichkeiten der österreichischen Nationalbank'. *Wirtschaftspolitische Blätter*, vol. 24, no. 3.

Kienzl, H. (1978), 'Währungspolitik in Konjunktur und Krise'. *Wirtschaft und Gesellschaft*, vol. 4, no. 2.

Lindbeck, A. (ed.) (1979), *Inflation and Employment in Open Economies* (North-Holland, Amsterdam).

OECD (1981), *Economic Survey* (OECD, Paris), p. 45.

Seidel, H. (1978), 'Der effektive Wechselkurs des Schilling', *Monatsberichte des österreichischen Instituts für Wirtschaftsforschung*, vol. 51.

Suppanz, H. and Robinson, D. (1972), *Prices and incomes policy. The Austrian Experience* (OECD, Paris).

Winckler, G. (1979), 'Probleme der Zinspolitik in Österreich'. *Wirtschaft und Gesellschaft*, vol. 5, no. 4.

The New Economic Environment in the 1970s: Market and Policy Response in Switzerland

RENÉ KÄSTLI
Swiss National Bank, Zurich

Introduction

How did Switzerland react to the many and sizeable shocks of the 1970s? This general question touches upon two separate issues: the market reactions to these shocks, and the response of economic policy.

Markets are constantly subject to changing conditions; but the shocks in the 1970s were probably sharper and more frequent than any in the preceding 20 years. The way in which the Swiss market participants and the Swiss authorities reacted to this situation is quite distinct from the issue of how the restrictions for economic policy changed, and is therefore treated separately.

With regard to economic policy, the most important event in the 1970s was certainly the emergence of a system of floating foreign exchange rates. The new system brought about entirely new conditions for operating monetary policy. While fiscal policy was more and more restricted by the growing concern about budget deficits, a monetary policy much more independent of events abroad came into being in small open economies. Therefore monetary policy was put in a new position in Switzerland. It is for this reason that I have chosen to focus mainly on monetary policy. This does not mean that the policy mix in Switzerland is now dominated by monetary policy; it only indicates that conditions have changed basically for monetary policy but have not altered for other forms of economic policy.

The shocks of the 1970s

Accelerations and decelerations of money supply

It is evident that monetary policy was responsible for some of the heavy shocks to Switzerland in the 1970s (compare tables 3 and 4 for the exact figures). Following the heavy inflow of foreign capital in the early 1970s, money growth was up sharply in 1971 and 1972. After the switch to floating exchange rates early in 1973, however, M1 growth rates two years later were down to approximately zero from a figure well in the two-digit range. In retrospect, it seems that in early 1973 the shock to the Swiss economy of having to adjust to rapidly changing growth rates of the money supply was too heavy to bear. The announced targets of a 6 per cent growth in the money supply for 1975 and 1976 and 5 per cent for 1977 and 1978 reflected the policy of gradually lowering the growth to rates that would lead to price stability. The deviation from the country's money supply goal, and again the subsequent return to the control of the monetary base, implied drastically changed financial conditions for the Swiss economy.

The oil shocks of 1973–74 and 1978–79

The oil shocks of the 1970s are only one example of changing relative prices. What makes them unique, apart from their political implications, is the size of the displacement and the fact that energy is an important factor of production. But it has to be noted that there were not only oil shocks in the 1970s but also, for example, raw material shocks. One should therefore keep in mind that oil serves as an example for the other shocks, too.

The effect of the oil shocks in Switzerland differed somewhat from that over the world as a whole. This is due to two different reasons. The first concerns the relevant US dollar prices. Switzerland's oil is purchased mainly in Rotterdam. Prices in Rotterdam relative to official OPEC prices were low during the first shock but high in the second. Therefore the 1973–74 price hikes were rather dampened for Switzerland, but were accentuated in 1978–79. The same holds true for the foreign exchange rate movements: the Swiss franc was very strong in 1973–74 but has been rather weak since the second major adjustment in the oil price.

On the whole, the first oil shock was (measured in relative price changes) much more severe worldwide than the second one; but in Switzerland the differences between the two were much smaller.

Fig. 1 Index of oil prices in Rotterdam and in Switzerland (beginning of 1973 = 100)

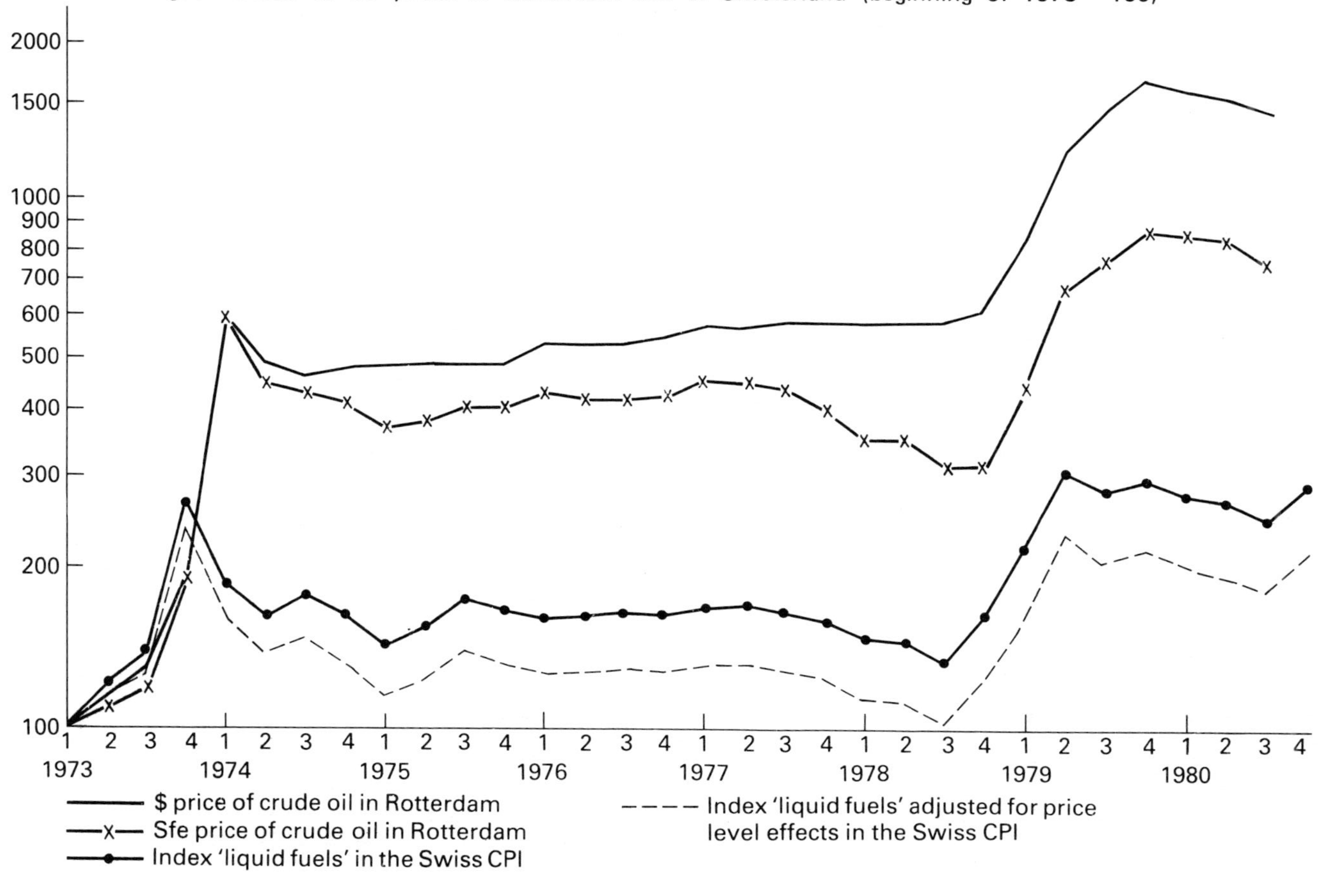

Figure 1 shows how the US dollar and Swiss franc prices for heating oil moved in Rotterdam. This graph exaggerates the oil shock, because the prices charged to the consumer moved less in relative terms since the costs of delivery, such as transport and taxes, did not move in line with the prices in Rotterdam. In order to show the magnitude of the change in relative prices the position 'liquid fuel' in the Swiss consumer price index, adjusted for the rise in the price level, is also shown. The oil shock calculated in this way shows more or less the same pattern in 1973–74 and in 1978–79. In fact, if the shock is measured in terms of petrol and not heating oil prices, the relative change is nothing like a 'shock'. Owing to heavy taxation, these prices moved only some 15 per cent in 1973–74 and some 20 per cent in 1978–79.

For monetary policy the question arises of whether external shocks of such a magnitude should have an influence on money supply. It is quite evident that a policy that does not respond to these price rises will force the necessary adjustment of relative prices through unexpected movements in money prices. This would, for example, imply that a money supply goal that aims at a zero inflation rate would force certain money prices to fall. It can be expected that adjustments of this type will have a contracting effect on the real economy. But this policy would minimize the effects on the price level. If monetary policy accommodates the shocks fully it must be expected that the oil price hikes will be translated into inflation rates substantially above the original goal. But such a policy will tend to reduce the real effects of the monetary policy, at least in the short run. Needless to say, the massive shifts in relative prices connected with the oil shocks will cause substantial adjustment costs either way.[1]

The Swiss monetary authorities tried to steer a middle course in this situation. While the Swiss National Bank was willing to let the price level move beyond the original goal, the money supply was not expanded to such an extent as to show the full price level effect of the oil price differences.

Foreign exchange rate movements

In early 1973 there was a widespread belief that after some initial adjustments foreign exchange rates would in general follow the actual inflation rate differential. This means that the index of the foreign exchange rate in real terms was expected to move around 100.[2]

Table 1 Index of the Swiss franc rate in real terms, 1973–80 (average 1974 = 100)

		Index vis-à-vis		
Monthly average		*$*	*DM*	*Total**
1973	June	98.2	93.7	95.8
	December	93.2	95.4	96.4
1974	June	98.8	96.0	97.8
	December	112.6	109.7	108.9
1975	June	117.3	108.1	105.9
	December	107.8	114.0	106.1
1976	June	112.8	116.5	114.0
	December	112.2	108.5	108.4
1977	June	106.3	103.1	101.6
	December	125.9	113.0	115.4
1978	June	133.9	119.2	120.3
	September	159.5	136.0	136.7
	December	145.5	120.4	123.8
1979	June	139.3	119.8	120.5
	December	140.9	116.2	117.9
1980	June†	129.5	113.7	109.2
	December†	115.5	117.1	107.0

* *Vis-à-vis* 15 important trading partners (trade-weighted)
† Provisional data
Source: Monatsbericht der Schweizerischen Nationalbank

Table 1 shows that this was not the case, certainly not in the short run. In autumn 1978 the appreciation of the Swiss franc in real terms reached nearly 40 per cent within four years and amounted to some 20 per cent within one year.

These movements created heavy adjustment problems for the Swiss economy. Exporters and domestic producers alike were faced with a situation in which their competitive situation worsened almost from day to day.

The extreme developments in the autumn of 1978 led the Swiss National Bank to abandon temporarily its money supply target. In this situation the Swiss National Bank remedied the situation so that, by announcing a foreign exchange rate goal *vis-à-vis* the Deutschmark and heavy interventions on the foreign exchange markets, the Swiss franc could be depreciated substantially within a relatively short time.

Real development outside Switzerland

It has already been pointed out that the Swiss economy is very open. Therefore developments in countries that buy Swiss exports are bound to influence the domestic economy. Table 2 shows the well-known fact that the most severe shock since 1961 took place in 1974 and 1975: growth rates of the OECD countries declined from 6.3 per cent in 1973 to 0.7 and −0.5 per cent in 1974 and 1975, respectively.

Table 2 Growth rates of real GNP of selected OECD countries

	USA	*Germany*	*France**	*OECD*
	%	%	%	%
1961	2.3	5.1	5.5	4.1
1962	5.6	4.4	6.7	5.3
1963	4.1	3.0	5.3	4.9
1964	5.1	6.7	6.5	6.3
1965	6.0	5.6	4.8	5.2
1966	6.0	2.5	5.2	5.4
1967	2.7	−0.2	4.7	3.9
1968	4.5	6.3	4.3	5.9
1969	2.6	7.8	7.0	5.4
1970	−0.1	6.0	5.7	3.9
1971	2.9	3.2	5.4	3.7
1972	5.8	3.7	5.9	5.5
1973	5.4	4.9	5.4	6.3
1974	−1.3	0.5	3.2	0.7
1975	−1.0	−1.8	0.3	−0.5
1976	5.6	5.2	5.2	5.3
1977	5.1	3.0	2.8	3.7
1978	4.4	3.3	3.6	3.9
1979	2.3	4.5	3.3	3.3
1980†	−0.1	1.8	1.6	1.0

* GDP
† Estimates
Source: OECD *Main Economic Indicators*

Market adjustments to the shocks

From what has been said above, it is evident that the Swiss economy had to adjust to a number of sizeable shocks during the 1970s. While it would be interesting also to examine the events that had an expansionary effect, we focus on the economically more intriguing adjustment to negative shocks. These were: an enormous deceleration of the growth rates in the money supply from 1972 to 1974; two oil shocks in 1973–74 and 1978–79; heavy appreciations of the Swiss franc in real terms up to 1978; and a slowing down of the economic activity of our main trading partners in 1974 and 1975.

In figure 2 the effects on the inflation rate and the growth rate of real GDP are shown. The most striking development is the slowing down of the inflation rate, from close to 10 per cent in 1974 to under 2 per cent in 1976.

The Swiss National Bank kept the money stock more or less constant during 1973 and 1974. That this monetary policy would eventually have effects on the price level had to be expected. But it is interesting to note that the lag between the shift in monetary policy and the price level response was, judging from international experience, quite long. This may have to do with the behaviour of the banks, which still held ample reserves owing to the very big increases in the monetary base of 1971 and 1972.

It is not surprising that such an anti-inflationary policy has also real effects. The old wisdom that these real effects show before the price level reacts is corroborated quite clearly in the experience of the mid-1970s in Switzerland. What is surprising is that the negative

Fig. 2 Inflation rate and growth rate of real GDP, 1961–80

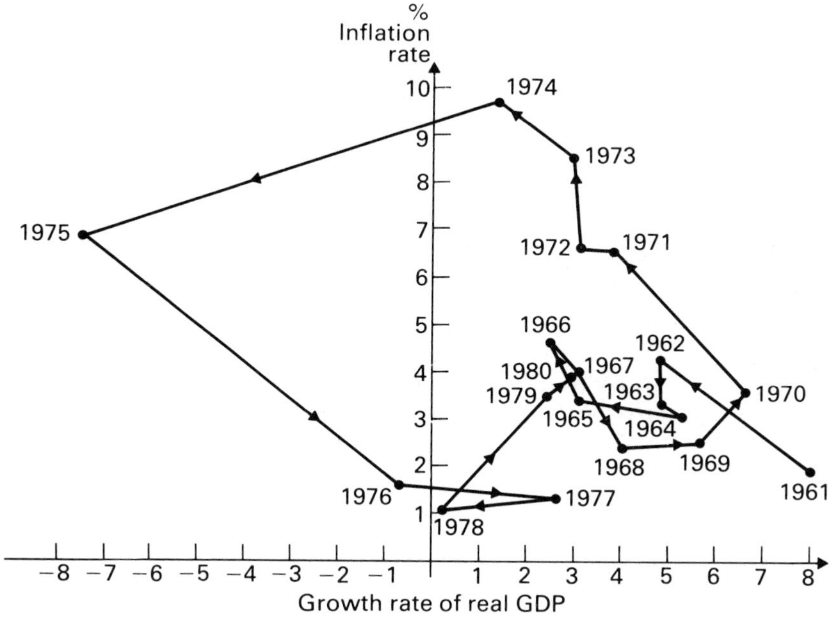

growth rates in 1975 – Switzerland recorded the sharpest decline in economic activity of all OECD countries in that year – and 1976 did not show up accordingly in the employment figures. Only for two months in the beginning of 1976 were unemployment rates slightly over 1 per cent, and they dropped below this figure afterwards.

There are several reasons for this. The one cited most often is that unemployment was exported. While the foreign active population dropped by some 200 000 people from its peak in 1973 to its trough in 1977, this figure clearly overstates the export of unemployment because the foreign active population declined substantially also by naturalization. It should be noted that a large part of the foreign working population has labour contracts that, owing to legal requirements, expire after nine months. These so-called seasonal labour contracts require the worker to emigrate after the expiration of his contract. The worker who enters into such a contract does therefore not seek permanent residence in Switzerland. Moreover, the decline of foreign workers certainly does not fully explain the drop of the active population by some 300 000 in the period from 1973–77.

Another reason why Okun's law did not work the same way in Switzerland as it did in the United States was the generally tight labour markets, which had led to the employment of many workers beyond their normal retirement age. When these people dropped out of the labour force they did not show up in the unemployment figures. A similar argument applies to female participation.

For these reasons, one might conclude that Switzerland was in a special position in 1974–76, and could not hope to have similarly low unemployment figures in other troughs of economic activity. This is only partly true. Certain factors lead one to believe that the Swiss situation may be somewhat more manipulable than that in other countries. One of these is the quick response of the labour force and of wages to changed conditions. In certain sectors – especially construction and some parts of textile industries – it is not uncommon for not only real but even nominal wages to be cut. Many of the problems connected with wage stickiness do not seem to show as clearly in Switzerland as in other countries. This is certainly due to a large part to the marked willingness of both parties on the labour market to find a mutual beneficial long-run solution to temporary problems, and to the recognition of the labour unions that structural changes have to take place in order to keep the economy sound. One example of these special labour relations is the so-called peace treaty in the machine industry. This treaty dates back to 1937 and explicitly excludes strikes in labour disputes.

Some institutional reasons should also be mentioned in this connection. First, the labour force in Switzerland is to a large part highly skilled. New employment will therefore normally cause high initial training costs. It will therefore not pay to vary the labour force with only slight and judged-to-be temporary reductions of demand. Second, unemployment insurance is conceived in such a way that it is not possible to live permanently off unemployment benefits. Third, after their mandatory schooling youths normally enter into long-run contracts providing a combination of formal schooling and on-the-job training. This apprenticeship arrangement takes care of the integration of newly entering workers, making youth unemployment almost non-existent.

Taking all these factors into consideration, one comes to the conclusion that Switzerland probably would have higher unemployment figures during a recession of the size of 1975–76, but would still be better off than many other countries.

Another reason why Switzerland had adjusted comparatively well to the recent changes may be the general confidence in the market mechanism. The 1975–76 downturn triggered some government programmes aimed at stimulating the economy by means of fiscal policy. But these programmes were designed to be temporary, and did not try to prevent necessary structural changes in the market. Owing to the, at times, heavy appreciation of the Swiss franc, these structural changes had to take place quite rapidly. While profit margins deteriorated substantially during these forced adjustments, it can be said that the necessary changes have taken place and, moreover, that the Swiss economy is probably in a better position to recognize and react to new shocks than it was ten years ago.

As in other countries, the oil shocks led to a substantial deterioration in the balance on current account. In 1980, for the first time since 1965, there was a deficit in the current account. Since Swiss financial markets are working well, the country did not have any problems financing this deficit domestically. Swiss firms or government therefore had no need to use the Euromarkets to a greater extent than before in order to finance their needs.

New conditions for economic policy under a system of flexible exchange rates

Switzerland's small and very open eonomy presents several problems with respect to monetary policy. Under a system of fixed exchange rates the money supply could not be controlled effectively; while under flexible exchange rates, the movements of the foreign exchange rate play a much greater role in determining the actual course of monetary policy than would be the case in a more closed economy.

Monetary policy in a small open economy under a regime of fixed exchange rates

Under the regime of fixed exchange rates, Switzerland was very reluctant to adjust the foreign exchange rate. Between 1946 and the beginning of 1973, when floating exchange rates were adopted, the Swiss franc was revalued only twice, in May 1971 and in the general realignment in December 1971. Since the Swiss franc tended to be strong, there was substantial short-run capital flowing into Switzerland when either a devaluation of other currencies or the revaluation of the Swiss franc was expected. Furthermore, Switzerland ran a surplus on its current account from 1966 on. Since the official foreign exchange rate would not clear the market, a large part of the inflow of foreign currencies had to be purchased by the Swiss National Bank.

Creation of base money is dominated by the foreign reserve component in Switzerland. Large inflows of foreign capital under a regime of fixed exchange rates were therefore reflected in respective growth rates of the monetary base. This means that under these institutional arrangements the monetary base was determined endogenously and not by a decision of the Swiss National Bank.

Even during the 1960s, this system had created problems with respect to a monetary policy geared to price stability. Given the circumstances, the Swiss authorities – not being willing to adjust foreign exchange rates – had to take measures against capital inflows or to try to prevent the, at times, excessive growth rates of the monetary base from being translated into respective growth rates of other monetary aggregates. This was done either by minimum reserve requirements or by restricting the growth of credits granted by Swiss banks.

Not surprisingly, the efficacy of these measures was limited. While different measures were in force between 1960 and early 1967, and again in different forms from autumn 1969 to 1980, the growth rates of the monetary base and of the money supply M1 moved remarkably close together. From this it follows that not only the monetary base but also M1 was factually determined endogenously and not by the central bank. This means, in other words, that the monetary aggregate M1 that best reflects the course of monetary policy[4] could not be controlled by the Swiss National Bank.

The situation of Switzerland under a regime of fixed exchange rates was typical for a small open economy. Monetary policy was made abroad; therefore, up to the end of 1972 the growth rates of the monetary base shown in table 3 do not reflect a well-defined

Table 3 The growth rate of net foreign assets and of the monetary base, 1961–80

	$\frac{\Delta RES_t}{RES_{t-1}} \times 100^\dagger$	$\frac{\Delta B_t}{B_{t-1}} \times 100^\dagger$
	%	%
1961	26.9	9.3
1962	2.3	5.9
1963	3.9	7.1
1964	7.8	6.7
1965	4.7	6.3
1966	1.6	2.2
1967	4.6	6.8
1968	3.3	12.5
1969	3.7	6.9
1970	10.2	6.7
1971	30.3	22.0
1972	20.2	15.8
1973	3.9	−1.0
1974	−5.3	7.0
1975	7.8	5.7
1976	8.7	3.8
1977	2.1	6.4
1978	18.1	9.6
1979	−15.1	9.1
1980	−19.0	−2.1
Averages		
1961–80	6.0	7.3
1961–72	10.0	9.0
1973–80	0.2	4.8

Notes

RES_t = net foreign assets (including gold) held by the Swiss National Bank at time t

B_t = monetary base at time t

† Yearly averages of the 12-monthly year-to-year growth rates

Sources: 'Revision der Geldmengenstatistik', *Beilage zum Monatsbericht der Schweizerischen Nationalbank* (August 1975); Monatsberichte der Schweizerischen Nationalbank. The figures are currently revised. In order to facilitate comparisons, only published figures are used

money supply policy of the Swiss National Bank. This led to difficulties, with respect to a monetary growth, that were considered to be unacceptable, especially in the early 1960s and early 1970s (see table 4).

Table 4 Inflation rates and growth rates of the money stock M1, 1961–80*)

	$\frac{\Delta M1_t}{M1_{t-1}} \times 100$	$\frac{\Delta GDP_t}{GDP_{t-1}} \times 100$	$\left(\frac{\Delta M1_t}{M1_{t-1}} - \frac{\Delta GDP_t}{GDP_{t-1}}\right) \times 100$	Inflation rate
1961	14.7	8.1	6.6	1.9
1962	10.5	4.8	5.7	4.3
1963	7.6	4.9	2.7	3.4
1964	5.9	5.3	0.6	3.1
1965	4.5	3.2	1.3	3.4
1966	2.7	2.5	0.2	4.7
1967	3.0	3.1	0.1	4.0
1968	9.5	3.6	5.9	2.4
1969	5.4	5.6	−0.2	2.5
1970	5.0	6.4	−1.4	3.6
1971	16.4	4.1	12.3	6.6
1972	17.9	3.2	14.3	6.7
1973	2.3	3.0	−0.7	8.7
1974	0.1	1.5	−1.4	9.8
1975	4.3	−7.3	11.6	6.7
1976	7.7	−1.4	9.1	1.7
1977	5.4	2.4	3.0	1.8
1978	16.2	0.3	15.9	1.0
1979	9.0	2.2	6.8	3.6
1980	−9.0	3.0	−12.0	4.0
Averages				
1961–80	6.9	2.9	4.0	4.2
1961–72	8.6	4.6	4.0	3.9
1973–80	4.5	0.5	4.0	4.6

* Yearly averages of the monthly year-to-year growth rates
Source: Monatsberichte der Schweizerischen Nationalbank

Monetary policy under a regime of floating exchange rates

The transition from a foreign exchange rate policy to a money supply policy[5]

In early 1973 Switzerland decided to abandon the exchange rates fixed in the Smithsonian Agreement. This decision was taken when it became apparent that capital inflows would be of unprecedented size if fixed exchange rates were to be maintained. The transition meant that it was possible from then on to influence at least the amount of

Swiss francs newly put in circulation. But this also meant that the Swiss National Bank had to take full responsibility for doing this.

This responsibility was interpreted in such a way that a money supply policy consistent with the long-run goal of price stability had to be created. The first step towards such a policy consisted of a decision with respect to the adequate monetary target.

Two criteria determined the choice of the optimal monetary target: the closeness of its relationship to other more basic goals of economic policy, and the possibility of exercising control over the monetary aggregate chosen.

It would be pretentious to say that every possible link between several key variables and different monetary aggregates was tested thoroughly. The results of research done abroad and in Switzerland, and the rather casual observation that inflation rates have tended to accelerate whenever growth rates of M1 also have accelerated, led the Swiss National Bank to concentrate on M1 from the beginning. Since inflation rates are the main concern of monetary policy, this observation meant that M1 had one of the two necessary properties to qualify as a monetary target.

The link between a monetary aggregate and other economic key figures is of no use if the monetary aggregate cannot be influenced appropriately by the central bank. Empirical research revealed that the money multiplier could be predicted quite accurately up to 1978. Therefore it was possible to establish a money supply target in terms of M1 and to use the monetary base to keep the target in line. This approach worked quite well from 1975 to 1977. Money supply targets of 6 per cent growth were established for 1975 and 1976 and of 5 per cent for 1977. The actual growth rates were very close to the goals, and seemed to indicate that the problems of controlling the money stock had been solved. Therefore a goal of 5 per cent growth of M1 for 1978 was expected to create no difficulties.

In 1977–78 however, Switzerland experienced two unprecedented foreign exchange rate movements, unprecedented both in size and closeness to each other. The first wave started in autumn 1977 and the second in summer 1978. The appreciation of the Swiss franc in real terms between the beginning of the year and end of September amounted to more than 18 per cent. This was – especially for our exporting industries – a very severe shock, which could have led to long-lasting damage to the whole economy if the situation were not remedied. The Swiss National Bank decided therefore to abandon the monetary target temporarily and pursue a foreign exchange target *vis-à-vis* the Deutschmark. (The Deutschmark was chosen because the

Federal Republic of Germany is our main trading partner and our main competitor on world markets.) Consequently, heavy interventions took place and the target for 1978 was overshot by a wide margin.

These developments show that monetary policy under a regime of flexible exchange rates is also complicated by the fact that an economy is small and open. Exchange rate considerations play a much greater role in policy decisions in such an economy than in a more or less closed economy. In view of the still disturbed situation on the foreign exchange markets, the Swiss National Bank decided not to announce a money stock target for 1979.

The foreign exchange market disturbances had a further effect relating to monetary policy. It turned out that the money multiplier had become less predictable. Since this implied also a greater danger of a too restrictive or too expansive monetary policy relative to the ultimate goals, the Swiss National Bank decided to switch from a M1 target to a base target. Both for 1980 and 1981 the target was set at a 4 per cent average growth rate.

Having established the monetary aggregate that would serve as a target, the next step consisted of setting a concrete figure for this target. This decision was reached in several steps.

The expected real growth of the economy was the starting point of the considerations to be made. Then the inflation rate target for the coming year was set. It was evident that this could not be done without taking into account the actual inflation rate. Since decelerations and accelerations of the price level also have temporary real effects; cutting down inflation from 10 to 0 per cent within one year, for example, would have a tremendous impact on the real economy in terms of growth rates and unemployment figures. Past inflation rates had therefore also to be taken into consideration in order to pursue a responsible monetary policy. This policy would consist of a gradual and not abrupt lowering of the quantitative money supply targets in order to achieve price stability.

Out of the three elements expected – real growth, expected (or targeted) inflation, and actual inflation – the quantitative target for the money aggregate under consideration was set. If this aggregate was not fully controlled by the central bank, a link to concrete policy actions – creation of base money – had to be established. Therefore, in the years when an M1 target was aimed at the money multiplier had to be predicted. Today the procedure is simpler still, since the policy is geared directly to the monetary base.

It may now seem that such a policy is bound to ignore foreign exchange rate movements since one could conclude that there would be no room for deviating from an established growth path of the monetary base. But this is not the case. It can be assumed that banks distinguish quite clearly between transitory and permanent changes in the monetary base and will therefore change money creation only in reaction to a movement in the monetary base judged to be permanent.

This assumption – which did rather well when put under empirical scrutiny – also has important policy implications. Since there is no one-to-one relationship between changes in the monetary base and changes in these monetary aggregates that trigger price and real movements, temporary deviations of the monetary base from its trend do not lead to substantial disturbances in the economy. The banks will in this case only vary their reserve position without accelerating or decelerating monetary growth, thus helping to even out the development. This is especially important in decisions with respect to our foreign exchange policy.

But the described mechanism will also lead to substantial lags of M1 growth if changes in the trend rate of the monetary base occur. Since the banks can see only the monetary base as a whole, they will first misjudge the new trend as a temporary deviation from the old trend and act accordingly. Only if the deviations are of the same direction for a certain time will the banks start to realize that the shift has been permanent, and only then will they start to adjust to the new restrictions.

The third step in the formulation of a money supply policy consisted of decisions concerning the day-to-day enactment of the policy. After the Swiss National Bank had adopted its first monetary target for the calendar year 1975, the growth rate of the monetary base was targeted quarter by quarter and controlled and if necessary adjusted monthly. At the end of 1976 a weekly meeting for the control of the monetary base was instituted.

As said before, the Swiss National Bank does not aim at a stable growth rate of the monetary base from week to week. The main concern is the behaviour of the base in the medium and long run. Consequently, the monetary base will tend to grow at larger than average rates when the foreign exchange rate situation is calm and to pick up when heavy interventions in the foreign exchange markets are necessary, thus creating additional liquidity for the banks.

The means of controlling the monetary base are mainly foreign exchange transactions consisting of outright sales, purchases of US dollars, or swap operations. This is not due to an explicit policy but rather the result of historical and institutional factors. Since it has been felt that upward pressure on our currency could be eased at least temporarily by buying foreign currency, and situations of heavy Swiss franc appreciations were quite frequent, there was not much room left for other types of transactions. But even if this room had been provided, the possibilities of engaging in open market transactions were quite limited because of legal restrictions. These restrictions were lifted in August 1979, but so far there has been no substantial shift towards more domestic money creation.

The influence of the 'Snake' and of the EMS on Swiss monetary policy

Switzerland was the first country in 1973 to opt for a system of floating exchange rates because the restrictions placed on a small open economy endangered more and more a monetary policy geared to price stability. This does not mean that foreign exchange rate movements did not matter any more from then on; it is well known that the Swiss National Bank had to abandon its monetary goal in 1978 because of foreign exchange considerations.

With respect to the 'Snake' and the EMS, however, it was felt that the differences in inflation rates between member countries were still too big for a new system of fixed exchange rates and were therefore bound to create difficulties. Moreover, it was felt that Switzerland – having paid dearly in terms of real effects on its economy for its stabilization efforts (see pp. 147–8 above) – should keep its relative monetary independence for the time being.

Starting from these basic considerations, Switzerland took the position of an interested observer. The Swiss authorities are eager not to abandon an inflation rate that, while considered too high, nevertheless compares favourably with other countries. In an environment of large differences in inflation rates, Switzerland opted for a relatively low inflation rate. The Swiss authorities knew that this implied in the long run an appreciation of the Swiss franc, which was expected to amount more or less to inflation rate differentials. Since it was not at all clear if in new fixed exchange rate systems such adjustments could take place, the Swiss authorities feared that the built-in mechanisms would sooner or later force the low-inflation countries to lead a more expansionary monetary policy, eventually bringing about the necessary adjustment by means of higher average inflation rates.

While more or less fixed exchange rates in a stable economic environment were and still are a desirable goal of economic policy, the 'Snake' and the EMS seemed not to be the appropriate means of reaching this goal. Besides, it may be pointed out that it is not at all clear that Switzerland would have been welcome to take part in the newly emerged systems.

Since Switzerland stayed outside the 'Snake' and the EMS, the new developments did basically not change the situation the country was in, since it had adopted floating exchange rates. The Swiss authorities had to decide how far they were willing to let foreign exchange rates move beyond what was considered to be a 'realistic' level and pursue a money supply policy within these limits. As was already mentioned, the money supply goal had to be abandoned once, in autumn of 1978, in favour of a foreign exchange rate goal. It is very likely that the money supply policy would have been restricted more often if Switzerland had been member of a new system of fixed exchange rates, even considering the co-ordinated foreign exchange interventions of all members in emergency cases.

Switzerland is not entirely independent of the EMS. There is an indirect link through the foreign exchange rate policy of the Swiss National Bank. As already mentioned, a foreign exchange rate goal *vis-à-vis* the Deutschmark was announced in autumn 1978. Since this goal of 'well over 0.8 francs for one Deutschmark' is still valid, there is a loose connection to the EMS. But Swiss experience seems to indicate that the limits within which the foreign exchange rates were allowed to move are too narrow to absorb the random shocks emerging in such a system. The movement of the Swiss franc/Deutschmark rate, which moved between 75 and 95 within two years without any big real changes, would illustrate that point.

Fiscal policy measures

While fiscal policy was used to a large extent to soften the impact of the recession of the 1970s in many countries, Switzerland could not use this instrument as effectively as others, for several reasons.

Switzerland's fiscal policy is highly decentralized. The federal government itself stands to collect only about one-third of total tax revenues. Since cantonal and local governments normally do not gear their fiscal policy to the business cycle, the scope of demand management is quite limited in size.

In the 1970s there was growing concern of the people over increasing budget deficits of the federal government. Since sizeable measures have to be put to the people in a referendum, this concern was translated into several negative votes on proposals that would have enlarged the government deficit. A fast and sizeable response to a slackening in economic activity is therefore very difficult.

This does not mean that the federal government did not react at all to the recession of 1975 and 1976. Since the construction industry is traditionally hardest hit by a slow-down, the measures centred on construction. Three so-called investment programmes were initiated in 1975 and 1976. It is estimated by the federal government that these programmes initiated additional orders of some 4.2 billion francs at a cost of some 1.6 billion francs. The programmes provided bonuses for construction projects of state and local governments started in the recession years. In addition, federal construction activity was stepped up. There were some other measures taken too, such as the intrcduction of mandatory unemployment insurance, and training programmes for persons becoming unemployed because of structural changes in the economy. The federal programmes did not try to prevent these structural changes, but rather aimed at absorbing the socially undesirable effects of the market adjustment processes.

Summary and conclusions

The most important change with respect to Swiss economic policy in the 1970s was certainly the transition to a system of flexible exchange rates. This enabled the Swiss National Bank to pursue a monetary policy of its own. The newly won independence was used to put a money supply policy into effect. The actual policy actions led to severe monetary shocks for the Swiss economy, since growth rates of the money stock were brought down from almost 20 to 0 per cent within two years.

This shock came in addition to several other changes. The Swiss franc appreciated heavily; several production factors, especially energy, became much more expensive; and worldwide economic activity slowed down substantially.

The policy aim of the sharp deceleration of the money supply was a reduction in the inflation rate to close to zero. This aim was reached for 1976–78, but an unprecedented upward move of the Swiss franc forced the Swiss National Bank to abandon its money supply goal temporarily. In 1981 the inflation rate stood at 5 per cent, which is considered too high for Switzerland.

The Swiss economy did comparatively well in adjusting to the shocks of the 1970s. While the recession was the sharpest of all OECD countries in terms of GDP growth, unemployment rates stayed relatively low. While some factors are shown to be special for the mid-1970s, others give rise to some hope that the Swiss unemployment rate will not respond so strongly to changes in the growth rates of GDP as in other countries in the future.

Despite some fiscal policy measures, the adjustment process in Switzerland went on basically without government aid. It is felt in Switzerland that it may be harder in the short run to let the markets adjust themselves, but that the real cost of such a policy is smaller in the long run.

Notes

1 For Japan the loss in real GDP in 1973–74 was estimated to be around 3%; for Western Europe and the United States around 2 per cent. See Fried and Schultze (1975), p. 21.

2 This statement, naturally, holds only if real changes are neglected.

3 The GDP in Switzerland was some 175 billion Swiss francs in 1980 and the export share was some 35 per cent.

4 There are some doubts that this still holds. This question is the subject of theoretical and empirical research at the Swiss National Bank.

5 The comments made in this section follow partly an address by F. Leutwiler, governor of the Swiss National Bank, at the Bank of Israel's Anniversary International Symposium (Leutwiler, 1979).

References

Fried, E. R. and Schultze, C. L. (1975). *Higher Oil Prices and the World Economy: the Adjustment Problems* (Washington, DC).

Leutwiler, F. (1979). 'Monetary policy and the wetting of money stock targets – the case of Switzerland'. Address given at the Bank of Israel's Anniversary International Symposium, 20 November 1979.

Ireland in the European Monetary System: the Effects of a Change in Exchange Rate Regime

BRENDAN M. WALSH
University College, Dublin

Introduction

During the 1970s Ireland experienced increasingly severe inflation. This prompted serious discussion of the costs and benefits of the long-established exchange rate link with the United Kingdom. In the event, the break with sterling took place as a consequence of the Irish commitment to join the European Monetary System (EMS) and the UK's ultimate unwillingness to do so, rather than as a result of a conscious decision to alter the exchange rate regime. The implications of entry into EMS have been far-reaching, and are only beginning to be evaluated by Irish economists. In reviewing the first two years of Ireland's membership of EMS, I have chosen first to take an historical perspective on Irish exchange rate policy.

Nineteenth-century floating

When Ireland and Great Britain were united by the Act of Union in 1800, the Irish pound had been floating against the British currency since the restriction of gold payments against the note issues of the Bank of Ireland and the Bank of England in 1797. The normal parity between the two currencies was 12:13, or IR£1 = £0.923. In the immediate aftermath of the suspension of convertibility, the exchange between the two currencies remained stable, disrupted only for a brief period in 1801 when the English pound depreciated on continental exchanges and the Irish pound remained firm.

The sharp fall in the Irish pound in 1803 was blamed for many 'evil effects', such as the rise in the price of imported goods and, 'as a consequence', in the price of home-manufactured goods. According to a contemporary pamphleteer, 'exchange engrosses the public mind and there seems to be some lowering cloud over the commercial atmosphere'.[1] In fact, the Irish pound only depreciated to IR£1 = £0.81, 12 per cent below the old parity – a relatively minor fall by present-day standards.

The debate that this depreciation occasioned became part of a wider controversy that engaged the leading British economists of the day. A Parliamentary Inquiry was established which issued its Report in 1804.[2] Although overshadowed by the more famous Bullion Committee Report of 1810, the Irish Currency Report contained many of the ideas that were incorporated in the 1810 Report, which became one of the main sources for nineteenth-century British monetary orthodoxy (Fetter, 1965). While it was acknowledged that certain real factors played a role in the depreciation of the Irish currency, among them the payment of rents to absentee English landlords,[3] most of the blame for the sudden fall of the Irish pound was placed on an excessive expansion of supply: it was 'highly probable' that 'this depreciation in Ireland arises almost entirely, if not solely, from an excess of Paper. . . . Comparing the issues of the Bank of Ireland with the rates of Exchange, a strong presumption arises of the connection between an increased Issue and a high Exchange' (Fetter, 1955, p. 61). On the strength of this analysis, the Report concluded that it lay within the power of the banks to stabilize the foreign exchanges by the use of their reserves and by appropriate credit policies.

After 1804, the Irish pound quickly regained its old value relative to the English pound. Following the sharp fall of the latter on continental exchanges, the Irish currency was above the old parity during most of the period 1813–15. It lost ground during the economic recession of 1815, falling to lower levels than had been reached before, but this depreciation provoked little debate, perhaps because the fall in the pound 'must have appeared as a blessing that gave some small relief in a period of economic distress' (Fetter, 1955, p. 55). Between 1816 and 1821 the value of the pound was gradually stabilized at the old 12:13 parity, so that when gold payments were resumed in 1821 at this rate the Bank of Ireland was willing to accept responsibility for maintaining a stable exchange.

The assimilation of the Irish and British currencies

The financial provisions of the 1800 Act of Union not only abolished all tariffs between Ireland and Great Britain, but also provided for the eventual assimilation of the Irish with the English pound. The stabilization of the exchanges in 1821 paved the way for this move, which was completed in 1826 simply by converting all transactions, debts, contracts, etc., from Irish to British currency on the basis of twelve-thirteenths the amount reckoned in Irish currency. This operation caused some confusion at the time (Hall, 1949, p. 110), but, in the words of one historian, 'after that date no exchange problems between the two countries could arise' (O'Brien, 1921, p. 534).

It has been claimed, however, by Lynch and Vaizey (1960) that by 'the suppression of [Irish] paper money in 1826 the effects of the Great Famine twenty years later were made inevitable' (p. 26). According to this view, the imposition of a one-to-one parity between the Irish and English pounds involved a contraction of the Irish money supply, and delayed the monetization of the economy of the more remote rural districts whose dependence on subsistence monoculture was thereby prolonged. The deflation of the Irish economy led to hardship, unemployment and the virtual elimination of several sectors of Irish industry. These authors see in Ireland's experience after 1826 a rehearsal of Britain's difficulties following the return to the prewar gold standard a century later.

Others take the view, however, that Ireland suffered little as a direct result of the currency changes in the early nineteenth century (cf. Cullen, 1972). According to this body of opinion, market forces had more or less restored the old relationship between the two pounds by 1821. The resumption of convertibility was delayed until the floating rate had settled at a level that made it relatively painless to restore specie payments. The change from an independent currency to the use of English pounds in 1826 was merely a change of unit of account that did not imply a forcible move to an overvalued parity. The long recession in Irish manufacturing after the end of the Napoleonic wars is attributed to the abrupt removal of tariff protection ('of which it stood in such urgent need on account of its comparatively undeveloped condition' – O'Brien, 1921, p. 419) and the emergent technical superiority of British industry (Cullen, 1972).

The following century and a half were uneventful as far as Irish exchange rate policy is concerned. The absence of an independent currency did not figure among the many grievances mentioned by the growing body of Irish opinion that voiced dissatisfaction at the union with Britain as the century progressed. The industrial protection argument made an appearance in the 1840s, when Isaac Butt adapted List's economic ideas to Irish circumstances. As the gap in living standards between Ireland and the rest of the United Kingdom became more glaring in the last quarter of the century, it was hoped that structural reforms, especially in land tenure, would alleviate the problem. A regional development board was established and a modest 'transfer of resources' occurred that could have been viewed among other things as compensation for the absence of an independent regional exchange rate.[4] But this interpretation is a bit fanciful, because there was no discussion of any penalties imposed on the Irish economy by the absence of an independent currency. The introduction of the old age pension and related developments in the social security area early in the twentieth century meant that Ireland began to receive more substantial net transfers from the rest of the United Kingdom. While none of these measures was explicitly addressed to the problems experienced by the less developed part of a currency union, they could be viewed as contributing to the conditions necessary for the continued smooth functioning of such a union.

The sterling exchange standard

So deeply ingrained was the monetary union in the thinking of Irish policy makers that when the Irish Free State was established in 1922 there was no serious questioning of the assumption that the British currency should continue to be the legal tender of Ireland. Not until 1926 was legislation introduced to permit the issue of Irish token coins.[5] In the same year a Commission was set up to consider if the foundation of the new state called for any changes in the laws on banking and note issue. Much of this Commission's work was concerned with the technicalities of replacing the commercial banks' note issue with a Consolidated Note Issue, but it also discussed the desirability of continuing to rely on the British legal tender. It recommended that a Currency Commission should be established with the power to issue Irish legal tender notes which would be backed one-to-one by gold and sterling liquid assets.[6] Thus, by the 1930s a distinctive Irish coinage and note issue were in circulation alongside British money in Ireland, and the two currencies were treated as perfect substitutes by the Irish public.

A more extended discussion of the appropriate basis for the Irish currency took place in the Commission on Banking, Currency and Credit that was established after a change of government in 1934. Many witnesses urged this Commission to adopt some of the radical approaches to currency and credit that were in vogue during the Great Depression. Views such as that 'the failure to take control of its own credit' was a reason for the poor economic performance of the new State, or that 'the Bank of England is working through its agents in Ireland to pauperise the country' (para. 214), were argued by witnesses before the Commission, but the Majority Report rejected such ideas out of hand. This Report stressed that maintaining the link with sterling was of paramount importance in view of the close integration of the two economies and the need to maintain international confidence in the Irish currency. Moreover, the existing one-to-one parity was deemed appropriate. It was argued that any change in this parity 'would introduce an element of uncertainty for the future, as it would be impossible to prevent the anticipation of further changes. The existence of such a feeling is in the highest degree upsetting and a grave deterrent to enterprise' (para. 211). In its recommendations the Commission confined itself to some technicalities regarding the note issue and the powers that should be given to the Monetary Authority.[7]

Ireland's departure from the Commonwealth and the declaration of a Republic in 1948 led to no change in the currency arrangements. The devaluation of sterling against the US dollar in 1949 caused a few politicians to wonder about the wisdom of keeping virtually all our foreign exchange reserves in sterling. In 1971, legislation was enacted that made it feasible to terminate the one-to-one link with sterling by government order. It could therefore be claimed that, when sterling floated in 1972, the Irish pound floated in unison as a result of an explicit decision rather than as a consequence of legal obligation (Whitaker, 1973, p. 67).

A feature of Irish economic policy during the 1950s was the use of deflationary fiscal policy to reduce balance of payments deficits and of monetary restraint to maintain a high level of foreign exchange reserves. In 1951 the balance of payments deficit rose to 15 per cent of GNP under the impact of rising dollar prices for raw materials and declining agricultural exports. The authorities responded by deflating the economy severely in 1952. Another balance of payments crisis in 1956 led the government to reduce its borrowing requirement from 6 to 3 per cent of GNP. While these measures proved adequate to achieve a slight balance of payments surplus by 1957, unemployment rose to 9 per cent of the labour force, and net emigration from the country amounted to over 2 per cent of the population – the highest rate recorded since the famine years of 1879–80.

The appropriateness and timing of these deflationary measures were questioned by some at the time and have been criticized by economists writing about the period (Kennedy and Dowling, 1975). The authorities may be faulted for not accepting that under a fixed exchange rate a balance of payments deficit would have been self-correcting so long as they refrained from trying to offset the deflationary effects on bank liquidity of the loss of reserves. Perhaps they were fearful that the adjustment period would have been too long to prevent a crisis of confidence precipitating even more severe measures than those actually taken. What is important in the present context is that Ireland played by the rules of the game of a fixed exchange rate, and despite the cost in terms of unemployment and emigration, no coherent body of opinion emerged to advocate devaluation as a less painful way of re-establishing external balance.

While the link with sterling seemed unassailable, and a devaluation of the Irish pound was not considered as a policy option, a wide range of protectionist measures were put in place with a view to fostering Irish industry. McAleese (1978) has shown that by the 1950s the level of effective protection enjoyed by the Irish industrial sector was exceptionally high by European standards. He calculates that the average nominal tariff of 25 per cent amounted to an effective tariff of 79 per cent, compared with an average effective tariff of 19 per cent in the six original member states of the EEC. In addition to these protective tariffs, special import levies were imposed for balance of payments reasons during the mid-1950s. However, these high tariffs were rapidly dismantled under the Anglo-Irish Free Trade Area Agreement (in 1965) and following entry into the EEC (in 1973). Reliance was henceforward placed on a variety of 'supply-side' measures, including incentives to foreign investment and export subsidies.

McAleese points out that devaluation as an alternative to protection appears to have been ruled out on the grounds that it would have entailed a loss of discipline and set in train the sequence of events feared by the 1934 Commission, namely, the expectation that one devaluation would lead to further downward adjustment. Thus the exchange rate regime, and even the parity, recommended for Ireland by the Committee of 1804 survived the emergence of an independent republic and the major difficulties experienced in maintaining external balance during the 1950s.

The costs and benefits of the sterling link

Surprisingly little attention has been devoted by Irish economists to analysing the costs and benefits of maintaining the historic exchange rate arrangement. For a century the exchange rate was not available as a policy instrument, and for a further half-century its use was not seriously contemplated. Widespread dissatisfaction with the slow growth in living standards, plus high unemployment and emigration rates, prompted relatively little interest in the scope for an independent exchange rate policy. The first systematic discussion of the potential gains from establishing a currency area is to be found in an essay by a governor of the Central Bank (Whitaker, 1973). The author examined Ireland's situation in the light of the growing literature on optimal currency areas. He concluded that the very high degree of economic interdependence between Ireland and the UK, including the free mobility of capital and labour, was ample justification for maintaining the link with sterling. In view of the importance of imported goods in Irish consumption patterns, he doubted whether sufficient money illusion existed for a devaluation to bring about any lasting change in the ratio of domestic to foreign factor prices. He therefore tended to accept Corden's (1972) verdict that Ireland, like Luxembourg, did not meet the criteria for an independent currency area. He demurred, however, from the inference that there was no cost to Ireland in sacrificing the use of exchange rate policy because of the possible gains that might be obtained through a revaluation that reinforced domestic policies aimed at curbing inflation; 'to the extent that tradeable goods constitute a large proportion of domestic expenditure, revaluation would tend to be a powerful anti-inflationary weapon' (Whitaker, 1973, p. 72). Thus he held out the hope that there might be something to be gained from a revaluation as an anti-inflationary policy, but warned against devaluation as a means of restoring balance of payments equilibrium. This line of thought was to reappear in subsequent debates on the problem of inflation in Ireland's small open economy.

Official thinking continued to reflect cost-push theories of the inflationary process. Attempts to mitigate the problem took conventional forms. The main emphasis was placed on a centralized system of wage negotiations that was inaugurated in 1970. In 1971 a National Prices Commission was established in the hope that tighter controls on prices would lower the inflation rate. In an influential article, Geary, Henry and Pratschke (1970) used input–output analysis to show how increases in the aggregate price level could be related to increases in the unit prices of the primary inputs to GNP. It became popular to apply the weights taken from this analysis to a vector of price increases in the primary inputs (making due allowance for productivity gains) to allocate the inflation rate between domestic and imported components. While this approach documented the impact of higher world commodity prices on the Irish economy, it also allowed commentators to claim that a significant proportion of our inflation was 'our own fault', especially by pointing to the 45 per cent weighting of wages and salaries in the primary input vector. Thus the Central Bank, in its Annual Report for 1971–72, warned that 'inflation in Ireland is largely home-produced and its immediate cause is money income increases far in excess of productivity gains' (p. 8). In the same vein, the Annual Report for 1973–74 stated:

> It is a fallacy, even for the open Irish economy, that inflation is due more to external than to internal causes. ... Even during 1973, when basic commodity and energy prices soared spectacularly, ... imported inflation accounted directly for no more than half the rise in Irish retail prices. ... [p. 10]

By the mid-1970s our thinking came to be dominated by the contrast between the high inflation to which the UK seemed prone and the low inflation that the Deutschmark zone of countries had maintained despite their dependence on imported oil. This contrast undermined the hitherto almost unquestioned belief that the sterling link was the most beneficial exchange rate arrangement open to this country. Changing currents of economic theory also influenced the debate. In 1975 the Irish Council of the European Movement held a conference on 'Currency Realignments and European Economic Integration', which provided a forum for Irish economists to debate the relationship between exchange rates, inflation and domestic economic policy. The growing influence of the small open economy (SOE) paradigm is evident from the proceedings of this conference. For example, Geary quoted with approval Caves's view that, 'given a fixed exchange rate and inflation abroad, [a small open economy] will suffer increases in domestic prices through *some* mechanism, the particular sequence of events depending on the country's internal economic structure' (Geary, 1975, p. 47).

Econometric support for the view that the Irish inflationary process was consistent with the SOE model and evidence as to the nature of the transmission mechanism were provided by Geary (1976). He concluded that the evidence supported the view that world (*viz.* UK) inflation *directly* influenced domestic price inflation, rather than working through the wage formation equation: 'wage inflation simply *adjusts* to price inflation, given the level of excess demand' (p. 398). The force of the qualification about the level of excess demand was diminished by the finding that an unemployment variable lacked statistical significance in both the wage and price equations. On the basis of a cross-spectral analysis of the Irish and UK time series, Bradley (1977) concluded that only very short lags (one quarter at most) existed between, for example, the UK retail price index and the Irish consumer price index. Thus in the mid-1970s the evidence was overwhelming that Irish inflation was almost entirely a reflection of UK inflation.

The most extended theoretical treatment of the exchange rate issue in an Irish context is provided by Ryan (1978). He cites the studies by Geary and others to support the view that the Irish inflation rate is determined by external factors:

> this is not to say that the rate of inflation in Ireland in any one year will be precisely equal to the rate prevailing in the United Kingdom. There can be divergences of a few percentage points in either direction for a short time. ... [p. 12]

Ryan concluded that 'domestic anti-inflationary measures, such as price controls, will be impotent', while, on the other hand, 'the only lasting effect of changing our exchange rate policy is that in doing so we change our domestic rate of inflation' (p. 77).

Discussion of the options that might be availed of in the light of this view of the Irish inflationary process was provided by Geary (1975). He stressed the positive contribution that could be made by a change of exchange rate regime. Moving from union with the UK, where inflation was running at over 20 per cent annually, to the 'Snake', where inflation was averaging less than 10 per cent, would not entail unacceptably high costs. To believe so would, in his view, be 'unduly pessimistic', because it amounted to ignoring

> the fact that given the high ratio of tradeable to non-tradeable goods in the Irish economy the decline in the inflation rate could be evident in less than a year ... it also ignores the possibility that in such circumstances the acceptability of Government measures to facilitate the transmission of the reduced inflationary impulses and reduce the costs of adjustment would be widespread. ... [p. 50]

In similar vein, Kennedy (1975, p. 105) pointed out that one of the reasons why Denmark had experienced a lower inflation rate than Ireland since 1968 was its decision to break with sterling and subsequently to enter the 'Snake', although he also stressed the role of moderation in wage demands in the Danish experience. Some economists went further and argued that 'it is not possible to get our rate of price increase down without changing the current exchange rate policy' (McDowell, 1975, p. 77).

At the risk of over-simplification or even distortion, the SOE view of inflation that gained ground in Ireland around this time can be modelled as follows:

e = domestic price of foreign exchange,

P = domestic price level,

P_w = world price level,

and $\dot{e}, \dot{p}. \dot{p}_w$ denote $\Delta \ln E$, $\Delta \ln P$, $\Delta \ln P_w$. Assuming perfect arbitrage for a single tradable commodity, then

$$\dot{p} = \dot{p}_w + \dot{e}. \tag{1}$$

A small country is a price-taker for the single commodity, and hence its inflation rate can be said to be determined by world inflation and the exchange rate. This model can be refined to allow for non-tradable goods, with the result that, even when the rate of increase in factor prices is equal in the two sectors of the domestic economy, differentials in productivity growth can cause domestic inflation to diverge from world inflation (this is the 'Scandinavian model' outlined by Lindbeck, 1979). But although factors such as differentials in productivity growth between sectors can influence the domestic inflation in this class of models, the main message is that the small country can succeed in lowering its inflation rate below the world rate only by appreciating its currency. If we assume that the exchange rate can be set by domestic policy-makers, whereas world inflation clearly cannot, the inference is obvious: a change in exchange peg can be used to moderate domestic inflation. In the Irish context, if we substitute the UK for 'the world', the policy prescription is to break the sterling link in order to lower our inflation rate below that of the UK.

It is interesting to relate this theory of inflation to the purchasing power parity (PPP) view of exchange rates. According to PPP, under floating exchange rates changes in domestic price levels lead to changes in exchange rates:

$$\dot{e}_i = \dot{p} - \dot{p}_i \qquad \text{or, more realistically,} \qquad \dot{e}_i = f(\dot{p} - \dot{p}_i). \tag{2}$$

The SOE model turns one of the countries into a price-taker and makes the exchange rate an exogenous variable, so that causation must flow from foreign prices to domestic inflation. Both theories share the prediction that there will be no (significant) real exchange rate movements, where a real exchange rate movement is defined as the difference between the exchange rate change and the inflation differential.

That Ireland was a small economy, open to international trade, could hardly be contested. This led to the acceptance of the assumption that Ireland was also a price-taker for traded goods. The view that commodity maıkets would operate quickly to eliminate divergences between the price of traded goods was taken to be self-evident. All these assumptions made the logic of the SOE theory of inflation inevitable:

> so long as we maintain a fixed exchange rate with *any* major country with which there is relatively free trade, we will tend in the long run to have that country's rate of inflation. The reasoning amounts to little more than recognising that markets do exist. ... [Norton, 1980, p. 190]

Moreover, the empirical evidence was, as we have seen, wholly consistent with this view of Irish inflation, although it was drawn entirely from a period when the Irish currency had been pegged to sterling and contained no information on the actual consequences of a change in the exchange peg.

The decision to join EMS

Inflation in Ireland and the UK reached a peak in the second half of 1976, when the annual rate of price increase was close to 20 per cent. The German inflation rate at that time was in the region of 4 per cent. Advocates of the view that a change in the exchange peg was a precondition for reducing Ireland's inflation rate were influenced by the enormous gap between British and German inflation at this time, and by the absence of an immediate prospect that this gap would narrow. In fact, British inflation moderated during 1977, and, as had always been the case in the past, Ireland's inflation followed the British rate closely. By early 1978 the annual rate of inflation had fallen to just over 6 per cent. The prospects for maintaining the sterling link and enjoying a return to moderate inflation rates looked better during early 1978 than they had for many years. Inflation in Germany had, however, abated to an annual rate of little over 2 per cent, so the gap between British and German inflation remained substantial.

An important new element in the situation was the gathering momentum for a new initiative on European monetary co-operation which culminated in the decision taken at the Brussels summit meeting in December 1978 to launch the EMS. The positive attitude of the Irish authorities to this initiative can be understood in the light of our firm commitment to the European Community and the considerable benefits to us of membership. A dilemma however arose from the possibility that the United Kingdom might remain outside the new system. If this were to occur, Ireland would be presented in the starkest manner with the choice between the traditional considerations of close integration and trading links as reasons for remaining linked with sterling, on the one hand, and the 'communautaire' considerations and the hope for benefits on the inflation front from joining the EMS, on the other. The continued importance of our trading links with the UK should be recalled. Despite a notable diversification of the destinations of our exports since joining the EEC, 46 per cent of our exports were still sold in the UK, while slightly over half our imports come from there (table 1). To join the EMS if the UK stayed out implied switching our currency peg from the country with which about half our trade was conducted to a group of countries that accounted for less than a quarter of our trade. This would place us in the situation of being the member of EMS to whom intra-EMS trade was of least relative importance.[8] On the other hand, if the UK joined the System, then over three-quarters of our trade would be intra-EMS.

The considerations that led us to take the step of joining, even as it became clear that the UK was likely to remain outside, were summarized by the Governor of the Central Bank as follows:

1 the inappropriateness of an indefinite prolongation of the sterling link;
2 the benefits in terms of a reduction in inflation to be obtained from adherence to a hard currency regime;
3 a commitment to a major Community initiative;
4 Community support in the form of a significant transfer of resources (Murray, 1979, p. 101).

As the final point indicates, we naturally sought compensation from the Community for the sacrifice of our exchange rate or, more precisely, for agreeing to switch from the lax hegemony of the UK (as it was then perceived) to the sterner discipline of what we viewed

Table 1 Irish merchandise trade by area, selected years, 1961–80

	1961	*1971*	*1972*	*1973*	*1976*	*1977*	*1978*	*1979*	*1980*
	%	%	%	%	%	%	%	%	%
Origin of imports									
UK	50.7	49.5	51.0	50.7	49.2	48.2	49.5	50.0	50.7
Other EEC (incl. Dk)	14.2	16.8	17.5	21.0	20.1	19.9	20.8	21.6	19.7
Others	35.1	33.7	31.5	28.3	30.7	31.9	29.7	28.4	29.6
Total	100.0	100.0	100.0	100.0	100.0	100.0	100.0	100.0	100.0
Destination of exports									
UK	74.3	65.9	60.8	54.7	48.7	47.0	47.3	46.4	46.2
Other EEC (incl. Dk)	6.4	10.1	16.8	21.3	27.1	29.2	30.2	31.1	31.3
Other	19.3	24.0	22.4	24.0	24.2	23.8	22.5	22.5	22.5
Total	100.0	100.0	100.0	100.0	100.0	100.0	100.0	100.0	100.0

Source: Trade Statistics of Ireland, various issues

as in essence a Deutschmark zone. The transfer of resources was to compensate for the deflationary bias to which we believed we were about to subject our economy. Our hesitancy about joining early in 1979 was finally overcome by increasing the size of this subsidy.

That sterling was a soft currency relative to the EMS was not doubted. The Governor of the Central Bank pointed out that the trade-weighted exchange rate index of sterling had fallen 25 per cent over the period 1973–78. While discretion did not allow him to make a public forecast of a particular exchange rate, he stated that ‘it would be prudent for us to proceed on the assumption that, in the longer run at any rate, membership of EMS involves a harder currency regime than non-membership’ (Murray, 1979, p. 105). In taking this view of future exchange rates, Irish economists reflected the prevailing international consensus. Three major forecasting units – the National Institute for Economic and Social Research, the London Business School, and Exchange Rate Outlook – were predicting that sterling would depreciate by between 3 and 7 per cent during 1979 (O’Connor, 1980). (It actually appreciated by 12 per cent.) There was, however, some hope on the part of Irish officials that, even if the UK remained outside, our entry into EMS would not entail a break in the sterling link for some time at least, ‘depending on the degree of success of the policy of the United Kingdom Government with regard to maintaining the exchange rate stability of sterling’ (White Paper on EMS membership, p. 18). Earlier one economist had, however, raised the question of how Ireland would fare if sterling began to reflect the effects of oil earnings on its balance of payments (Honohan, 1978).

By participating in the EMS from its inauguration Ireland was committed to a radically new departure in economic policy. Hopes were high that the inflation imported from the UK would rapidly be replaced by the moderating effects of the lower rate of inflation prevailing in continental Europe. There was a great deal of talk about the 'convergence' of our inflation and interest rates on the EMS rates. An economist with the Central Bank claimed that, 'after a decade of inflation we can now contemplate the prospect of an early and sustained return to inflation rates comfortably back into single figures' (McCarthy, 1979, p. 109). With an unconscious echo of the earlier comparison between Ireland's experience after the loss of an independent currency in 1826 and Britain's return to the gold standard in 1926, Keynes's comment on Britain's departure from the gold standard in 1931 was quoted: 'The romantic phase is over, and we can begin to discuss realistically what policy is for the best' (McCarthy, 1979, p. 109).

To be fair to those who held out the prospect of a rapid convergence to low inflation rates as the reward for joining EMS, they were explicit as to what policies were 'for the best' in the new environment. Despite their occasional tendency to write as if the line of causation flowed unidirectionally, and inexorably, from the choice of exchange rate regime to the domestic inflation rate, there was a widespread awareness of the indispensible need to support our decision to enter EMS through appropriate fiscal and monetary policies designed to curb the balance of payments deficit. It was stressed that we would no longer be justified in seeking rates of increase in nominal income of the order of magnitude that had become normal during the 1970s. During 1979 strenuous attempts were made to obtain an agreement on an incomes policy based on the expectation of inflation falling to single figures. The failure to obtain such an agreement was a clear indicator that expectations about inflation had not been radically changed as a result of EMS entry.

The government was urged to adopt a more stringent fiscal policy in order to protect our foreign exchange reserves, already depleted by large balance of payments deficits during the 1970s. We were told that our currency was now to be quoted daily on foreign exchanges in contrast with the situation where it was merely a regional variant of sterling. This would focus 'the searchlight of the market's judgement on our overall macroeconomic strategy' (McCarthy, 1979, p. 113). We were warned that 'ultimately, of course, technical exchange rate arrangements are not decisive, but rather how prudently we manage our affairs domestically' (McCormack, 1979, p. 110).

The experience in EMS

Ireland joined the EMS at its inauguration in March 1979. We opted for the narrow $2\frac{1}{4}$ per cent margin within the grid, rather than the 6 per cent band chosen by Italy. For two weeks following our entry sterling remained inside the Irish pound's intervention limits and the Central Bank of Ireland maintained the one-to-one parity with sterling. However, by the end of March sterling's unanticipated strength led the Bank to abandon this parity and, for the first time in a century and a half, the Irish pound was quoted at a discount against sterling. The continued strength of sterling relative to the EMS currencies meant that, even if we had opted for the 6 per cent margin within the system, we would have delayed the break only until 10 April 1978.

The ending of the one-to-one no-margins parity with sterling immediately imposed costs on the Irish economy. About one half of our trade by value, and probably a higher proportion of the number of transactions, was suddenly subject to foreign exchange costs from which they had formerly been exempt. It has been estimated on conservative assumptions that this cost equalled about IR£5.5 million in 1979 alone (McCarthy, 1980, p. 36).

Uncertainty regarding the exchange rate with sterling imposed substantial additional costs that are not fully measured in the cost of obtaining forward cover in the market. Furthermore, the traditional freedom of movement of capital between Ireland and the UK was restricted by the imposition of exchange controls, and there was no compensating reduction in the controls between Ireland and the EMS countries. On the other hand, the transfer of resources from the Community materialized in the form of an interest subsidy on loans mainly from the European Investment Bank. The value of this subsidy has been placed at IR£45 million a year for five years. Additional subsidies were made available on a bilateral basis, mainly from Germany and France, with an estimated value of IR£25 million a year for two years. The present value of this package has been estimated as 3 per cent of 1979 GNP (McCarthy, 1979, p. 35), which hardly covers the present cost of additional transaction costs involved in breaking the sterling link.

The course of the effective (trade-weighted) exchange rate index of the Irish pound since 1977 is shown in table 2 and figure 1. For the period since March 1979 a hypothetical index is also shown, calculated to illustrate what would have happened if the link with sterling had been maintained (making no allowance for changes in

Table 2 Effective (trade-weighted) exchange rate index of the Irish pound, 1976–81
(December 1971 = 100)

End month	*1975*	*1976*	*1977*	*1978*	*1979** *(a)*	*1979** *(b)*	*1980** *(a)*	*1980** *(b)*	*1981** *(a)*	*1981** *(b)*
Jan.	88.6	84.3	77.2	79.7	77.50		77.50	81.92	66.1	88.7
Feb.	88.6	84.2	76.9	78.8	77.67		75.88	82.54	67.5	86.3
Mar.	88.9	82.1	77.1	76.7	78.44	78.89	74.72	83.05	67.3	86.8
Apr.	88.0	80.6	76.7	76.4	77.74	79.68	74.44	82.56		
May	86.8	79.0	76.6	76.6	76.82	79.70	74.67	82.83		
Jun.	84.7	79.4	76.6	76.9	76.26	80.43	75.03	82.92		
Jul.	86.3	79.4	76.7	77.8	75.37	82.32	75.39	83.21		
Aug.	85.5	79.0	77.1	77.5	75.41	81.97	74.59	83.92		
Sep.	85.0	76.2	77.1	77.6	76.88	82.01	73.94	84.41		
Oct.	84.6	74.3	77.4	77.28	77.65	79.95	72.22	85.34		
Nov.	84.0	75.4	78.0	77.41	77.81	79.61	70.27	86.37		
Dec.	84.1	76.3	78.6	77.76	77.66	80.20	69.62	86.27		
Mean	86.2	79.1	77.1	77.5	77.11	79.99	73.97	83.79		
St. dev.	1.87	3.27	0.6	0.941	0.981	1.56	2.18	1.52		
Coefficient of variation (%)	2.2	4.1	0.8	1.2	1.3	1.95	2.9	1.8		

* Series (a) is the actual index; series (b) is a hypothetical value based on IR£1 = £1.
Source: Central Bank of Ireland *Quarterly Bulletin*

Fig. 1 Effective exchange rate index of the Irish pound, 1977–81, based on monthly averages

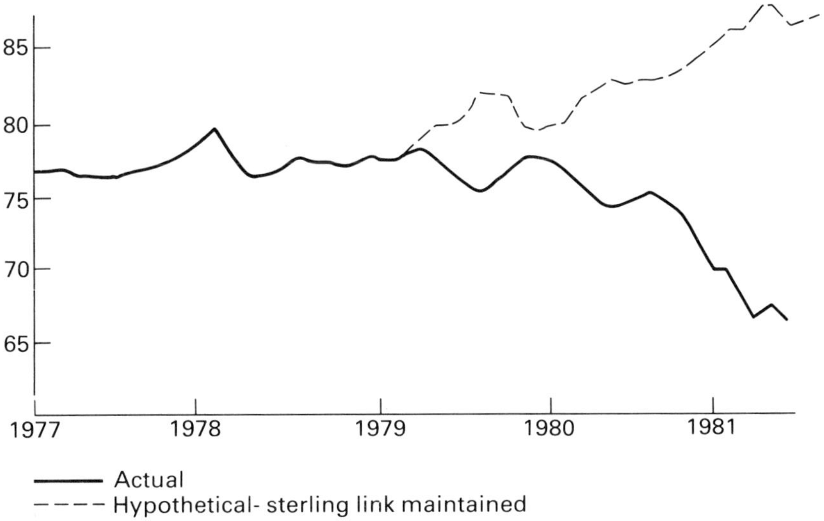

trade patterns as a consequence of the different exchange rate regimes). The instability of the exchange rate is summarized by the coefficient of variation calculated for each year on the basis of the monthly values of the exchange rate. (The use of weekly values would, of course, have shown much greater variability.) By this measure, 1980 was the most unstable year for the Irish pound since 1976. Even more disappointing is the fact that our entry into a 'zone of monetary stability' resulted in a less stable exchange rate during 1980 than would have existed if the link with sterling had been maintained.

The sharp fall in the value of the Irish pound since early 1970 is, of course, mainly a reflection of the decline in the value of the EMS currencies relative to sterling and more recently the US dollar. The Irish currency has so far maintained its value within the EMS. Initially, the Central Bank contained to within 0.25 per cent the spread between the buying and selling rate for the pound sterling and the US dollar, but by the beginning of 1980 this was widened to allow the pound to fluctuate as widely as was permitted under the parity grid rules.

Although during the course of the first half of 1981, the Irish pound has fallen towards the lower end of the band around its central rate, its value within the EMS has not been realigned.

The extraordinary contrast at the end of May 1981 between the 16 per cent depreciation of the Irish pound since the entry into the EMS and the 11 per cent appreciation that would have occurred if the link with sterling had been maintained summarizes the extent to which the consensus expectation that we had switched to a harder currency peg in March 1979 was falsified. Predictions about the repercussions for domestic inflation that had been made on the expectation that the EMS would appreciate against sterling cannot be evaluated on the basis of our experience in the System. On the other hand, predictions that were simply based on what would happen when we pegged to a bloc of currencies that were inflating at a slower rate than sterling can be evaluated by reference to the events of the last two years. Comparing the outcome since 1979 with the predictions derived from the SOE models, in which causation is assumed to run from the rate of inflation in the countries to which the currency is pegged to the domestic inflation rate, it is clear that this process has proved far less automatic and much slower than was widely believed. The very high correlation between movements in the Irish and British price levels in the past presumably reflected not only the fixed exchange rate between the two currencies, but also the very close trading, financial, and institutional links between the two countries, and did not carry over into the same close relationship between Ireland and the EMS countries during the first two years of our membership of the new exchange rate bloc.

Figures 2 and 3 show for West Germany and the UK a comparison of movements in the exchange rate relative to the Irish pound and movements in the ratio of inflation rates. Little would be gained by showing the data for the UK prior to 1977, because the exchange rate was pegged at one-to-one and the two inflation rates never deviated by as much as 2 per cent in a year. Despite the relatively crude nature of these price data, it is clear that before 1979 there was no evidence of significant changes in the Irish real exchange rate relative to sterling. The parallel movement of the two price levels over the entire period for which data are available was one of the comforting facts of history for those who viewed Ireland as a classical example of an SOE.

After entry into the EMS, however, the story is dramatically different. The Irish and UK price levels have continued to move in tandem (apart from deviations caused by the switch to indirect taxation in the UK in 1979–80), but the exchange rate has fallen, slowly at first and then rapidly during the last half of 1980. A longer

Fig. 2 Sterling-Irish pound exchange rate and ratios of UK-Irish price indices: quarterly observations, 1977–81

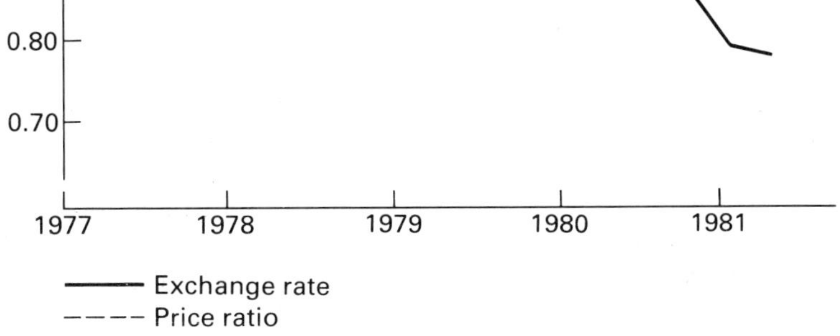

Fig. 3 Deutschmark–Irish pound exchange rate and ratio of West German–Irish price indices: quarterly observations, 1975–81

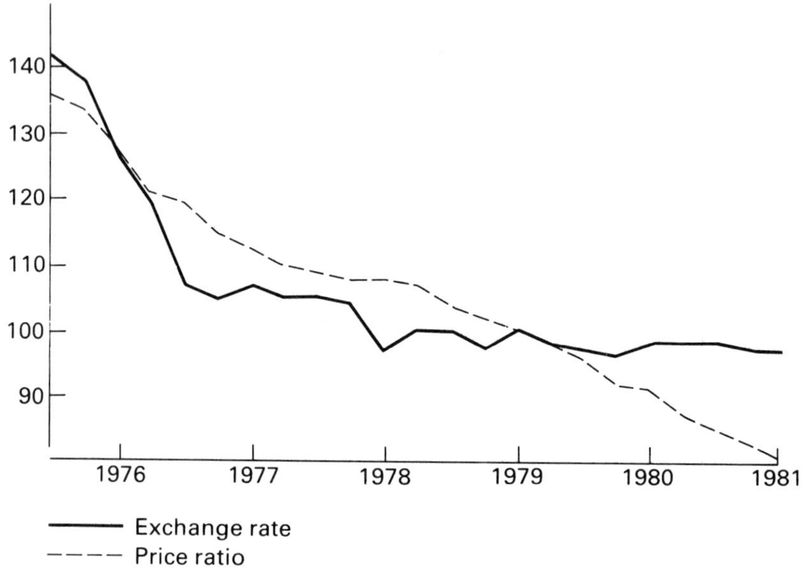

pre-EMS perspective on the relationship between Irish and German prices and exchange rates is shown in figure 3 to illustrate how, even in the case of a country with which our trade and general economic links are relatively weak, the purchasing power parity view of exchange rates is reasonably consistent with the evidence prior to entry into EMS. This presumably reflects the Irish–UK links shown in figure 2, and the sterling–Deutschmark exchange market. Following entry into EMS the Irish pound–Deutschmark exchange rate flattened out (except for the revaluation of the mark within EMS in September 1979) but the Irish inflation rate has continued to out-pace the German rate.

The Irish experience since joining EMS may be seen as another example of a significant and relatively enduring change in real exchange rates, to be added to the list that has already been compiled by, for example, Frenkel (1981). It also demonstrates that it is possible to maintain an exchange rate peg with countries whose inflation is considerably lower than domestic inflation rate for much longer than most adherents to SOE theories would have predicted. Finally, it implies that the SOE view of inflation does not fit the facts over the short to medium run in Ireland.

With hindsight, it is not difficult to enumerate reasons why the long-run predictions based on SOE models have not proved correct over a two-year period. As already mentioned, these models tended to ignore the role played by close trading links and a high degree of integration in maintaining equality of inflation rates between two countries that had fixed exchange rates. Furthermore, the assumption that Ireland is a price-taker in all tradable markets is not accurate. Irish industrial export firms are relatively highly specialized, and may exercise some market power in particular markets. Finally, it should be recalled that the effects of the substantial real depreciation of the Irish currency relative to sterling have been offset in the market for most agricultural products by the operation of the Common Agricultural Policy, which has resulted in very little change of the Irish pound price of agricultural exports to the UK.

Under a fixed exchange rate, a country with more rapid inflation and decreasing competitiveness relative to its trading partners is expected to incur balance of payments deficits whose deflationary consequences lead eventually to the elimination of the deficit. In recent years, however, it has been feasible for countries such as Ireland to finance a persistent deficit on current account by foreign borrowing. In fact, entry to EMS increased Ireland's access to foreign credit and improved the terms on which it is available. Foreign borrowing has been used to replenish stocks of foreign reserves that would otherwise have been exhausted, and to finance very substantial current account deficits.

In the absence of such borrowing, it would have long since proved necessary to deflate the level of domestic absorption, to devalue the currency substantially, or to use some combination of these policies in order to move towards balance of payments equilibrium. Thus, foreign borrowing on an unprecedented scale has played a crucial role in the course of macroeconomic events in recent years. The magnitude of this role was not anticipated by commentators at the time of our entry into EMS, which helps account for why many of their predictions about the effects of entry have not yet materialized.

Irish economic policy in EMS

The recognition by economists of the need to use fiscal policy to reinforce the price-moderating effects of the new exchange rate regime was not fully shared by the Irish government. This much was clear from the passages in the White Paper, which discussed the prospects facing Ireland on entry to EMS. It was accepted that participation in the System would involve a formal commitment to hold the exchange value of the Irish pound within narrow limits, but it was argued that:

> In order to attain this, the balance of payments deficit on current account might well have to be reduced to lower levels more rapidly than envisaged in the Government's strategy. It would be completely at variance with economic and social needs in Ireland to do this by deflationary action, which would have the effect of reducing output and increasing unemployment beyond its existing level, which is already high by Community standards. [p. 10]

The case was made instead for Community aid on a significant scale to help Ireland in the adjustment period and to bring living standards closer to the European average. The outcome was, as we have seen, a substantial transfer of resources, the effects of which may well have been to raise expectations of significant increases in real living standards in the period immediately following entry. It is also significant that to avail itself of this aid, the Irish government had to borrow substantial sums from the European Investment Bank.

During the 1970s, Irish macroeconomic policy departed from the conservative practices that had been normal up to then. In the wake of the first oil price increase, a significant deficit emerged on the government's current budget. Although some progress was made towards eliminating the deficit during 1976 and 1977, it rose again in 1978 and ran at over 6 per cent of GNP in 1979 and 1980. These deficits, and the government's additional borrowing for capital purposes, were financed to an increasing extent through foreign borrowing, as may be seen from table 3. In contrast with the situation in the mid-1970s, when much of government borrowing could be financed from domestic sources, in recent years the private sector's financial supply has fallen to a low level, and most of the government borrowing has been financed from abroad. The result has been that, whereas at the beginning of the 1970s Ireland was a net creditor (on official balances), by 1980 net external indebtedness amounted to about 20 per cent of GNP and was growing rapidly. While a significant proportion of the current budget deficit in 1975 could be attributed to the depressed level of economic activity (Dowling, 1978), the increase in this deficit during 1978 and 1979 occurred at a time when the economy was severely constrained by domestic supply shortages, especially of skilled workers. Hence, the high level of borrowing undoubtedly contributed to the very striking increase in

Table 3 Budget deficits, public sector borrowing requirements balance of payment current account, external assets and liabilities, 1971–80

	Current budget surplus	*Net borrowing by public authorities*	*External govt debt*	*External debt of semi-state companies*	*Official external reserves*	*Balance of payments on current A/C*
	(% of GNP)		*(IR£ million)*	*(IR£ million)*	*(IR£ million)*	*(IR£ million)*
1971	+2.2	5.2	89	83	281	−71
1972	+1.4	5.3	107	112	432	−48
1973	+0.9	6.6	126	134	435	−82
1974	+1.3	12.3	312	160	495	−280
1975	−5.5	13.3	471	187	676	−6
1976	−2.8	10.3	1040	217	955	−157
1977	−2.5	9.75	1038	229	1201	−115
1978	−4.4	12.2	1064	240	1252	−149
1979	−6.1	13.6	1607	485	975	−730
1980	−6.3	14.9	2108	792	1346	−725

* Budget data are on a national account basis
Source: Central Bank of Ireland *Quarterly Bulletin*: National Income and Expenditure

the balance of payments deficit that occurred in those years. At the same time, of course, it helped to finance this deficit.

The standard response to criticisms by economists of the way macroeconomic policy has been conducted in the recent past has been to accept that retrenchment is inevitable sooner or later, but to plead that deflation would be inappropriate and unacceptable at a time when the level of unemployment is already high and increasing owing to the world recession and the rapid growth of the working-age population. The behaviour of the main monetary aggregates during the 1970s is shown in table 4. Domestic credit expansion (DCE), which has been advocated as the most relevant monetary target in a small open economy, is broken down into private and public sector credit growth. The latter consists of monetary financing of the public sector borrowing requirement and comprises total government borrowing less sales of government debt to the Irish non-bank public. A separate sub-total for foreign borrowing by government (equal to the 'government capital' item in the balance of payments) is shown. The accounting identity that underlies table 4 is the basic relation for an open economy:

Increase in credit = increase in money supply ± change in reserves.

This identity can be thought of as reconciling the *ex ante* increase in

Table 4 Changes in monetary aggregates, 1973–80
(all variables expressed as % of GNP)

	1973	*1974*	*1975*	*1976*	*1977*	*1978*	*1979*	*1980*
(1) Increase in private sector credit	6.6	6.5	6.3	9.0	10.1	13.5	12.3	6.1
(2) Government monetary financing	6.0	9.4	6.4	5.8	5.5	8.3	9.4	10.2
(foreign borrowing)	(1.1)	(4.6)	(4.3)	(6.6)	(3.8)	(5.5)	(6.7)	(6.9)
(3) = (1) + (2) = domestic credit expansion	12.6	15.9	12.7	14.7	15.7	21.8	21.7	16.4
Changes in:								
(4) Net external liabilities of public authorities	—	2.6	−0.6	0.4	−0.9	4.6	10.4	2.5
(5) Net external liabilities of commercial banks	−1.0	—	0.6	2.1	5.0	—	0.3	2.4
(6) Net non-monetary liabilities of commercial banks	0.8	1.5	2.1	4.5	0.3	2.1	—	0.8
(7) = (3) − (4) − (5) − (6) = change in M3	12.8	11.4	11.4	7.8	8.6	15.1	11.0	10.7

Sources: Kelleher (1981); Kenneally (1980); Central Bank of Ireland *Quarterly Bulletins*; National Income and Expenditure

the money supply, that is, DCE, with the *ex post* increase in domestic money supply via changes in reserves. If DCE exceeds the amount that the public wishes to hold given the rate of growth of income and the level of interest rates, the result is a decline in external reserves. Thus, the relevant target variable for monetary control is not the growth in money supply, but rather the increase in credit. This has long been recognized in the Irish context (Oslizlok, 1967), but has been given new emphasis recently by several economists (Ryan, 1978; Kelleher, 1980; Kenneally, 1980). The impact of DCE on output, expenditure and the balance of payments has not yet, however, been explicitly studied in the context of an econometric model. The macro-model of the Irish economy constructed at the Central Bank has a strongly 'Keynesian' orientation, in the sense that the level of activity is demand-determined and the monetary sector is relatively underdeveloped and unrelated to the main model.[9] We need further research to establish how variables such as DCE influence the main macroeconomic variables. Dowling (1973–74) has provided some econometric support for the view that government borrowing tended to be closely associated with the current account balance of payments deficit during the period 1953–72. The experience since 1974, summarized in tables 3 and 4, suggests this relationship has held over recent years.

It is clear from the evidence in table 4 that during the 1970s there has been a spectacular growth in net external liabilities, which can be attributed to the need to accommodate the excess of the growth in DCE over the growth in the cash balances held by the public.

An increasing proportion of foreign borrowing is now taking the form of issues of Irish government debt denominated in foreign currencies. Earlier in the 1970s, and again following entry into EMS, there were substantial purchases of domestic Irish government securities by non-residents, but in 1980 the main source of foreign credit has been the increase in debt denominated in US dollars, Deutschmarks and sterling (see table 5). The cost of debt service on this borrowing includes movements in the exchange rate as well as current interest charges; and, owing to the depreciation of the Irish pound during the 1970s, foreign borrowing has proved to be a very expensive source of funds. The average cost to an Irish borrower of a one-year loan over the period 1974–79 ranged from 12 per cent in sterling or Irish pounds to 19 per cent in Deutschmarks or 25 per cent in Swiss francs (Walsh, 1980). The sharp fall in the Irish pound relative to the US dollar and sterling since our entry into EMS has made loans denominated in these currencies expensive over the last two years.[10] The virtual stability of intra-EMS exchange rates since 1979 has allowed us to borrow in other EMS currencies at nominal interest rates, which have been significantly lower than those prevailing in Ireland, but the longer-run implication of our exposure in these currencies can perhaps be anticipated from figure 3.

Table 5 External government debt*
(IR£ million at current exchange rate)

	1976	*1977*	*1978*	*1979*	*1980*
Sterling	50.5	76.8	139.4	141.2	236.9
US$	686.9	685.6	661.5	764.7	1102.0
DM	177.5	180.4	209.8	741.9	1134.6
Others	147.5	119.7	380.4	379.4	426.8
Total	1062.4	1062.5	1391.1	2027.2	2900.3

* Including debt of state-sponsored bodies
Source: Central Bank of Ireland *Quarterly Reports*

Conclusion

The failure of the UK to participate in the EMS resulted in a dramatic new departure in Irish exchange rate policy. In March 1979 we changed our currency peg from the country with which we conducted about half our trade to a group of countries that account for less than a third of our trade. Part of the motivation for this change in exchange rate regimes was the belief that the EMS peg would prove more beneficial in terms of imported price stability than the sterling link had proved to be during the 1970s.

The course of events was very different from that anticipated or hoped for at the time of our entry into EMS. In the first place, the UK's reluctance to enter EMS has turned into a more or less permanent independent exchange rate policy. Second, this independent UK exchange rate policy has been pursued in the interests of facilitating measures of domestic monetary control that now appear to be showing success in reducing inflation, although at enormous costs in terms of unemployment and lost output. To have retained the sterling link during the period of sterling's strength on foreign exchanges would have entailed serious problems for Ireland, resulting in higher unemployment and slower growth of output than has been recorded during the last two years. We would by now, however, be closer to coming to terms with the factors underlying our inflationary processes. Instead, the continued fall in the external value of our currency has reinforced the inflationary spiral and fuelled expectations of further price rises. The failure of domestic macroeconomic policy to reinforce the opportunity offered by the new exchange rate peg must take much of the blame for this outcome.

The lessons that should be learned from our post-EMS experience also have a bearing on the use of economic models in formulating policy advice. In retrospect, it is now obvious that a majority of commentators anticipated benefits to Ireland from EMS entry in terms of a highly simplified model of inflation in an SOE. The reality proved different because of several institutional and other rigidities to which the theories paid too little heed. While it is still possible to maintain that 'in the long run' the predictions of the theories will be validated, the interim has proved much longer than most people anticipated, and the theories provided little guidance to our experience during this interim. Specifically, while in due course it is very likely either that our inflation rate will converge with that of the main EMS countries or, failing this, that we shall prove unable to hold our exchange rate within the System, it is now evident that too little attention was paid in 1979 to the precise mechanisms that will eventually dictate which of these outcomes materializes.

The focus of this paper has been on the problems posed for Ireland by its position as a small economy very open to international shocks during a period of global inflation. During the 1970s the high rate of inflation experienced in the UK eroded the benefits that for so long had attached to pegging the Irish pound to sterling. The creation of the EMS in 1979 appeared to offer Ireland an opportunity to achieve a more stable internal and external value for the currency. This hope has not been realized: domestic inflation has continued unabated, despite the two-year interval of stable exchange rates *vis-à-vis* the EMS currencies. The contrast between our inflation rate and that of the low-inflation members of the EMS is increasingly glaring, and will inevitably exert pressure on our exchange rate within the System. The danger is now that a realignment within the EMS of an Irish pound that is already floating against sterling can be presented as a technical and relatively minor change, compared with which an explicit decision to devalue against sterling would have been a highly visible and controversial action. If this sequence of events materializes, then with hindsight it will be clear that Irish entry into EMS had the effect of removing an important external discipline on the conduct of domestic economic policy.

Notes

I would like to thank Paul de Grauwe for his comments on this paper as read at the Colloquium in Florence in 1981. In the course of preparing this paper I received helpful comments from several sources, including P. T. Geary, D. A. G. Norton, M. McDowell and John Murphy of University College Dublin, John Martin of the OECD, K. A. Kennedy, J. Durkan and several of their colleagues at the Economic and Social Research Institute, Dublin, and Patrick Honohan of the Central Bank of Ireland. The views expressed in the paper, and any remaining errors, are of course solely my responsibility.

1 The quotations are from O'Brien (1921), p. 531.

2 *Report from the Select Committee on the Circulating Paper, the Specie and the Current Coin of Ireland*; reprinted in Fetter (1955).

3 The Irish bankers argued that the fall in the currency was due mainly to Ireland's unfavourable 'balance of remittances'.

4 The Congested Districts Board promoted agriculture, fishing and cottage industries along the western seaboard between 1891 and 1922. The modest scale of this 'transfer of resources' may be gauged from the fact that its budget was the interest from a £1.5 million endowment (Micks, 1925, p. 181).

5 The Institute of Bankers in Ireland 'doubted if any real demand for a distinctive coinage can be said to exist among the majority of the people'

(quoted in Pratschke, 1969, p. 52). A discussant of the Currency Bill in 1927 claimed that there were 'only two national calamities that we have been spared from. One was an earthquake and the other a rate of exchange' (quoted in Meenan, 1970, p. 362).

6 This legislation was amended in 1930 to allow for the inclusion of suitable non-sterling assets in the legal tender note fund, but this facility was not availed of until 1956.

7 The Commission was not too happy with the idea of an Irish Central Bank. Among the 'possible dangers from the setting up of a Central Bank is that people will expect too much from it'. Its main function should be to 'safeguard the integrity of the national monetary unit', not 'to attempt to solve social problems through any facile device of monetary manipulation' (para. 372).

8 Moreover, the share of foreign trade in the Irish national accounts exceeds that of all other EMS countries.

9 This model has yielded very low fiscal policy multiplier estimates, but some of this pessimism may be reduced in the light of recent substantial upward revisions of population, employment and (possibly) output growth estimates for the late 1970s.

10 The cost of foreign borrowing to business firms is increased by the fact that amounts attributable to exchange rate losses on the capital sum are not tax deductible: better incur high domestic interest charges, which are fully tax deductible, than low foreign interest charges and high exchange losses.

References

Bradley, J. (1977), 'Lags in the transmission of inflation'. *Economic and Social Review*, vol. 8, no. 2, pp. 149–54.

Corden, W. M. (1972), 'Monetary integration', *Princeton Essays in International Finance*, no. 93.

Cullen, L. M. (1972), *An Economic History of Ireland Since 1660* (Batsford, London).

Dornbusch, R. (1980), 'Exchange rate economics: where do we stand?' *Brookings Papers on Economic Activity*, vol. 1, pp. 146–94.

Dowling, B. R. (1973–74), 'The development of the financial sector in Ireland, 1949–72'. *Journal of the Statistical and Social Inquiry Society of Ireland*, vol. XXIII, part 1, pp. 57–107.

Dowling, B. R. (1978), 'Budget deficit and fiscal policy'. In *Economic Policy: A Review of Major Issues* (Economic and Social Research Institute, Dublin).

Fetter, F. W. (1955), *The Irish Pound in London: 1797–1826* (Allen & Unwin, London).

Fetter, F. W. (1965), *Development of British Monetary Orthodoxy 1797–1876* (Harvard University Press, Cambridge, Mass.).

Frenkel, J. A. (1981), 'The collapse of purchasing power parities during the 1970s'. *European Economic Review*, vol. 16, pp. 145–65.

Geary, P. T. (1974–75), 'The causes of inflation', *Statistical and Social Inquiry Society of Ireland*, vol. XXIII, part II, pp. 1–7.

Geary, P. T. (1975), 'Ireland's policy option'. In *European Monetary Union and the Sterling Link* (Irish Council of the European Movement, Dublin).

Geary, P. T. (1976), 'World prices and the inflationary process in a small open economy – the case of Ireland'. *Economic and Social Review*, vol. 7, no. 4, pp. 391–400.

Geary, R. C., Henry, E. W. and Pratschke, J. L. (1970), 'The recent price trend in Ireland'. *Economic and Social Review*, vol. 1, no. 3, pp. 345–56.

Hall, F. G. (1949), *History of the Bank of Ireland* (Hodges Figgis, Dublin).

Honohan, P. (1978), 'Some effects of North Sea oil on the Irish economy'. *Economic and Social Review*, vol. 9, no. 2, pp. 147–56.

Irish Council of the European Movement (1975), *European Monetary Union and the Sterling Link*, Record of the Symposium held by the European Movement (Dublin).

Jonson, P. D. (1976), 'Money and economic activity in the open economy: the United Kingdom, 1880–1970'. *Journal of Political Economy*, vol. 84, pp. 979–1012.

Kelleher, R. (1980), 'Recent trends in monetary policy'. *Quarterly Economic Commentary*, Dublin, (Economic and Social Research Institute, Dublin), pp. 25–32.

Kelleher, R. (1981), 'Monetary and financial implications of deficit financing'. Paper to Dublin Economics Workshop, 23 January 1981 (mimeo).

Kenneally, M. (1980), 'Recent trends in monetary policy: some further observations'. *Quarterly Economic Commentary*, September (Economic and Social Research Institute, Dublin).

Kennedy, K. A. (1975), 'Impressions of a visit to Denmark'. *Central Bank of Ireland Quarterly Bulletin*, Autumn, pp. 89–115.

Kennedy, K. A. and Dowling, B. R. (1975), *Economic Growth in Ireland: The Experience Since 1947* (Gill and Macmillan, Dublin).

Lindbeck, A. (1979), 'Imported and structural inflation and aggregate demand: the Scandinavian model reconstructed'. In Assar Lindbeck (ed.), *Inflation and Employment in the Open Economies* (North Holland, Amsterdam).

Lynch, Patrick and Vaizey, John (1960), *Guinness's Brewery in the Irish Economy, 1759–1876* (Cambridge University Press).

McAleese, D. (1978), 'Outward-looking policies, manufactured exports and economic growth: the Irish experience'. In M. J. Artis and A. R. Nobay (eds), *Proceedings of Association of University Teachers of Economics Conference, 1977* (Basil Blackwell, Oxford).

McCarthy, C. (1979), 'The European Monetary System and Irish macroeconomic policy'. *Central Bank of Ireland, Annual Report, 1979*, pp. 109–21.

McCarthy, C. (1980), 'EMS and the end of Ireland's sterling link'. *Lloyds Bank Review*, no. 136 (April), pp. 30–42.

McCormack, D. (1979), 'Policy-making in a small open economy: some aspects of Irish experience'. *Central Bank of Ireland Quarterly Bulletin*, Winter, pp. 92–113.

McDowell, M. (1975), 'Discussion'. In Irish Council of the European Movement (1975).

Meenan, J. (1970), *The Irish Economy Since 1922* (Liverpool University Press).

Micks, W. L. (1925), *History of the Congested Districts Board* (Eason and Sons, Dublin).

Murray, C. H. (1979), 'The European Monetary System: implications for Ireland'. *Central Bank of Ireland, Annual Report, 1979*, pp. 96–108.

Norton, D. A. G. (1980), *Economic Analysis for an Open Economy: Ireland* (Irish Management Institute, Dublin).
O'Brien, George (1921), *The Economic History of Ireland from the Union to the Famine* (Longman Green & Co, London).
O'Connor, P. (1980), 'The EMS – Ireland's Experience and Prospects'. Paper read to Statistical and Social Inquiry Society of Ireland, 13 November 1980 (mimeo).
Oslizlok, J. (1967), 'Towards a monetary analysis of aggregate demand'. *Central Bank of Ireland Quarterly Bulletin*, November, pp. 53–71.
Pratschke, J. L. (1969), 'The establishing of the Irish pound: a backward glance'. *Economic and Social Review*, vol. 1, no. 1, pp. 51–76.
Ryan, T. M. (1978), *An Economic Analysis of Irish Exchange Rate Policy*, Research Paper no. 2 (European League for Economic Cooperation and Irish Council of European Movement, Dublin).
Walsh, M. (1980), 'Foreign currency borrowing: the cheap money myth'. *Journal of Irish Business and Administrative Research*, vol. 2, no. 2, pp. 20–8.
Whitaker, T. K. (1973), 'Monetary integration: reflection on Irish experience'. *Moorgate and Wall Street Review*, Autumn; reprinted in *Central Bank of Ireland Quarterly Review*, Winter 1973, pp. 64–80.

Macroeconomic Adjustment and Exchange-rate Policy in Middle-income Countries: Greece, Portugal and Spain in the 1970s

LOUKA T. KATSELI
Yale University, New Haven, Connecticut

Southern Europe: differences and similarities

A paper on comparative economic behaviour always runs the risk of over-simplifying complex internal processes for the sake of comparisons, of overlooking important country-specific developments, or of assuming away social and historical determinants of economic actions.

It is all too frequent for countries that are quite dissimilar in their traditional structures and social characteristics to be lumped together under such elusive titles as 'less developed' or 'newly industrialized countries' (LDCs or NICs) or, within the context of this conference, as 'southern Europe'. In most of these cases, the emphasis on a few common characteristics such as income per capita, level of industrialization or even geographical location creates the misleading impression that a group of countries is in fact homogeneous.

In past discussions and memoranda over the second enlargement of the European Economic Community (EEC), for example, all three southern European countries were portrayed as essentially agricultural producers and exporters of food and labour whose continuous internal development would be a drain for the Community as a whole. It is by now well documented that this characterization does not apply equally to all three candidates and that the net benefits of entry into the EEC both for the Community and the new members are quite different across countries (Seers and Vaitsos, 1981). Spain is a large country of approximately 37 million where agriculture contributes less than 10 per cent of GDP and around 20 per cent of civilian employment;[1] industry and construction's share is over 30 per cent in GDP and around 36 per cent in employment. Portugal and Greece, smaller and more open to trade,[2] depend more than Spain does on their agricultural sectors as a source of income and employment and have substantially more limited industrial bases and financial markets. Despite these similarities, Greece's per capita income in 1979 was over $4000 while Portugal's was under $2000. In all three cases, but especially in Portugal and Greece, 'development' and 'underdevelopment' coexist on any number of definitions. These are growing dual economies where the state has been traditionally powerful both politically and economically and which have in the past (especially Greece and Portugal) looked upon Europe and/or the United States as arbitrators of internal political developments and guarantors of export markets.

In the 1970s all three countries underwent important political transformations overthrowing long established dictatorships, surprisingly around the same time: 25 April 1974 in Portugal, July 1974 in Greece, and November 1975 in Spain. All three new governments had to meet rapidly rising expectations and to deal with rather similar internal pressures: a push for real wage increases, general uncertainty with negative repercussions on investment and international capital flows, and last but not least growing demands for expansionary policies on the part of the government to correct long-standing injustices. This transition period coincided with a period of grave external shocks. The four-fold increase in the price of oil and other intermediate goods in 1973–74 caused a dramatic worsening of the terms of trade and increased the internal stagflationary pressures not only in the southern European countries but in all of their major trading partners. Furthermore, the instability in the international monetary system and the growing volatility of the major currencies imposed additional costs on these countries and required a careful exercise of exchange rate policy.

The 1970s therefore represent an exceedingly interesting juncture in the economic and political evolution of these countries which lends itself to comparative analysis. It is the exposure to similar internal and external shocks, rather than geographical proximity or common structural characteristics, that makes such an undertaking worthwhile, however difficult. This paper represents only a start in that direction.

Transmission of internal and external disturbances

Despite important differences in their economic structure, all three southern European countries were confronted in the past decade with a number of common disturbances both of internal and external origin. In the middle of the 1970s these included a substantial increase in real wages (table 1), largely as a result of internal pressures towards income redistribution and a dramatic worsening of the terms of trade that was induced by the increase in the price of imported intermediate goods. As can be seen in table 2, the deterioration of the terms of trade in all three countries during 1974–75 was significantly worse than the average for industrial countries or for that matter the non-oil developing countries. Furthermore, the combination of internal political and economic uncertainty and the adverse effects of the oil crisis on most OECD countries resulted in a precipitous fall in tourism and emigrant remittances (table 3).

Table 1 Change in real wage
(annual percentage change)

	1970	*1971*	*1972*	*1973*	*1974*	*1975*	*1976*	*1977*	*1978*	*1979*
	%	%	%	%	%	%	%	%	%	%
Greece*	3.1	5.7	5.0	0.7	−0.5	11.3	15.3	8.6	11.1	1.6
Portugal†	5.4	−1.2	−2.1	1.1	7.0	3.4	−9.2	−12.4	−11.5	−9.0
Spain‡	14.0	7.3	6.7	5.7	17.7	13.7	15.2	5.8	6.3	8.0

* Hourly payments for workers in industry and handicraft deflated by the consumer price index
† *Source:* S index of average daily wages of industry and transportation employees in Lisbon deflated by the consumer price index
‡ *Source:* B index of hourly wages deflated by the consumer price index
Source: IMF Yearbook (1980)

Table 2 Terms of trade
(annual percentage change based on unit values)

	1970	*1971*	*1972*	*1973*	*1974*	*1975*	*1976*	*1977*	*1978*	*1979*
	%	%	%	%	%	%	%	%	%	%
Greece*	−1.7	−3.9	−4.3	7.1	−13.2	−6.8	−0.1	3.5	−4.9	−9.4
Portugal†	7.3	60.2	−0.8	0.9	−7.3	−29.6	58.0	−41.6		
Spain*	−7.1	−2.8	5.6	−7.8	−29.3	−1.3	1.8	6.5	7.4	
Industrial countries‡				−1.0	11.0	2.5	−1.0	−1.0	3.0	−2.5
Oil-exporting countries				15.0	137.0	−5.0	4.5	1.0	10.5	28.0
Non-oil developing countries				7.5	−8.0	−9.5	3.5	3.0	−4.0	−2.5

* IMF *International Financial Statistics Yearbook* (1980)
† UN *Yearbook of International Trade Statistics* (1978)
‡ IMF *Annual Report* (1980)

Table 3 Selected current account balance developments (annual percentage change of millions of SDRs)

	1972	*1973*	*1974*	*1975*	*1976*	*1977*	*1978*
	%	%	%	%	%	%	%
Greece							
Travel (credit)	18.7	19.3	−16.0	42.1	38.5	17.3	25.6
Emigrants' and workers' remittances	13.2	16.3	−13.4	13.5	14.2	14.2	−1.5
Portugal							
Travel (credit)		19.7	−7.4	−31.0	−4.4	21.9	35.6
Emigrants' and workers' remittances		13.4	0.3	−4.8	−4.8	16.0	33.8
Spain							
Travel (credit)	12.5	18.4	−3.1	8.3	−6.9	27.9	28.2
Emigrants' and workers' remittances	5.1	46.8	−19.4	0.3	4.8	−1.8	17.4

Sources: IMF *Balance of Payments Yearbook,* vol. 30 (December 1979)

Table 4 Ratio of government consumption expenditures to GDP

	Greece	*Portugal*	*Spain*
1970	12.6	14.2	8.5
1971	12.5	13.9	8.7
1972	12.2	13.8	8.6
1973	11.4	13.2	8.6
1974	13.8	14.5	8.8
1975	15.2	15.4	9.2
1976	15.1	14.1	9.8
1977	16.0	14.2	10.1
1978	16.0	14.3	10.5
1979	16.2		11.0

Source: IMF *International Financial Statistics* (1980)

On the policy side, all three countries experienced faster than average growth of government consumption expenditures during most of the period, and increases in the government budget deficit which were largely monetized. Thus government consumption expenditures rose to an increasingly larger fraction of GDP (table 4), while with few exceptions money supply grew at an average annual rate of 20 per cent (table 5). In terms of exchange rate policy, by the end of 1975 all countries abandoned their previous practices and devalued their currencies *vis-à-vis* most trading partners.

Table 5 Money supply
(annual percentage change)

	1970	*1971*	*1972*	*1973*	*1974*	*1975*	*1976*	*1977*	*1978*	*1979*
	%	%	%	%	%	%	%	%	%	%
Greece										
M1	11.7	16.6	19.2	23.4	19.8	16.4	22.4	16.9	22.3	17.4
M2	18.8	22.1	23.1	15.8	20.5	25.0	24.5	22.7	24.0	17.5
Portugal										
M1	7.0	4.9	16.6	35.4	10.2	24.5	12.7	11.7	14.2	36.2
M2	14.9	13.5	24.2	28.3	13.6	12.6	20.9	16.9	20.6	38.0
Spain										
M1	6.0	23.8	24.1	23.5	17.3	18.7	21.9	18.6	17.3	8.5
M2	15.1	24.1	23.1	24.1	18.9	18.9	19.7	18.7	20.3	17.8

Source: IMF *International Financial Statistics Yearbook* (1980)

The aim of this section is simply to suggest a consistent framework of analysis that captures the essential features of these economies and that highlights the likely effects of particular disturbances on the domestic price component, the income level and the balance of payments. The model used for this purpose is basically an extension of earlier work by the author (Katseli-Papaefstratiou 1979; 1980), which itself built upon a rapidly growing literature on the responsiveness of small and open economies to external disturbances. The main underlying assumptions are (1) that the country in question is a price-taker in export and import markets, (2) that the country is an importer of intermediate goods[3] for which there is no domestic production but which are used in fixed proportions to domestic factors in the production of non-traded goods and services; (3) that nominal wages and exchange rates are exogenously determined but variable depending on the overall targets of unions or monetary authorities; and (4) that domestic financial markets are not adequately developed so that excess demand for money holdings[4] translates into a reduction of demand for goods.

Some indirect evidence on degrees of market power seems to suggest that, in fact, southern European countries could be characterized as price-takers in international markets especially on the import side (Branson and Katseli-Papaefstratiou, 1981a).[5] Similarly, tables 6 and 7 on the commodity composition of trade support the argument that these countries can be characterized effectively as importers of intermediate goods and exporters of labour- and land-intensive final goods despite growing diversification of their export sectors.

Table 6 Imports by broad economic category (percentage of total value)

	Greece			Portugal			Spain		
	1973	*1975*	*1979*	*1973*	*1975*	*1979*	*1973*	*1975*	*1979*
	%	%	%	%	%	%	%	%	%
M/GNP or *M/GDP*			25.9*			32.1†			14.0†
1 Food, beverages	10.7	6.5	8.1	11.9	16.7	11.3	9.4	11.3	10.6
2 Industrial supplies	35.0	31.3	26.9	42.7	36.8	39.3	44.1	35.6	34.5
3 Fuels	12.0	21.8	21.0	6.1	15.1	19.3	12.8	25.7	29.6
4 Machinery	20.8	15.3	13.6	17.2	14.4	16.8	21.8	18.8	13.8
5 Transport	16.0	20.4	24.9	13.1	8.8	8.8	6.1	3.8	5.2
6 Consumer goods	5.6	4.6	5.5	9.0	8.2	4.5	5.8	4.7	6.3
7 Goods NES	0.0	0.0	0.1	0.1	0.0	0.1	0.0	0.0	0.0
Intermediate goods (111+121+2+3+4+521+53)	83.7	88.1	84.7	81.3	82.9	90.5	88.6	90.4	88.2

* Imports of goods and invisible payments
† Imports of goods and services as a percentage of GDP (1978 figure)
Source: UN *Yearbook of Trade Statistics* (1979)

Table 7 Exports by industrial origin (percentage of total value)

	Greece			Portugal			Spain		
	1973	*1975*	*1979*	*1973*	*1975*	*1979*	*1973*	*1975*	*1979*
	%	%	%	%	%	%	%	%	%
X/GNP or *X/GDP*			20.1*			20.3†			15.00†
1 Agriculture	23.6	22.6	17.4	3.9	2.7	2.5	14.1	12.6	11.4
2 Mining, quarry	5.0	5.3	4.8	6.7	4.8	2.7	0.9	1.2	0.8
3 Manufacturing	71.4	72.1	77.8	89.4	92.5	94.8	85.0	86.2	87.8
31 Food, bev., tob.	15.2	13.1	15.3	16.3	15.1	12.7	16.1	10.5	9.6
32 Textiles	17.1	17.7	21.9	29.8	29.3	34.2	13.1	12.8	10.7
33 Woods	0.6	0.5	0.5	8.1	7.5	9.6	1.4	1.1	1.1
34 Paper & paper products	0.4	0.5	1.0	5.3	7.4	5.9	3.3	3.7	3.8
35 Chemicals	19.8	17.4	16.8	7.9	9.5	6.8	12.0	12.4	12.9
36 Non-metal min.	1.1	5.0	5.5	2.6	2.6	2.7	2.2	3.6	4.0
37 Basic metals	12.8	10.6	11.0	1.1	2.0	3.5	7.1	7.9	11.4
38 Metal manuf.	3.7	6.8	5.6	16.9	17.8	18.3	27.6	32.7	32.9
39 Other manuf.	0.7	0.4	0.3	1.4	1.3	1.0	2.1	1.5	1.5

* Exports of goods and invisible payments
† Exports of goods and services as percengage of GDP (1978 figure)
Source: UN *Yearbook of Trade Statistics* (1979)

Finally, in the absence of careful econometric studies, a casual look at the workings of the financial markets seems to validate their assumed interdependence with commodity markets.[6] These links are made even stronger in the context of Greece and Portugal because of the presence of strict exchange controls.

Table 8 presents in summary form the qualitative solutions of the model; these include the responsiveness of home goods prices ($\hat{P}_h$), value-added (dV) and the current account, $e\hat{R}^*$, to a number of exogenous or policy-induced disturbances such as changes in real wages ($\hat{w}$), changes in the foreign prices of imported inputs ($\hat{P}_r^*$) or exported final goods ($\hat{P}_x^*$), changes in the exchange rate ($\hat{e}$) and emigrant remittances ($\hat{F}^*$), or finally changes in autonomous expenditures such as government expenditures on non-traded (dG_h) or imported commodities (dG_m).

Increases in real wages or in the price of imported goods have similar effects on the economy. Under both circumstances, the net real wage in the non-traded goods sector rises and the supply of home goods decreases. An increase in the real wage will also reduce output in the export goods sector. In either case, value-added or income is reduced while the effect on the price of non-traded goods is ambiguous. The stronger the contractionary supply-side effect, the

Table 8 Effects of selected disturbances on non-traded goods prices, income and the balance of payments

Disturbance	$\hat{P}_h$	dV	$e\hat{R}^*$
$\hat{W} = \hat{w}$†	?‡	—	—
$\hat{P}_r^*$	?§	—	—
$\hat{P}_x^*$	+	+	+
$\hat{F}^*$	+	+	+
dG_h	+	+	—
dG_m	0	0	—
$\hat{e}$	?‖	?‖	?‖

† A caret above a variable indicates percentage change

‡ For this to be positive (or negative),

$$E_h P_h H^s \gtreqless [(P_h - P_r) R^d E_h + P_x X^s E_x] m_h (1-t)(1-\lambda k)$$

§ For this to be positive (or negative),

$$E_h P_h H^s \gtreqless (P_h - P_r) R^d (1 + E_h) m_h (1-t)(1-\lambda k)$$

‖ For this to be positive the equivalent of the Marshall–Lerner conditions must hold, namely that

$$P_x X^s (1 + E_x) + eF^* \geq P_r R^d (1 + E_h)$$

more inflationary the outcome. Given a decrease in value-added and savings and the absence of autonomous changes in domestic absorption, the balance of payments deteriorates.

Improvements in the terms of trade or increases in emigrant remittances produce, as might be expected, markedly different results. Value-added increases either directly through the foreign exchange inflow, or, in the case of a terms of trade improvement, indirectly through the supply response of the exportable sector. In either case demand for the non-traded good increases through both substitution and income effects and the price of the non-traded commodity unambiguously rises. The increase in value-added and savings improves the balance of payments.

On the policy side an increase in government spending on non-traded goods has the normal expansionary effects on output and prices and deteriorates the balance of payments as the ratio of non-traded to traded goods prices rises.[7] Increased spending on imported goods, on the other hand, has a zero multiplier effect.

A nominal devaluation of the currency has both substitution and income effects since the increase in the domestic price of traded commodities induces both a shift in consumption towards non-traded goods and an expansion of domestic supply. Imports of intermediate goods also rise. The net effect on value-added is positive so long as the increase in the value of exports and transfers from abroad exceeds the increase in the value of imports. These conditions are in fact identical to the Marshall–Lerner conditions.

The analytical framework presented can be used as a reference point to understand the historical experience of the southern European countries in the 1970s. The abrupt increase in the cost of production owing to increases in the real price of imported intermediate goods and domestic labour resulted, as expected, in a substantial decline in the growth rate of output in 1974–75 (table 9). It is interesting to note that in the latter part of the decade Greece and Portugal grew faster than most industrial or European countries; Spain's economy, on the other hand, continued to stagnate. This differential performance could be probably attributed to the substantial drop in investment demand which, as can be seen in table 10, occurred right after 1974 in Greece and Portugal but three years later in Spain. The drop in net transfers from abroad in the latter part of the decade rather than in the middle might also have contributed to these differences.

The inflation rate measured by the annual percentage change in the consumer price index (CPI) was 25 per cent in Greece and Portugal in 1974, but reached that level only in 1977 in Spain

Table 9 Growth of real GDP
(annual percentage change, 1975 prices)

	1971	*1972*	*1973*	*1974*	*1975*	*1976*	*1977*	*1978*	*1979*
	%	%	%	%	%	%	%	%	%
Greece	7.1	8.9	7.3	−3.6	6.1	6.4	3.4	6.2	3.8
Portugal	6.6	8.0	11.2	1.1	−4.3	6.2	5.4	3.2	4.1
Spain	5.0	8.1	7.9	5.7	1.1	3.0	2.6	2.5	1.5
Total OECD*	3.6	5.5	6.3	0.6	−0.5	5.3	3.8	4.0†	3.4†
Total OECD Europe*	3.6	4.3	5.9	2.2	−0.9	4.6	2.3		
EEC*	3.5	4.0	6.0	1.7	−1.4	5.0	2.4		

* GDP weights: centred three-year moving average
† These are real GNP growth rates for all industrial countries from IMF, *Annual Report* (1980)
Sources: OECD Economic Outlook, vol. 27 (July 1980); IMF *Annual Report* (1980)

Table 10 Shares of expenditures in national income

	1973	*1974*	*1975*	*1977*
Greece				
C/GNP	61.524	65.298	65.548	64.175
I/GNP*	34.835	28.414	26.222	26.569
GC/GNP	11.142	13.417	14.753	15.473
X/GNP	13.858	15.100	15.881	15.594
M/GNP	24.557	24.858	26.121	24.477
TR/GNP	2.635	3.075	2.777	3.048
X − M − TR/GNP	−8.065	−6.683	−7.579	−5.835
Portugal				
C/GNP	67.4	75.3	81.8	76.4
I/GNP*	26.1	24.7	16.4	25.7
GC/GNP	13.1	14.4	15.4	14.3
X/GNP	25.6	25.7	19.7	18.0
M/GNP	32.9	41.0	32.2	33.3
TR/GNP	0.7	1.0	−0.08	−1.1
X − M − TR/GNP	−6.5	−14.4	−12.6	−16.4
Spain				
C/GNP	67.7	67.8	68.3	69.9
I/GNP*	24.8	28.1	26.6	22.6
GC/GNP	8.6	8.8	9.3	10.2
X/GNP	14.4	14.4	13.3	14.6
M/GNP	15.5	19.2	17.3	16.8
TR/GNP	−0.05	+0.2	−0.1	−0.5
X − M − TR/GNP	−1.1	−4.6	−4.1	−2.7

* Includes gross fixed capital formation and change in inventories
Source: IMF *International Financial Statistics Yearbook* (1980)

Table 11 Change in consumer prices
(annual percentage change)

	1970	1971	1972	1973	1974	1975	1976	1977	1978	1979
	%	%	%	%	%	%	%	%	%	%
Greece	2.9	3.0	4.2	15.6	26.9	13.4	13.3	12.2	12.5	19.0
Portugal	6.4	11.9	10.6	12.9	25.3	15.2	21.1	24.4	22.5	23.8
Spain	5.8	8.1	8.3	11.4	15.7	16.8	15.1	24.5	19.8	15.6
Europe	6.6	11.7	10.9	16.0	22.2	18.3	15.1	19.7	25.1	
Industrial countries	5.5	5.2	4.7	7.6	13.3	11.1	8.3	8.5	7.1	9.4

Sources: IMF *International Financial Statistics Yearbook* (1980); *OECD Economic Outlook*, vol. 27 (July 1980)

(table 11). Thus the stagflationary effects of the 1974–75 disturbances were felt right away in the two smaller countries but only with a lag in Spain. This could be attributed partially to greater degrees of openness to trade in Greece and Portugal relative to Spain (tables 6 and 7) as well as to their markedly less competitive industrial structures. Increases in the real cost of production are thus passed on faster to the consumer than would be the case in a more competitive setting.

These hypotheses seem to be validated by some preliminary empirical results, which are presented in table 12. The complexity and interdependence of an economy, especially at a time of structural change, hampers the unambiguous specification of cause–effect relationships. Thus, these are only tentative estimates of the CPI elasticities with respect to current and lagged values of the money supply (M1), money wages (W) and import prices (P_m) for Greece and Spain.[8]

In both countries expansion of the money supply affects the CPI with a two- to three-quarter lag, but it has a stronger cumulative effect on prices in Spain than in Greece. A 10 per cent increase in M1 will raise the CPI by 8 per cent within a year in Spain and about 6 per cent in Greece. On an annual basis, the responsiveness of the CPI to a given increase in nominal wages is similarly higher in Spain than in Greece (8 per cent versus 5 per cent respectively for a 10 per cent increase in wages); their maximum effect, however, is only after three to four quarters, whereas in Greece increases in the cost of labour are passed on to prices within the same quarter.

The same can be said for changes in import prices: whereas on an annual basis the contribution to inflation of a 10 per cent increase in import prices is about the same in both countries (roughly

Table 12 Estimated elasticities of the consumer price index with respect to selected variables

Variables	*Greece* *1971(I)–1980(I)*	*Spain* *1971(II)–1979(I)*
C	−0.024 (1.5)*	−0.060 (1.5)
$M1_t$	0.134 (1.6)	0.163 (0.6)
$M1_{t-1}$	0.165 (1.9)	0.173 (1.0)
$M1_{t-2}$	0.299 (3.2)	0.277 (2.1)
$M1_{t-3}$	0.016 (0.2)	0.235 (1.6)
$M1_{t-4}$		−0.016 (1.0)
W_t	0.471 (3.2)	0.148 (1.2)
W_{t-1}	0.045 (0.3)	0.148 (1.2)
W_{t-2}		0.390 (3.6)
W_{t-3}		0.194 (2.2)
W_{t-4}		−0.026 (0.4)
$P_{m(t)}$	0.086 (1.8)	0.060 (1.2)
$P_{m(t-1)}$	0.068 (1.5)	0.012 (0.25)
$P_{m(t-2)}$		−0.002 (0.05)
$P_{m(t-3)}$		−0.005 (0.09)
$P_{m(t-4)}$		0.086 (1.4)
R^2	0.67	0.65
DW	1.51	1.8

* *t*-statistics in parentheses

2 per cent), the transmission process is markedly faster in the case of Greece than in Spain.

Exchange rate policies have also played a role in the transmission of external disturbances. Thus, inflation rates would probably have been higher in 1974 in Spain had monetary authorities not allowed the Spanish peseta to appreciate substantially relative to the US dollar up to the middle of 1975. The reversal of policies at the end of that year and the depreciation of the peseta relative to all major trading partners probably contributed to the adverse developments in the second half of the decade. The following section presents a more careful interpretation of these developments.

Exchange rate policy

Following the breakdown of the Bretton Woods system of fixed parities, all three countries sought to pursue a more flexible exchange rate policy.

Given the fact that the major currencies exhibited substantial fluctuations *vis-à-vis* each other, pegging the exchange rate to any single one of them meant substantial and continuous realignments *vis-à-vis* the others. Since all three countries have geographically diversified trade sectors (table 13), this implied analogous movements in the home currency price of traded commodities if not of the terms of trade.[9]

Figures 1 and 2 illustrate the bilateral exchange rate movements of the Greek drachma (DR), the Portuguese escudo (E) and the Spanish peseta (P) *vis-à-vis* two of the major currencies, the US dollar and the Deutschmark.

As early as the third quarter of 1971, Spain and, to a lesser extent, Portugal abandoned the dollar currency area and followed the Deutschmark in its upward trend against the dollar. This continued until the middle of 1975, at which time both countries, hit by rising prices and appreciating effective real exchange rates, started devaluing in nominal terms *vis-à-vis* both hard currencies. The escudo's devaluation against the dollar has continued ever since; the devaluation against the Deutschmark was halted around the end of 1979. Spanish authorities, probably sensitive to the inflationary consequences of further nominal devaluations against as major a trading partner as Germany, reversed that trend at the third quarter of 1977 and attempted to stabilize the peseta–Deutschmark price at around 36 pesetas to the Deutschmark. This lasted until about the end of 1979. Greece followed the dollar in its downward movement *vis-à-vis* the other hard currencies for a much longer period than either Spain or Portugal; the drachma price of the dollar continued to be 30 dr until the middle of 1975 at which time, and probably for the same reasons as in the other two cases, a basket peg was adopted and the drachma started devaluing *vis-à-vis* the basket. It is only towards the end of the decade and in view of the large increase in the price of imports and the CPI, that the rapid depreciation *vis-à-vis* the European currencies was mitigated. This policy shift was also prompted by increased trade prospects with the European Economic Community (EEC) in light of the imminent entry into the Community and the expected movement towards harmonization of monetary and exchange rate policies.

The experience of the three countries during the 1970s can be thus subdivided into three roughly comparable periods. In the first period, which lasted from the middle of 1971 to the middle of 1975, Spain and Portugal maintained rough parities *vis-à-vis* the Deutschmark and appreciated substantially *vis-à-vis* the dollar; in the

Table 13 Direction of trade: percentage of country's total exports to/imports from selected countries

	Greece						*Portugal*						*Spain*					
	Exports			*Imports*			*Exports*			*Imports*			*Exports*			*Imports*		
	1973	*1975*	*1979*	*1973*	*1975*	*1979*	*1973*	*1975*	*1979*	*1973*	*1975*	*1979*	*1973*	*1975*	*1979*	*1973*	*1975*	*1979*
	%	%	%	%	%	%	%	%	%	%	%	%	%	%	%	%	%	%
Industrial countries	70.6	62.9	59.4	76.3	70.5	67.3	78.6	78.8	81.8	76.3	70.0	71.1	70.2	63.2	62.3	70.4	60.4	56.7
United States	6.5	5.1	5.5	8.3	7.4	4.8	9.8	7.2	6.0	8.2	12.4	11.8	13.9	10.5	7.2	16.1	15.9	12.5
Japan	1.2	1.6	1.1	7.0	8.3	9.5	1.7	0.9	1.1	4.3	3.4	2.6	1.5	1.2	2.0	2.6	2.4	2.3
EEC (9)	54.9	49.7	49.1	50.1	42.5	44.3	48.6	50.1	56.9	45.4	40.3	41.6	47.8	44.7	48.0	42.9	34.7	35.9
France	6.6	7.3	6.1	7.6	5.9	6.3	5.1	6.6	10.0	6.9	7.6	8.3	12.7	13.6	16.1	10.3	8.3	9.7
Germany	21.5	21.1	19.3	19.5	15.9	15.9	7.6	10.2	12.7	14.5	11.4	12.4	11.7	10.7	10.3	13.6	10.3	9.6
Italy	9.5	8.3	9.8	9.1	8.2	9.3	3.2	3.3	6.0	5.2	5.0	5.1	5.3	3.4	6.5	6.0	5.1	5.6
United Kingdom	7.1	4.9	5.2	5.6	4.8	5.7	23.7	21.2	18.1	11.8	8.7	9.1	8.0	7.6	7.2	6.3	5.3	5.1
Oil-exporting countries	3.3	12.6	14.7	6.7	10.7	11.7	0.6	1.9	1.6	3.2	10.8	15.0	6.2	10.5	10.9	11.8	21.7	24.9
Non-oil developing countries	16.3	14.5	17.3	12.5	14.1	15.2	19.7	16.6	13.9	19.0	13.7	10.5	20.5	20.4	22.0	15.3	13.6	15.5

Source: IMF *Direction of Trade Yearbook* (1980)

Fig. 1 Home currency price of the dollar

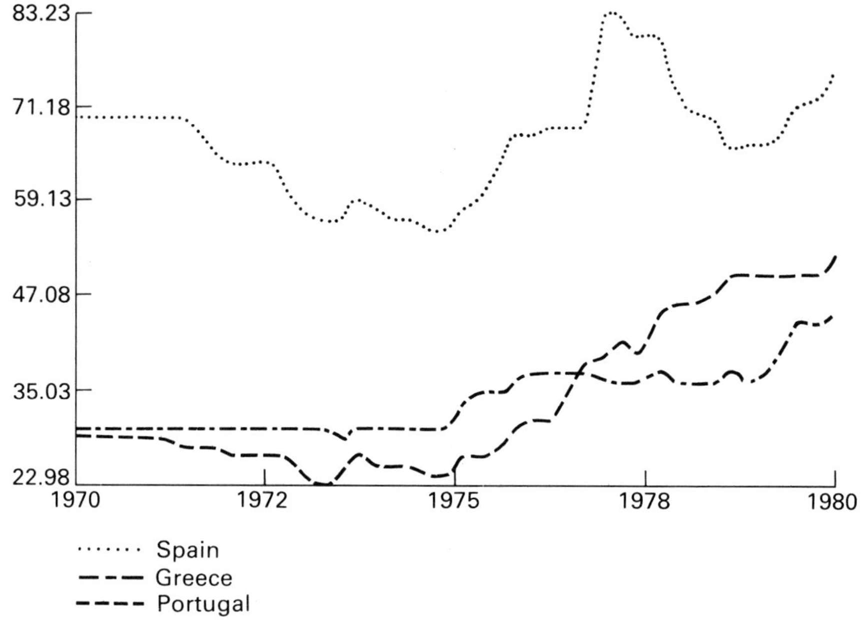

Fig. 2 Home currency price of the Deutschmark

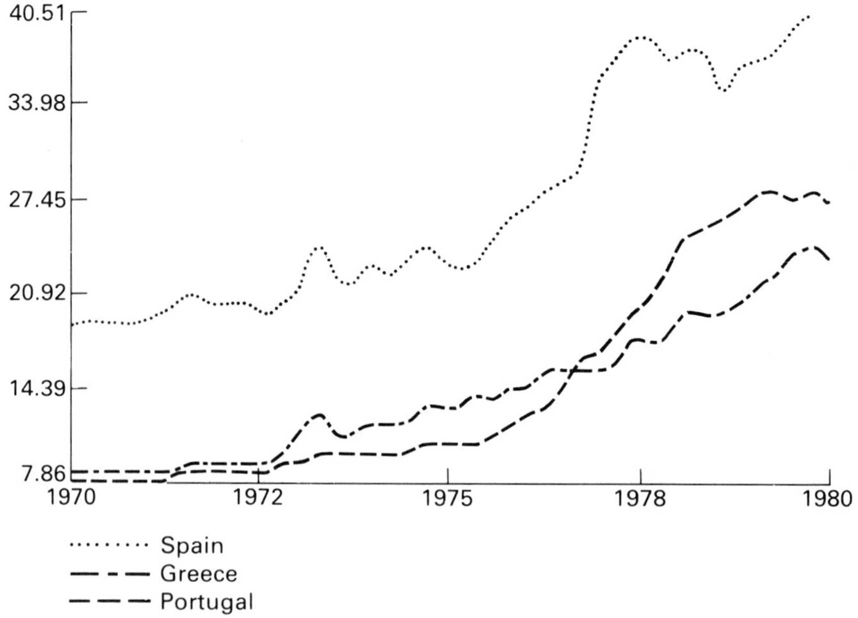

case of Greece the opposite held true. In the second period, which lasts from 1975(II) to 1977(III) in the case of Spain and until the end of 1979 in the other two countries, all three countries experienced substantial effective nominal devaluations *vis-à-vis* all major trading partners. Since that time, monetary authorities have attempted to maintain rough parities with the European currencies and to move accordingly with the dollar.

A clearer picture of the similarities and differences across countries in the exercise of exchange rate policy is provided in tables 14, 15 and 16, which present estimates of the relevant weights of each of the major currencies in the effective currency basket to which the Southern European countries pegged.

Pegging to a currency basket means stabilizing the own nominal or real currency price of an arbitrarily chosen *numeraire* (here the Deutschmark) to an average of other currencies relative to the *numeraire*. The basket peg can be either fixed or variable, in which case the own currency price of the *numeraire* is adjusted relative to the average in a more or less systematic manner. In the case where the adjustment is based on such indicators as the current account balance or the stock of reserves, the basket peg can be rigorously defined as

$$\dot{r}_j = F(B) - \sum_i w_i \dot{J}_i; \qquad F' < 0; F(0) = 0. \tag{1}$$

If authorities are in fact defining the basket over real exchange rates, then

$$\dot{r}_j + \dot{q}_N - \dot{p}_j = F(B) - \sum_i w_i(\dot{J}_1 + \dot{q}_i - \dot{q}_N) \tag{2}$$

where (for both equations)

j = home country

i ≠ j = all other countries including the *numeraire*

N = the *numeraire* country, here the USA

r_j = j currency units per dollar

J_i = $ per unit of i currency

w_i = weight to be assigned to the *i*'th currency

q_N = the appropriate US price index in dollars, here the CPI

q_i = country *i*'s CPI

Table 14 Movements of home-currency price of the Deutschmark (DM) relative to the DM price of selected currencies (quarterly data)

	C	$w_{\$}$†	w_Y	$w_{£}$	w_L	w_F	$w_{DM} = -(1+\Sigma w_i]$	R^2	DW
Greece (DR/DM)									
1970(II)–1974(IV)	−0.003	−0.778	0.025	0.120	−0.391	−0.097	0.121	0.932	2.7
	(0.6)‡	(4.9)	(0.1)	(0.6)	(1.8)	(0.6)	(1.0)		
1975(I)–1980(IV)	0.024	−0.288	−0.045	−0.154	0.026	−0.014	−0.525	0.420	1.7
	(4.4)	(1.9)	(0.5)	(1.3)	(0.2)	(0.07)	(3.1)		
Portugal (E/DM)									
1970(II)–1974(IV)	0.006	−0.287	−0.087	0.096	−0.022	−0.131	−0.569	0.722	2.9
	(1.7)	(2.3)	(0.6)	(0.6)	(0.1)	(1.0)	(5.8)		
1975(I)–1980(IV)	0.028	−0.549	0.187	−0.151	−0.176	−0.065	−0.246	0.416	1.4
	(3.3)	(2.3)	(1.2)	(0.8)	(0.7)	(0.2)	(0.9)		
Spain (P/DM)									
1970(II)–1974(IV)	−0.005	−0.667	−0.289	0.116	0.157	−0.362	0.045	0.984	1.4
	(2.7)	(11.0)	(4.5)	(1.7)	(1.9)	(6.0)	(0.9)		
1975(I)–1980(IV)	0.008	−0.366	0.125	−0.157	−0.393	0.011	−0.220	0.269	1.7
	(0.6)	(1.1)	(0.6)	(0.6)	(1.1)	(0.02)	(0.6)		

† This is the weight in the basket assigned to nominal movements in the *numeraire* price of each currency i, here the DM price of the dollar
‡ *t*-statistics are in parentheses

Table 15 Movements of real home-currency price of the Deutschmark relative to real DM price of selected currencies (quarterly data)

	C	$w_{\$}$†	w_Y	$w_£$	w_L	w_F	$w_{DM} = -(1+\Sigma w_i)$	$R2$	DW
Greece (DR/DM • CPIG/CPIGR)									
1970(II)–1974(IV)	−0.010	−1.07	−0.288	0.118	−0.020	0.063	0.197	0.69	2.3
	(0.8)‡	(1.9)	(0.6)	(0.2)	(0.2)	(0.1)	(0.5)		
1975(I)–1979(IV)	0.003	−0.305	0.129	−0.087	0.077	−0.169	−0.645	0.25	2.6
	(0.5)	(1.4)	(1.0)	(0.5)	(0.3)	(0.6)	(2.8)		
Portugal (E/DM·CPIG/CPIPO)									
1970(II)–1974(IV)	−0.012	−0.453	−0.195	−0.014	0.036	0.146	−0.520	0.74	2.3
	(2.5)	(2.1)	(1.1)	(0.8)	(0.1)	(0.7)	(3.3)		
1975(I)–1980(I)	0.006	−0.271	0.204	0.116	−0.661	0.224	−0.612	0.25	2.7
	(0.5)	(0.7)	(0.8)	(0.4)	(1.5)	(0.4)	(1.5)		
Spain (P/DM · CPIG/CPISP)									
1970(II)–1974(IV)	−0.011	−0.352	−0.340	0.225	−0.222	−0.365	0.054	0.95	2.7
	(3.9)	(2.8)	(3.4)	(2.2)	(1.3)	(3.2)	(0.6)		
1975(I)–1980(II)	−0.005	−0.239	−0.051	−0.167	−0.526	0.198	−0.215	0.32	1.6
	(0.5)	(0.7)	(0.2)	(0.7)	(1.3)	(0.4)	(0.6)		

† This is the weight in the basket assigned to real movements in the *numeraire* price of each currency i, here the DM price of the dollar
‡ *t*-statistics are in parentheses

Table 16 Movements of real home-currency price of the Deutschmark relative to the basket (quarterly data)

	C	CA†	F‡	$w_{\$}$§	w_Y	$w_£$	w_L	w_F	$w_{DM} = -(1 + \Sigma w_i)$	R^2	DW
Greece											
(DR/DM · CPIUS/CPIGR)											
1970(II)–1974(IV)	0.030	0.083	−0.003	−0.822	−0.156	−0.102	−0.439	0.251	−0.268	0.77	2.3
	(0.9)‖	(1.3)	(1.4)	(1.5)	(0.4)	(0.2)	(0.6)	(0.5)	(1.5)		
1975(I)–1979(IV)	0.010	−0.0002	0.0003	−0.336	0.073	−0.055	0.139	−0.185	−0.636	0.31	2.8
	(0.9)	(0.7)	(1.0)	(1.5)	(0.5)	(0.3)	(0.5)	(0.5)	(2.7)		
Portugal											
(E/DM · CPIG/CPIPO)											
1970(II)–1974(IV)	0.044	−0.130	−0.001	−0.454	−0.074	−0.298	0.129	0.141	−0.444	0.79	2.8
	(1.2)	(1.0)	(1.6)	(2.1)	(0.4)	(1.1)	(0,4)	(0.7)	(2.7)		
1975(I)–1980(I)	−0.004	−0.023	−0.0003	−0.214	0.255	−0.062	−0.720	0.389	−0.648	0.40	2.5
	(0.3)	(1.4)	(1.6)	(0.6)	(1.1)	(0.2)	(1.6)	(0.8)	(1.6)		
Spain											
(P/DM · CPIG/CPISP)											
1970(II)–1974(IV)	0.004	−0.020	−0.0001	−0.305	−0.304	0.117	−0.248	−0.350	0.090	0.96	2.9
	(0.4)	(0.9)	(1.5)	(2.4)	(2.9)	(0.9)	(1.4)	(3.1)	(0.9)		
1975(I)–1980(II)	0.017	−0.0001	−0.0002	−0.103	−0.312	−0.167	−0.566	0.735	−0.587	0.46	1.9
	(1.1)	(0.7)	(1.7)	(0.3)	(1.2)	(0.6)	(1.5)	(1.4)	(1.5)		

† Percentage change of net foreign assets
‡ In billions of home currency units
§ This is the weight in the basket assigned to real movements in the *numeraire* price of each currency i, here the DM price of the dollar
‖ *t*-statistics are in parentheses

P_j = country j's CPI in home currency

B = the current account or basic balance

$\dot{x} = dx/x$, the proportional change in x, for any variable x

Tables 14 and 15 respectively present estimated elasticities of each country's nominal and real home currency price of the Deutschmark with respect to the nominal and real Deutschmark price of a number of currencies. As one would expect, the choice of the *numeraire* is completely arbitrary and does not influence the estimated coefficients. Thus, when the dollar was chosen as the *numeraire* the coefficients remained unchanged. The only difference was in the estimated R^2, i.e., in the explained variation of the dependent variable.

Given the direction of trade data (table 13), the currencies chosen include the Deutschmark, the yen, the pound, the Italian lira and the French franc. Despite the high collinearity between the Deutschmark and the yen,[10] the estimated elasticities do not vary significantly when the latter is excluded.

In the absence of any well formulated hypothesis as to the process by which the home currency price of the dollar is adjusted relative to the basket, a constant is included in the regression equations. In table 16 two alternative hypotheses are tested, namely that the adjustment relative to the basket is based on the current account balance (CA) as well as on the stock of net foreign assets (F). This latter term captures past current account developments that affect current exchange rate policy. For each country, the weight of the Deutschmark in the basket is derived by subtracting the sum of the reported weights from unity.[11] The t ratios reported under the Deutschmark weight come from the regressions that involved the dollar as the *numeraire* currency.

A number of tentative but interesting conclusions can be drawn from the results.

1 Over the whole period of the 1970s, the weight of the dollar in the basket is remarkably high in all three countries. This is hard to explain in terms of relative trade shares (table 13), but has to be understood in light of the inertia of the early period and possibly a misplaced emphasis on currency of denomination weights rather than actual trade shares.[12]

2 Between the first and second period the weight of the dollar declines in the Greek and Spanish case both in nominal and real terms; in Portugal the nominal/real distinction seems to be important.

3 In the first period the weight of the Deutschmark is highest in the case of Portugal, while in the second it is highest in the case of Greece (over 0.50 in both cases). This is consistent with trade shares if the Deutschmark weight represents trade with the European Economic Community as a whole. Maintaining a relatively stable rather than declining home currency value of emigrant remittances might also be an important aspect of that choice.

4 In all three cases the share of the Italian lira is quite high. This probably reflects the preoccupation with competitive export positions in third markets.

5 It is unclear from the data whether the basket in these three countries was determined over nominal or real exchange rates. The results are generally better in table 14, and this tends to confirm our intuition that inexperience with managing a basket and a lack of an analytical framework resulted in nominal rather than real basket formulations.

6 With the exception of Portugal, the first period was characterized by nominal and real appreciation of the currencies relative to the basket. In the second period all currencies were nominally devalued. The nominal devaluation was strongest in Portugal (12 per cent on an annual basis) compared with Greece (approximately 8 per cent) and Spain (around 4 per cent). This resulted in a real devaluation relative to the basket in the two smaller countries but a real appreciation in Spain (around 4 per cent).

7 Inclusion of the current account balance and the level of net foreign assets as potential determinants of the adjustment *vis-à-vis* the basket seems to improve the overall results. The new variables have in general the expected signs (there are two exceptions), and the stock of foreign assets seems to be an important determinant of the authorities' reaction to third-country exchange rate movements.

The above results suggest a general pattern: confronted with inflationary pressures in the mid-1970s of both domestic and foreign origins, the monetary authorities in all three countries attempted to safeguard their competitive position internationally through a process of nominal effective devaluations. In the face of domestic inflation rates, which at least in Spain and Portugal exceeded 20 per cent by 1977, the policy of nominal devaluations resulted in small real devaluations in the case of Greece and Portugal and a small real appreciation in the case of Spain (table 15). As we have shown in the preceding section, however, nominal effective exchange rate devaluations are partly responsible for domestic inflationary pressures.

Thus by the end of the 1970s these countries found themselves caught in the classic dilemma associated with exchange rate policy, namely the dilemma between balance of trade *v.* domestic inflation targets. The econometric evidence, however sparse, seems to suggest that in small open economies the effects of exchange rate movements on the price ratio of non-traded to traded goods is higher than the effect on the terms of trade; hence exchange rate policies need to be evaluated in that light. The experience of these countries in the 1970s and the switch in policies in the early 1980s seem to substantiate that claim.

The decision of Greece and the potential new members of the EEC to join the European Monetary System (EMS) has to be judged accordingly. Joining the EMS would limit the potential flexibility of these countries in the exercise of exchange rate policy. This would be especially true if they continue to maintain a geographically diversified trade.

Given the historical experience of the 1970s, the necessary adjustment will be relatively bigger in the case of Greece, which followed the dollar for most of the past decade. It is clear that participation of the new members in the EMS is in the interest of the traditional members. A policy of nominal devaluations *vis-à-vis* the Deutschmark currency area by the southern European countries provided in the past some competitive advantage over France and Italy in the export market of agricultural goods, and caused some redirection of trade on the import side towards non-community members. It will be up to the new members to decide whether or not; having given up the flexibility of commercial policy by joining the EEC, they should also give up the flexibility of exchange rate policy.[13]

Notes

1 The source of these data is the OECD *Economic Surveys* (OECD, 1980a, b, c).

2 See tables 6 and 7.

3 The model allows for imports of final goods which are substitutes in demand to home goods.

4 These include high-powered reserves and foreign exchange reserves.

5 For a proxy of world market power, a weighted average of the country's export shares in total world exports for four main exportables was used. The same was done on the import side. The table shows the numbers pertinent to the three countries and the average for the EEC countries.

Indices of market power, 1974

	Export side	Import side
Greece	0.0091	0.0027
Portugal	0.0337	0.0019
Spain	0.0144	0.0140
Average EC (8)	0.0331	0.0169

6 The weakest part of the model is the treatment of international capital movements and the role of speculation in the foreign exchange market. For an interesting analysis of the workings of 'parallel' foreign exchange market and its implications, see de Macedo (1979).

7 The government expenditure multiplier is equivalent to the open economy multiplier (Katseli-Papaefstratiou, 1979).

8 All data are quarterly data and are derived from the IMF, *International Financial Statistics*. Money supply data refer to M1 (line 34 in *IFS*); wages are hourly earnings (line 65); import prices are unit value indices in domestic currency units (line 75). Government expenditures were excluded as they are highly correlated with the growth of money supply (for Greece, p. 82; for Spain, p. 84).

9 For a detailed analysis of the effects of third-country exchange rate movements on a country's terms of trade or the price of traded goods, see Branson and Katseli-Papaefstratiou (1981a, b).

10 Correlation coefficient is 0.92.

11 This procedure might overestimate slightly the weight of the Deutschmark since other currencies might be included in the basket.

12 For a detailed analysis of this problem see Branson and Katseli (1981b).

13 This is precisely Corden's (1972) argument against monetary integration of countries that have formed a customs union.

References

Branson, W. H. and Katseli-Papaefstratiou, L. T. (1981a), 'Exchange rate policy for developing countries'. In S. Grassman and E. Lundberg (eds), *The World Economic Order* (Macmillan, London).

Branson, W. H. and Katseli, L. T. (1981b), *Currency Baskets and Real Effective Exchange Rates.* Economic Growth Center Discussion Paper no. 372, April.

Corden, W. M. (1972), *Monetary Integration, International Finance Section.* Princeton University Essay on International Finance no. 93, April.

Katseli-Papaefstratiou, L. T. (1979), *Transmission of External Price Disturbances in Small Open Economies* (Garland Press, New York).

Katseli-Papaefstratiou, L. T. (1980), 'Transmission of external price disturbances and the composition of trade', *Journal of International Economics*, vol. 10, pp. 357–75.

Katseli-Papaefstratiou, L. T. and Marion, N. P. (1980), *Adjustment to Variations in Imported Input Prices: The Role of Economic Structure.* National Bureau of Economic Research Working Paper no. 501, July.

Macedo, J. (1979), *Exchange Rates in Portugal 1973–1978: A Portfolio Model of an Inconvertible Currency.* Economic Growth Center Discussion Paper no. 324.

OECD (1980a), *Economic Survey: Spain* (OECD, Paris), April.

OECD (1980b), *Econimic Survey: Portugal* (OECD, Paris), July.

OECD (1980c), *Economic Survey: Greece* (OECD, Paris), August.

Seers, D. and Vaitsos, C., (eds) (1981), *The Second Enlargement of the EEC: Integration of Unequal Partners* (Macmillan, London).

A Portfolio Model of an Inconvertible Currency: the Recent Experience of Portugal

JORGE BRAGA DE MACEDO
Princeton University, Princeton, New Jersey

Introduction

As the example of Greece suggests, a freer foreign exchange market for the Portuguese escudo is likely to be set up soon, with quotation in at least one of the ten members of the European Economic Community. Aside from some form of convertibility, exchange rate policy in Portugal will be constrained by the impossibility of pegging to a major currency without floating against other major currencies. Indeed, since the advent of generalized floating in 1973, exchange rate policy has been based on a basket of currencies reflecting the structure of the Portuguese current account. Furthermore, since 1977 the inconvertible escudo has crawled relative to that basket peg. One question is thus whether a (managed) floating exchange rate regime is viable and whether it should be implemented instead of the present crawling peg regime. If the crawling peg is to continue, a view has to be taken as to the likely effects of membership on the basket of currencies to peg to as well as on the indicators for determining the rate of crawl.[1]

Given the constraints implied by the present international monetary system and the ones implied by the pattern of trade in goods, services and assets, the answer will depend on the macroeconomic objectives set by the Portuguese authorities rather than on community norms. In the recent experience, macroeconomic policy has largely been determined by the need to adjust to the serious external imbalance that followed the shocks of 1973–75, with unfavourable effects on long-run development prospects. Since it is not clear that membership of the EEC will in itself induce an accelerated growth process,[2] exchange rate policy becomes a central instrument for improving profitability in the export sector while preserving external balance.

The improvement in competitiveness is often cited as a major objective of exchange rate policy. Also, in 1980 exchange rate policy was successfully used to fight inflation. The extent to which the attainment of these objectives depended on the inconvertibility of the currency has not, however, been discussed. This paper analyses exchange rate policy in Portugal under the assumption that inconvertibility generates a black market for foreign exchange where the price of foreign currency is determined by portfolio balance. The econometric results suggest that inconvertibility was an important feature of the exchange regime because a 'free' foreign exchange market would probably have been unstable. Indeed, an historical perspective on the Portuguese currency experience suggests that exchange rate flexibility has been associated with political and economic instability.[3]

The recent macroeconomic experience

Overview

In the recent experience of Portugal, the usual polemics of macroeconomic policy are made more intriguing by the combination of deep ideological cleavages and severe data limitations. Some see the policy of wage restraint of the first Socialist government in 1976 as the first step in 'the restoration of capitalism', and look at the two devaluations of 1977 and the IMF stabilization package of 1978 as evidence that capitalism has been restored. In their view, the structural nature of the Portuguese balance of payments problem makes restrictive macroeconomic policies at best ineffective and at worst perverse. They further believe that administrative controls would have allowed Portugal to achieve external balance at less social cost. Others are more sceptical about controls and argue instead that the government was unwilling and unable to tackle the macroeconomic balance of payments problem effectively, even as the country was reaching the brink of bankruptcy. It is then easy to claim that a carefully negotiated standby agreement with the IMF was the superior alternative.[4]

The quick success in restoring external balance, in particular the spectacular recovery of the current account in 1978–79, showed that the structural rigidities were not such that they made an elasticity–optimist combination of expenditure-switching and expenditure-reducing macroeconomic policies ineffective. Despite its simplicity, the dependent economy model turns out to be useful in identifying phases in the macroeconomic adjustment process since the shocks that followed the export- and remittance-led boom of 1968–73. Focusing on the gaps between actual and potential output on the one hand and the actual and 'warranted' real wage on the other, under the assumption that an increase in output leads to a current account deficit if the real wage does not fall correspondingly, three phases suggest themselves. The first phase, 1974–75, is characterized by the opening of the two gaps relative to the situation of full employment and surplus prevailing in early 1973. While the increase in the labour force increased potential output and the terms of trade deterioration implied a decline in real income, the Revolution brought a decline in actual output and an increase in real wages. Stabilization policy succeeded in moderating the decline in output via increased government expenditure. On the other hand, price controls and a fixed exchange rate ensured that the substantial increases in nominal wages were not offset by increases in the price of goods. Because of the decline in imports, however, during this phase the reported current account deficits remained at a manageable 6 per cent of gross national product. One economic adviser suggested in the summer of 1975 that an immediate devaluation of about 20 per cent would be required to save the Revolution. Later that year, a more influential team recommended 'a disregard for external financing constraints',[5] while hinting that a crawling peg devaluation could be used 'to blunt the impact of inflation' and 'retain trade competitiveness'. By that time, there remained the abundant and undervalued gold reserves of the earlier regime, but the decline in remittances and widespread capital flight had virtually wiped out foreign exchange reserves.

Perhaps as a consequence of the advice, the expansionary policy stance continued in the second phase, 1976–77. In particular, aggregate real expenditure (including public administration) increased by 7 per cent in 1976, narrowing the output gap. Despite a sliding devaluation in the first half of the year, imports picked up from their depressed 1975 level while exports continued to decline. In the face of the worsening current account deficit, the influential economic advice in the summer of 1976 became a 30 per cent once-and-for-all effective devaluation, which would reduce real wages by 6 per cent and restore cost competitiveness to the 1973 level.[6] But the Socialist government did not take such unpopular measures before the December local elections, and indeed delayed them until the pressure to borrow foreign exchange made a policy package inevitable. At the end of February it announced the relaxation of price controls, ceilings on wage increases, modest increases in interest rates and an effective devaluation of less than 15 per cent. While these measures may have prevented a further worsening of the wage gap, they were not accompanied by a check on public sector borrowing and allowed a brisk expansion of aggregate demand. This narrowed the output gap but deteriorated external payments further, and a second 'policy package' was thus required six months later. The measures of August 1977 included another increase in interest rates and the announcement of a crawling peg regime based on inflation differentials with forward cover by the central bank. The current account deficit, $340 million in the third quarter of 1977, worsened to $380 and $430 million in the next two quarters. Domestic credit creation amounted to 7, 11 and 5 per cent per quarter these three quarters while the respective consumer price inflation rates were 1, 4 and 5 per cent.

As 'Cooper's law' would have predicted, the government fell before the year's end, but it was still a Socialist-led coalition that signed the letter of intent to the IMF in May 1978, initiating the third phase. The major feature of the IMF agreement was to recognize explicitly the connection between the rate of crawl and the rate of monetary expansion, and thus to set tight ceilings on domestic credit creation and the public sector borrowing requirement. The current account turned into a surplus in the third quarter, and so did the balance on non-monetary transactions, which has remained in surplus since. On the other hand, the rate of growth of output, while still above the OECD average, declined from 5.7 per cent in 1977 to 3.2 per cent in 1978 and to 4.5 per cent in 1979. Inflation declined from 28 per cent in 1977 to about 23 and 24 per cent in 1978 and 1979, and productivity increased but real wages continued to fall and probably closed the gap. The rate of crawl accommodated the domestic inflation rate in 1978 but declined to 1 per cent per month in April 1979 and to 0.75 per cent in June, in light of the improvement in the external position.

The first three phases can be inferred from figure 1, where the rate of growth of output is plotted together with the difference between the current account balance and the public sector borrowing requirement expressed in billions of escudos with 1980 purchasing power over goods and services produced in the four major trading partners.[7] From 1974 to 1977, government dissaving (excluding nationalized firms) was more than offset by foreign saving, so that private savings fell short of private investment (including nationalized firms). In

Fig. 1 Growth and the 'savings gap'

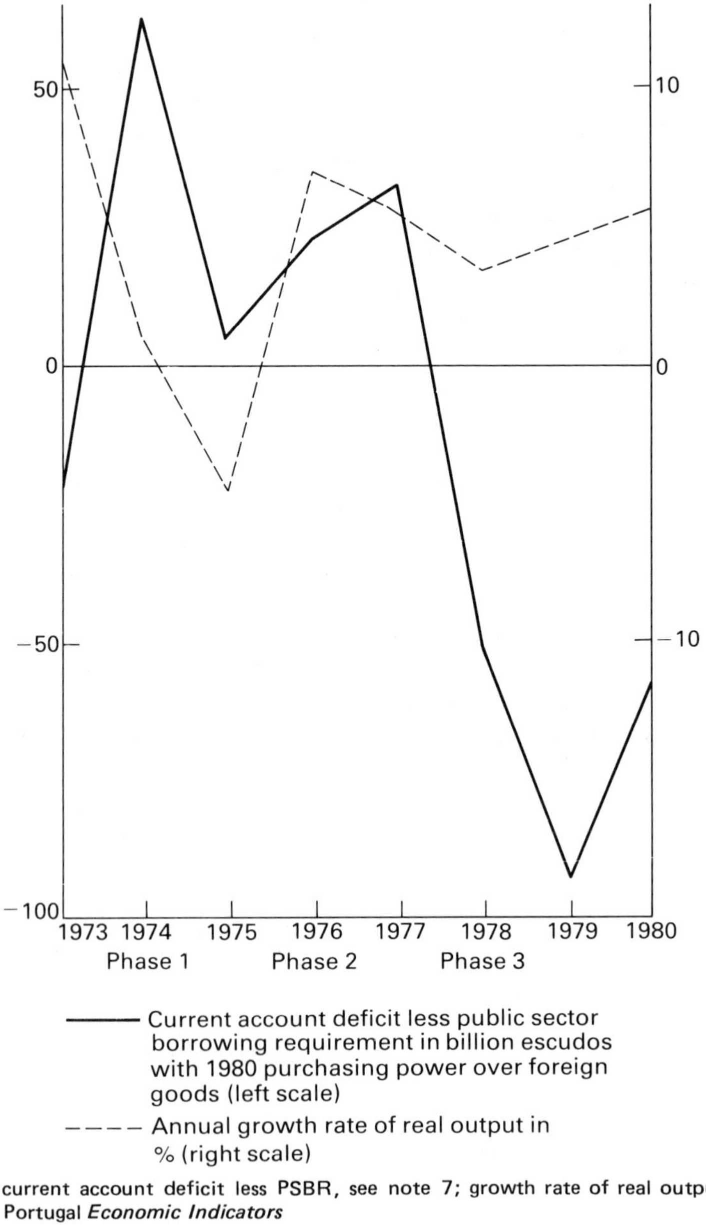

Sources: current account deficit less PSBR, see note 7; growth rate of real output, from Banco de Portugal *Economic Indicators*

1978–79 the recovery of the current account was accompanied by an increase in private savings while a worsening government deficit crowded out private investment. In 1980, the improved investment climate and a greater control over public spending might have begun to reverse the process, as suggested by the drop in the savings gap and a growth rate two points higher than the planned 3.5 per cent.

One consistent feature of the three phases of the macroeconomic adjustment process deserves emphasis here. This is the positive association between the rate of change of the escudo–dollar rate and the current account deficit, known as the 'acceleration hypothesis' and illustrated in figure 2.[8] In 1980, when the exchange rate was successfully used to fight inflation at the cost of worsening the current account, the relationship broke down. An effective revaluation of 5 per cent was decided in mid-February and the rate of crawl was decreased to 0.5 per cent in June. Inflation dropped to a remarkable 17 per cent, reversing the fall in real wages, while the growth rate increased to a remarkable 5.5 per cent. While these policies were basically continued in 1981 (the current account worsened again but the rate of crawl was nevertheless maintained), the increase in real wages and the budget deficit became excessive again, so that, as mentioned, a fourth phase may have been initiated in late 1980.

Fundamentals of exchange rate determination

In the five years between the beginning of 'generalized floating' and the agreement with the IMF, the purchasing power of the escudo over goods and services included in the consumer price index of the four major trading partners – France, Germany, the United Kingdom and the United States – fell by about 70 per cent while the purchasing power of a basket of these currencies – the Japanese yen, the Canadian dollar and the Swiss franc, weighted by the country's dollar income – fell by about 36 per cent.[9] Nevertheless, domestic consumer price inflation did not entirely offset this dramatic decline, thus restoring the competitiveness of Portuguese exports. Indeed, as mentioned above, changes in relative wages were a major feature of the recent macroeconomic experience of Portugal. This is evident in figure 3, which plots escudo unit labour costs in Portugal relative to the four major trading partners (using the same weights as in figure 1), together with the relative real-wage gap and the nominal effective depreciation of the escudo.[10] Even though changes in relative warranted real wages were probably substantial, relative actual wages

Fig. 2 The 'acceleration hypothesis'

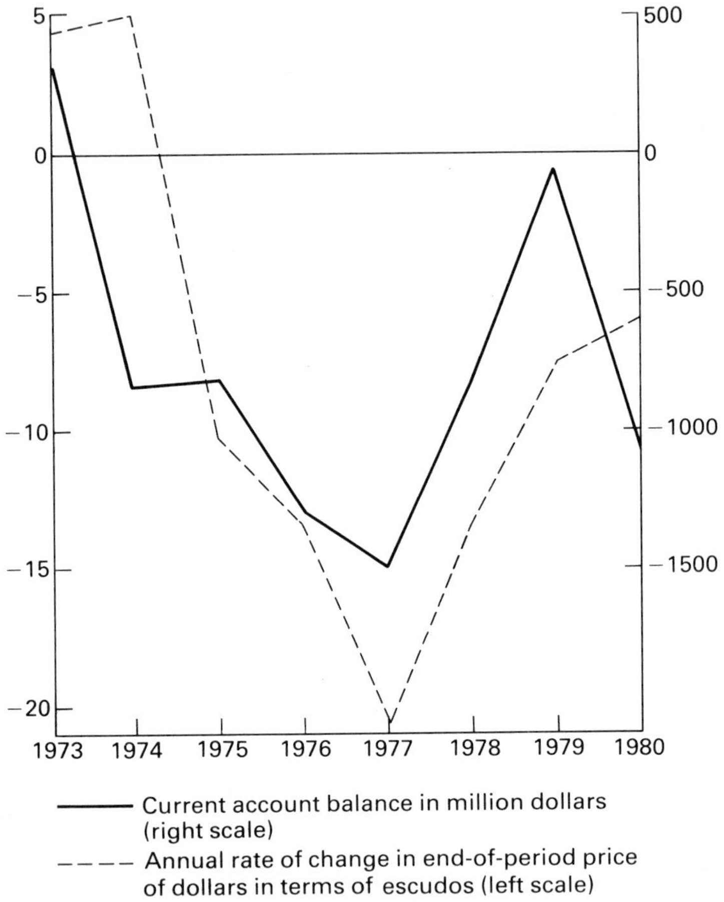

Sources: current account balance, from Banco de Portugal; price of dollars in terms of escudos, Banco de Portugal *Quarterly Bulletin*

in figure 3 also display the inverted-J pattern associated with the phases of macroeconomic adjustment described earlier. The distance between the two curves measuring labour costs, on the other hand, show a period of real (consumer price) appreciation until 1978 and a period of real depreciation since then. This remarkable improvement in competitiveness, difficult to reconcile with the standard monetarist approach to the exchange rate (see Appendix 2), has in turn been a major factor in the recovery of Portuguese exports.

Fig. 3 Relative unit labour costs (1973 = 100)

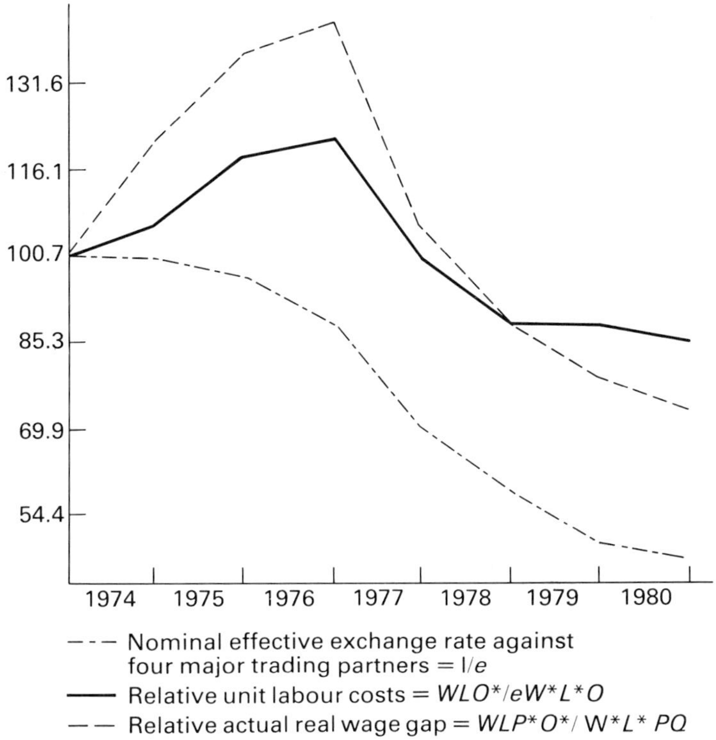

Sources: described in note 10

Given the trade deficit, however, the improvement in the current account was due largely to substantial remittances attracted by the increase in interest rates in 1978. While some believe that only a financial reform *à la* Korea or Taiwan could link the short-run success of monetary programming to a higher long-run rate of growth, a comparison between the recent performances of Argentina and Chile suggests that the combination of capital controls and trade liberalization is preferable to financial liberalization and trade restrictions.[11] Indeed, the success of the 1978 stabilization programme can also be seen in the fact that the Portuguese authorities were reluctant to liberalize interest rates entirely, so that the differential was not high enough to attract excessive capital inflows that would have exacerbated real appreciation via the foreign monetary base rather than reverse the process.

The reversal is further illustrated in table 1, which shows various measures of the change in relative prices.[12] Column (1) reports a measure of the relative price of non-traded goods, using the services item (excluding rent) in the consumer price index as a proxy for non-traded goods (weight in total about 1/4) and assuming that the remaining items in the consumer price index are traded goods. This measure shows a decline from 1973 to 1979, a pronounced drop in 1977 and a remarkable increase in 1980. Using the wholesale price index as a proxy for the price of traded goods, as in column (2), implies a decline in relative prices starting in 1976 and a substantial drop in 1978, but the change in relative prices from 1973 to 1979 is about the same. Using the wage in manufacturing as a proxy for the price of non-traded goods shows a much more dramatic increase

Table 1 Indices of relative prices (base 1973 = 100)

	(1) $\frac{CPI_{nt}}{CPI_t}$	(2) $\frac{CPI_{nt}}{WPI}$	(3) $\frac{WA}{WPI}$	(4) TOT	(5) $\frac{WPH}{WPM}$	(6) $\frac{WA}{WPM \cdot TOT}$
1974	91.8	94.5	113.0	92.4	88.1	108.2
1975	90.1	99.4	133.0	84.9	78.4	126.1
1976	87.6	96.0	132.4	80.8	83.6	137.2
1977	80.7	89.9	119.6	83.2	77.9	112.8
1978	80.3	82.8	103.7	82.5	91.5	108.2
1979	74.8	76.0	96.3	78.5	99.4	110.9
1980	79.9	86.8	113.5	74.7	81.6	123.0

Definitions and sources:

CPI_{nt}: index of non-traded goods in the consumer price index (CPI) excluding rent; Lisbon CPI to 1976, continental CPI thereafter. Includes mostly services, weight 23.5% (in continental CPI including rent, 18%). *Source:* INE, *Boletim Mensal*

CPI_t: index of traded goods in the CPI including food and clothing, weight 76.5%. *Source:* INE, *Boletim Mensal*

WPI: index of wholesale prices in Lisbon. *Source:* IMF *International Financial Statistics*, line 63

WA: index of total labour compensation in manufacturing. *Source:* Bank of Portugal (BP), *Boletim Trimestral*

TOT: index of the ratio of unit values of exports and imports. *Source:* BP, *Relatorio Annual* (1980)

WPH: index of home goods in the WPI, including mostly exportables, weight 55%. *Source:* IMF *International Financial Statistics*, line 63a

WPM: index of imports in the WPI, weight 30%. *Source:* INE, *Boletim Mensal*

(6): real wage in terms of the wholesale price index allowing for quantity changes: *WA* divided by *WPM* times *TOT* raised to the power of the share of exportables (including transformed imported raw materials) = 70%

to 1975–76 and a pronounced decline in 1977–79. To the extent that prices of non-traded goods are a constant mark-up over wages, the measure of column (3) is preferable because of the narrow coverage of non-traded goods in the consumer price index.

Emphasis on the relative price of non-traded goods, based as it is on the aggregation of import and export goods, should not obscure the fact that relative import prices increased sharply after 1973, as shown in column (4), which reports the ratio of export and import unit values. The usual caveats apply to this rough measure of the terms of trade deterioration. Also, the capacity to import in 1979 was above the 1973 level, owing to the recovery of export production. An alternative measure of the relative price of exportables and importables is shown in column (5) as the ratio of the price of 'home goods' included in the wholesale price index (weight about 1/2) to the price of imports included in the same index (weight about 1/3, excluding the other item, transformed imported raw materials). If these two measures are roughly comparable, the opposite movements from 1976 and 1979 can be used to infer the direction of quantity changes. Except in 1977, the volume of exports seems to have increased less than the volume imports, so that the index in column (5) increases while the index in column (4) declines. In column (6) we report a measure of the relative price of non-traded goods which accounts for quantity changes. It is constructed by deflating nominal wages by the import price index included in the wholesale price index adjusted for the ratio of unit values in column (4). The result is a more pronounced decline in 1979 and an increase in 1979.

All of the relative price indices reported in table 1 show a decline in 1977–78, confirming that exchange rate devaluation was effective in lowering real wages. As we proceed to show, furthermore, the 'equilibrium' relative price of traded goods also increased as a consequence of the increase in domestic interest rates.

Interest differentials and the capital account

Having examined the fundamental determinants of the value of the Portuguese escudo, we shall proceed to analyse how interest differentials have linked the fundamentals to the short-run value of the inconvertible escudo. Before doing so, however, we will describe the official and unofficial foreign exchange markets in some detail.

Exchange restrictions and the black market

Despite a regular summary in the IMF *Annual Report on Exchange Restrictions* since the 1951 *Supplement*, the operation of the Portuguese foreign exchange market is surrounded with some mystery. The central bank sets twice-daily spot rates of exchange of the escudo against 17 major currencies, and these rates are used in the transactions of commercial banks with the public. Transactions in foreign currencies are, in principle, restricted to authorized residents. Foreign holders of escudos and unauthorized residents are thus excluded from the 'official' exchange market. On the other hand, authorizations to residents are restricted to holders of import and export licenses granted less than 120 days previously. With respect to receipts from invisible trade, namely private remittances, no authorization is needed. Prior registration of imports and exports of goods is thus required in the form of a bulletin (BRI for imports, BRE for exports), granted by the Directorate General of Foreign Trade of the Ministry of Trade. For all exports and imports free of quantitative restrictions, the purpose of this registration is to enforce the surrender of foreign exchange to the monetary authorities. The commercial banks themselves can deal in foreign exchange only with the Bank of Portugal and are not expected to solicit foreign exchange transactions with banks abroad or to enter into arbitrage operations in foreign markets. The gross holdings of foreign exchange by commercial banks and their net foreign asset position are also subject to control by the central bank.

The official spot market for the escudo therefore relies on a two-tier structure: on one level the bulletin-holders and the commercial banks; on the other, the commercial banks and the Bank of Portugal, whereby the former balance flow demand and supply of foreign exchange given their working balances on foreign currency.

The rate set by the central bank is influenced both by the reported excess demand for and supply of foreign exchange by commercial banks and by the outlook on the cross-rates between the currencies quoted by the central bank. Excess demand for and supply of foreign exchange by the commercial banks is in turn related to the bulletins outstanding, with leads for imports and lags for exports. The central bank could balance these demands and supplies by changing the rate, but the practice has been rather to buy or sell reserves to the commercial banks, so that the daily balancing of commercial banks' demand and supply has not been determinant in the setting of the official rate by the central bank. The commercial banks are authorized to enter into swap transactions with the Bank of Portugal and also into forward transactions with individual customers, provided that the forward rate lies within the spot bid-ask spread, which is equivalent to suppressing a forward premium as such. Thus there was no official forward market before September 1977, when the Bank of Portugal began to provide forward cover in ten major currencies, and this operation was discontinued in the stand-by agreement with the IMF less than one year later.

In sum, the official market for foreign exchange has been devised to remain located predominantly in Portugal, and access to it has been tightly controlled by the central bank and the Directorate General of Foreign Trade, except for supply of foreign exchange associated with invisible trade and unrequired transfers. It can be argued that such a tightly controlled exchange regime provides strong incentives for the development of unofficial markets where the price of foreign exchange that equates desired to actual stocks of foreign exchange by domestic residents and of domestic currency by foreigners is determined. And even if bulletin-holders always surrendered (or requested) the authorized amount of foreign exchange, which is widely believed not to be the case, capital flight and invisible receipts from tourism and emigrants ensure a regular source of supply of foreign exchange in such markets.

In fact, unauthorized dealers in foreign exchange in Geneva, New York and Rio de Janeiro have created an unofficial spot market for the escudo, located chiefly in Lisbon:[13] some estimates of the black market rate against the dollar are reported in table 2. It is noteworthy that in some cases the percentage differences between the two sources are close to the black market premium using black market and spot rates from the same source. But this premium is not too large, except during the period of civil strife in late 1974 and in the second half of 1975. Thus it reached 113 per cent on 15 August, the week of the resistance to the Marxist Fifth Provisional Government, and 69 per cent on 28 November, when Lisbon was under a state of siege. Then, just before the introduction of the crawling peg in late August 1977, and when the negotiations with the IMF led to the fall of the First Constitutional Government in late 1977, the premium reached 20 per cent. In other cases, namely during early 1973 and in June 1978, the black market rate is below the official rate.

Data on black market transitions are notoriously unreliable. Pick's estimates of the capital flight in the immediate post-25 April period go as high as $400 million, slightly higher than the average monthly import bill in 1973–75 but 40 per cent of the record high of December 1974, while outflows in 1975 are guessed to be about

Table 2 Bid end-of-quarter escudo–dollar rates

	*(1)***	*(2)*	*(3)*
1973(I)	n.a.	25.64	25.12
1973(II)	n.a.	25.64	23.25
1973(III)	n.a.	23.75	23.31
1973(IV)	n.a.	25.97	25.91
1974(I)	n.a.	25.64	24.81
1974(II)	25.5 (1)*	24.25	25.19
1974(III)	n.a.	27.78	25.77
1974(IV)	27.5 (1)	25.97	24.69
1975(I)	32.0 (2)	26.67	24.24
1975(II)	37.0 (2)†	26.18	24.48
1975(II)	40.0 (2)	37.04	27.49
1975(IV)	n.a.	38.47	27.30
1976(I)	36.0 (1)‡	32.26	29.16
1976(II)	n.a.	35.09	31.47
1976(III)	n.a.	34.48	31.15
1976(IV)	n.a.	35.33	31.42
1977(I)	39.0 (1)‡	39.68	38.83
1977(II)	43.0 (1)	39.37	38.82
1977(III)	45.0 (1.5)	45.05	40.79
1977(IV)	46.5 (1.5)	47.62	39.50
1978(I)	46.0 (1.5)	41.15	41.14
1978(II)	47.0 (1.5)	45.45	45.74
1978(III)	47.5 (1)	47.00	45.46
1978(IV)	47.25 (1.25)	47.62	45.89
1979(I)	49.50 (1.50)	49.00	48.26
1979(II)	50.50 (1.50)§	50.00	48.88
1979(III)	49.75 (1.50)§	52.65	49.11
1979(IV)	51.25 (1.50)§	52.08	49.88
1980(I)	49.00 (1.50)§	51.00	50.86
1980(II)	49.00 (1.25)§	49.00	49.92
1980(III)	50.00 (1.50)§	52.10	50.08
1980(IV)	53.50 (1.50)§	56.20	52.93

** Spread between bid and offer in parentheses
* April † May ‡ January § mid-month

Sources:

Column (1): withheld by request; Lisbon black market. Records were destroyed before April 1977; the numbers reported are approximate

Column (2): *International Reports*: Lisbon black market, last Thursday of quarter. See Macedo (1979a, p. 43) for values in 1973(III), 1978(III) and 1979(I)

Column (3): *International Reports*: New York official market, last Thursday of quarter

$100 million at an annual rate. A major black market dealer quotes a figure on gross transactions in 1977–78 of about $50 million, 40 per cent of which were carried out in Lisbon. Other sources put the size of the market at $260 million, no less than 12 per cent of imports, whereas the analysis of partner country data has shown that under-invoicing of exports from 1973 to 1977 was about $225 million (with half for 1975 alone) or 2 per cent of f.o.b. exports over the same period.[14] Note that even if the flows in the black market are small, it does not follow that foreign exchange balances of Portuguese residents are negligible because the black market rate equilibrates a stock and the flows are basically a link between the official current account transactions and the unreported transactions that increase or decrease that stock.[15]

The forward markets

Quotations on the forward price of the escudo against the dollar in New York are also available,[16] but unauthorized foreign exchange dealers suggest that the market is quite thin and thus that arbitrage and speculative activity are likely to be small.[17] However, in table 3 data on the official record rates and those quoted in New York during the brief overlap show a fairly small spread, of the same order of magnitude as the spread between bid and offer in the official market. The free forward rates increased relative to the

Table 3 End-of-month forward rates against the dollar (average of bid and offer)

	1 month			*3 months*			*6 months*		
	Spot one-month lead	*Official**	*Free*	*Spot three-month lead*	*Official**	*Free*	*Spot six-month lead*	*Official**	*Free*
1977 (9)	40.48	41.25	41.72	39.86	42.10	43.51	40.95	43.42	44.37
1977 (10)	40.79	40.89	41.23	40.12	41.73	43.07	41.96	43.02	44.33
1977 (11)	39.86	41.26	41.65	40.11	42.19	43.70	45.72	43.59	44.83
1977 (12)	40.12	40.30	40.60	40.95	41.21	42.43	45.66	42.58	43.66
1978 (1)	40.11	40.55	41.12	41.96	41.41	43.08	45.36	42.69	43.98
1978 (2)	40.95	40.55	40.96	45.72	41.39	42.86	45.38	42.63	44.18
1978 (3)	41.96	41.35	41.86	45.66	42.16	43.85	45.38	43.38	45.26
1978 (4)	45.72	42.36	43.03	45.36	43.22	44.95	43.45	44.48	47.16

* Official forward quotations were discontinued on 4 May 1978

Sources: official: *Bank of Portugal Annual Report* (1977), p. 295; (1978), p. 339; 'free': computed from forward discounts in New York from *International Reports*

official ones in early 1978 when news of the probable termination of the official cover began to spread: in April 1978 there was a 6 per cent premium for the six-month forward rate. Table 3 also reports the realized future spot rate. Thus, at the end of the first month of crawl, as the effective exchange rate was expected to depreciate at an annual rate of 13 per cent, an importer would have bought dollars three months forward at a premium of 13 per cent even though at maturity the escudo had appreciated by 9 per cent against the dollar. The loss of the importer would have been a gain for the exporter who would have sold dollars forward. This pattern was reversed after November, and in February, March and April 1978 the realized depreciation was 5.5, 44 and 20 per cent respectively above the premium. On the basis of this evidence it cannot be ruled out that the forward operation was beginning to be a net loss to the central bank when it was decided that it should be discontinued.

Needless to say, the official forward market was not designed to encourage offsetting the substantial interest differential between Portugal and the world market. The 90–180 domestic deposit rates were only about 2 per cent higher than 90-day covered differentials (CDs) in New York, while the 90-day lending rate in Portugal was about 7 per cent over the prime rate. Accordingly, the averaged covered interest rate differential in favour of New York during the period was 6 per cent for borrowers and 10 per cent for lenders. The realized average differentials were 3 and 11 per cent respectively. The black market and the free forward market, however, do provide a channel for interest arbitrage. Assuming that expectations about the future black market premium were stationary, the averaged covered interest rate differential for lenders who use this alternative channel would have been 8 per cent and the realized average 3 per cent.[18]

The maturity structure of deposit rates in Portugal, however, has become very steep,[19] and the practice of limited penalties for early withdrawal of longer maturity deposits suggests that the relevant substitute for the three-month Eurodollar deposit might be a six-month deposit in Portugal.[20] If this latter comparison were made, the average covered differential in favour of New York using the free markets would decline by 7 percentage points to 1 per cent. This covered differential is of the same order of magnitude as the one generally observed in well developed forward markets, and could define a transactions costs 'band'.[21] Taking the average over the period of overlap, however, hides the very substantial variability that is to be expected in a thin market and is apparent in table 4. Plotting together the difference between the two deposit rates and the end-of-quarter three-month bid forward discount, as done in figure 4, shows large covered differentials until 1979, probably reflecting not only the expectation of a discreet devaluation of the official rate

Table 4 Annualized three-month forward discounts and black market premium

	Forward: offer	*Discount: bid*	*Black market premium*
	%	%	%
1973(I)	−0.5	−4.0	2.1
1973(II)	0.0	−7.0	10.3
1973(III)	−2.5	−10.5	2.6
1973(IV)	3.0	−0.3	2.3
1974(I)	10.0	9.0	3.3
1974(II)	9.6	9.1	−4.0
1974(III)	12.5	9.5	8.0
1974(IV)	23.5	21.5	5.2
1975(I)	10.0	−5.0	10.0
1975(II)	8.0	7.0	6.9
1975(III)	11.5	9.5	34.7
1975(IV)	15.6	13.6	40.9
1976(I)	18.5	17.5	10.6
1976(II)	18.0	16.5	11.5
1976(III)	18.1	17.1	10.7
1976(IV)	17.0	16.0	12.4
1977(I)	6.3	5.8	2.2
1977(II)	12.0	11.0	1.4
1977(III)	27.0	26.0	10.4
1977(IV)	34.7	16.9	20.6
1978(I)	34.5	21.0	0.0
1978(II)	29.0	12.9	0.0
1978(III)	18.0	16.0	3.4
1978(IV)	12.1	8.5	3.8
1979(I)	13.1	9.4	1.5
1979(II)	11.1	10.0	2.3
1979(III)	10.5	7.7	7.2
1979(IV)	6.0	4.3	4.4
1980(I)	3.1	−0.2	0.3
1980(II)	11.0	10.0	−1.8
1980(III)	6.9	4.6	4.0
1980(IV)	0.8	−3.0	6.2

Source: International Reports

Fig. 4 Three-month forward discount and deposit rate differential (end-of-period percentage per year)

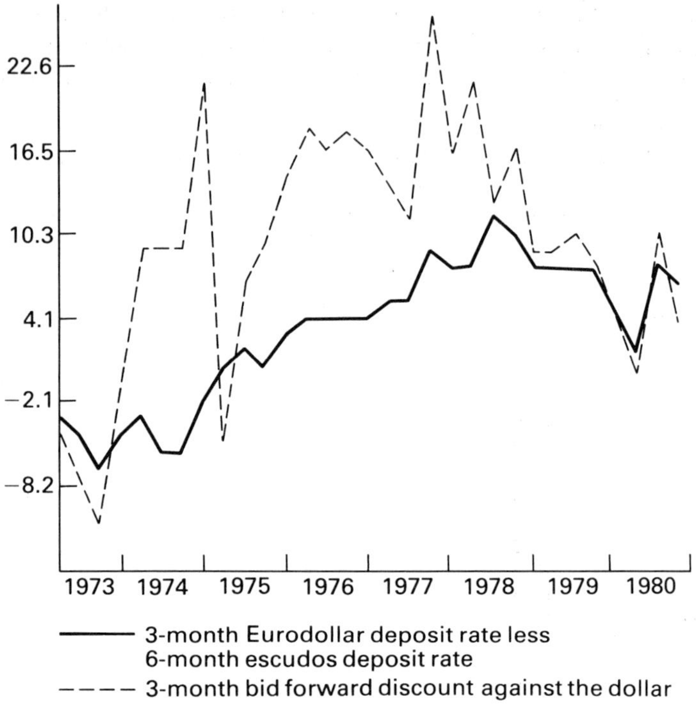

Sources: Eurodollar deposit rate, from IMF *International Financial Statistics*; six-month escudos deposit rate, from Banco de Portugal; three-month forward discount, from table 4

and a sizeable probability of default but also substantial changes in the variance of the purchasing powers of the two currencies, and hence in the risk premium.[22] The effect of the 'peso problem' is clear in the first quarter of 1977, when the covered interest differential went to zero.[23] The failure of the February measures is reflected in the steep increase of the forward discount. It was not until the improvements in the payments situation became apparent in the fourth quarter of 1978 that the covered differential narrowed, and indeed turned in favour of Lisbon in 1980. The emergence of a premium on the forward purchase of escudos at the end of March 1975 is more difficult to explain, but the widening of the spread (the sale of forward escudos faced a 10 per cent discount) accords with intuition.

On the whole, figure 4 shows the progressive awareness of the implications of capital mobility by the Portuguese authorities. Despite exchange controls, an administratively set interest rate has generated a small covered differential in the last few quarters.[24]

There is, however, no presumption that covered interest arbitrage is widely practiced through the official spot market, and the black market premium on the dollar introduces an extra cost for interest arbitrageurs. In figure 5 the end-of-quarter bid black market premium is plotted together with one rough measure of the covered interest differential relevant for borrowers. Neglecting the bid–ask spread in the Eurodollar market (typically about 0.125 per cent for three-month maturities), the measures also ignore credit rationing in Portugal by using the 90-day lending rate. When the black market

Fig. 5 Covered lending rate differential and the black market premium

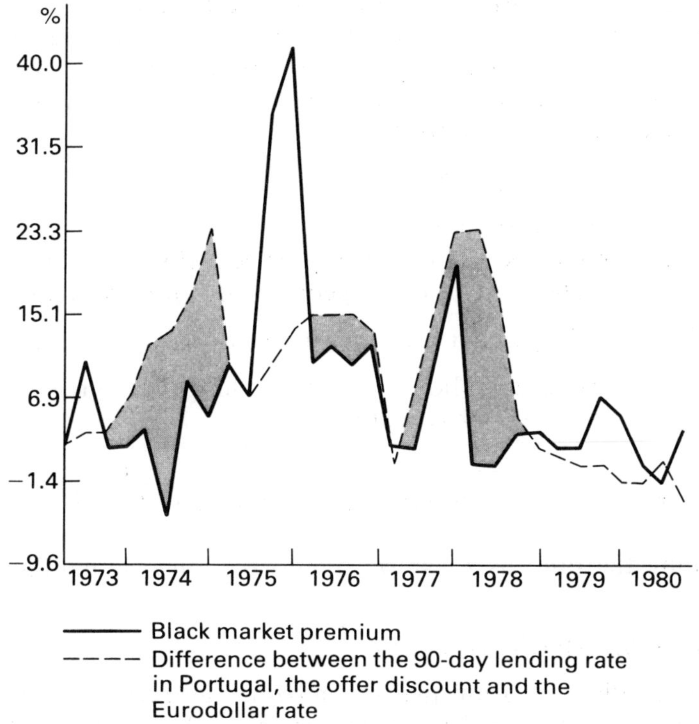

Sources: black market premium, from table 4; 90-day lending rate in Portugal, from Banco de Portugal; offer discount, from table 4; Eurodollar rate, from IMF *International Financial Statistics*

premium is smaller than the covered differential, the corrected differential remains in favour of New York (shaded area). The differential was in favour of Lisbon during the turbulent period of 1975 as well as during most of 1978–80. But the existence of the black spot market also introduces a new source of information on the future spot rate. Accordingly, while standard weak efficiency tests cannot reject the null hypothesis for the one- and three-month segments of the New York forward market when the official spot rate is used, they do reject 'efficiency' when the black market is used. Given the weakness of these tests, the importance of the black market in reflecting expectations about the spot market has to be investigated. Consider first a suggestive benchmark case.

An 'equilibrium' spot rate

The hypothesis of 'efficiency', suitably modified for an environment with long-run inflation differentials, can be used to construct the 'equilibrium' spot rate[25] implied by the real interest differential or the real forward discount. In fact, for comparable securities, neglecting transactions costs, the 'equilibrium' spot rate next period, $\tilde{S}$, is given by the Fisher equation:

$$\tilde{S}_{t,t+1} = (1 + d_{t,t+1})\, S_t$$

where d is the real forward discount.

Now, by recursive use of the Fisher equation, we can, if expectations are consistent, write the expected spot rate τ periods ahead as

$$\tilde{S}_{t,\tau} = (1+d_{t,t+1})(1+d_{t+1,t+2})(1+d_{t+2,t+3}) \ldots (1+d_{\tau-1,\tau})\, S_t.$$

If the discount follows a first-order autoregressive process, $d_t = bd_{t-1}$, we have approximately

$$\tilde{S}_{t,\tau}/S_t \simeq \exp\left(\sum_{i=0}^{\tau-1} d_{t+i,t+i+1}\right) = \exp\left(d_{t,t+1}\sum_{i=0}^{\tau-1} b^i\right).$$

Taking the limit as $\tau \to \infty$ we obtain the long-run equilibrium rate, $\tilde{S}_t$, as:

$$\tilde{S}_t = S_t \exp\,(d_{t,t+1}/1-b).$$

Empirically, a four-quarter moving average of inflation in Portugal and in the United States is used to construct the real discount and the real interest differential. Summary statistics of the variables used are in panel A of table 5. Averaging the measure of

Table 5 The real interest differential (quarterly data 1973(I)–1980(III))

A Summary statistics (% per annum)

		Mean	*Stand. dev.*	*Min.*	*Max.*
(1)	3-month Eurodollar deposit rate	8.98	2.95	5.11	17.11
(2)	6-month deposit rate in Portugal	12.05	5.49	4.50	19.00
(3)	US inflation	8.84	3.09	3.89	15.58
(4)	Portuguese inflation (four-quarter moving average)	19.65	4.96	6.96	27.07
(5)	Real differential	−7.74	5.78	−19.51	3.53
(6)	Real forward premium	0.33	6.49	−17.47	11.25

B Box–Pierce χ^2 with seven degrees of freedom (95% level = 14.07)

(5)	35.68
(6)	12.27

C Regression (5 in number per quarter)

$$RD_t = -0.0046 + 0.7552 RD_{t-1}$$

(st. error) (0.0032) (0.1293)

$R^2 = 55\%$

Durbin $h = 0.213$

Standard error of regression = 0.0101

inflation brings the coefficient of variation slightly below the US figure, while for quarterly changes it was almost 50 per cent above. As shown in lines (5) and (6), there is a substantial average real differential, while the real premium is close to zero. The stochastic behaviour of these two series is examined in panel B by means of the Box–Pierce χ^2 test for autocorrelation. While randomness is accepted for the forward discount with seven lags, there is substantial autocorrelation in the real differential. We then use the measure in line (5) to generate the long-run real forward discount. In panel C, the regression of the real interest differential on its lagged value gives an estimate of b between 0.63 and 0.88 and an insignificant constant.[26] Using the point estimate of b in table 5, the 'equilibrium' spot rate is obtained and plotted together with the end-of-quarter official and black market rates in figure 6. The persistent positive differential makes the equilibrium rate generally greater than both the spot and the black market rate. In the periods of turbulence (summer–autumn

Fig. 6 The 'equilibrium' spot rate (escudos–dollar)

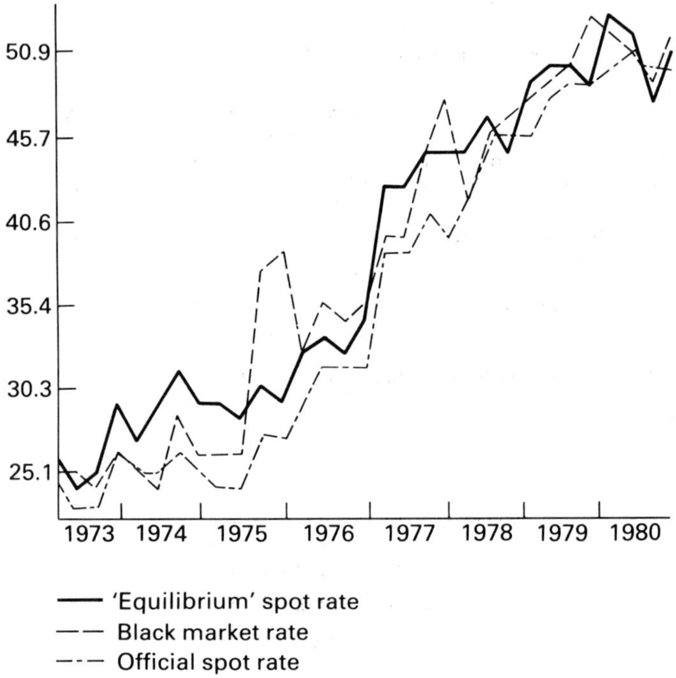

Sources: variables described in the text

1975 and spring 1978), and in the spring of 1979, the black market rate is greater than the equilibrium rate. The figure suggests that including a long-run inflation differential makes the equilibrium rate follow the black market rate more closely except in periods of intense turmoil. The implication is that it would be desirable to allow for a wider band in the official rate so as to incorporate the changes in valuation now confined to the black market. Similarly, the development of the forward market for the escudo is not likely to lead to 'destabilizing speculation' in periods of tranquil trading and should therefore be encouraged by the monetary authorities. This heuristic analysis of the 'good behaviour' of the unofficial markets has to be supplemented by an econometric analysis of the link with the official market. This is done in the following section in the framework of a simple portfolio balance model.

A portfolio model of the black market rate

The model

In this section, a simple portfolio model of the black market rate is presented and estimated. We begin with a model of a convertible currency, where the black market premium is always one and the exchange rate is flexible, then proceed to a model where the official rate is determined by the monetary authorities and the black market rate is flexible.

Consider a small country that trades a composite of goods as well as a non-interest-bearing asset – money for short – with the rest of the world. Private domestic financial wealth is thus divided between the domestic residents, M, and the domestic currency value of the stock of foreign assets held by domestic residents, F. The real asset demand functions of domestic residents have as arguments the expected rate of change of the real exchange rate, π, which captures the return differential; domestic real income, y, which captures transactions needs; and real financial wealth, A. Foreign real demand for domestic assets, on the other hand, will be taken to depend only on the return differential because the effect of an increase in foreign income or foreign wealth in the foreign demand for domestic assets is neglected.[27] If, furthermore, portfolio balance obtains continuously, then, writing the assumed signs of partial derivatives above the arguments, we have:

$$\frac{eF^{\mathrm{d}}}{P} \equiv f(\overset{+}{\pi}, \overset{-}{y}, \overset{+}{A}) = \frac{eF}{P} \tag{1}$$

$$\frac{M^{\mathrm{d}}}{P} \equiv m(\overset{-}{\pi}, \overset{+}{y}, \overset{+}{A}) = \frac{M}{P} \tag{2}$$

$$AP \equiv W \equiv M^{\mathrm{T}} - G + eF \tag{3}$$

$$\frac{G^{\mathrm{d}}}{eP^*} \equiv g(\overset{-}{\pi}) = \frac{G}{eP^*} \tag{4}$$

where

e is the domestic currency price of foreign currency;
$P(P^*)$ is the domestic (foreign) price level;
π is the expected rate of change of $e_{\mathrm{r}} = eP^*/P$, the real exchange rate;
$M^{\mathrm{T}} = M + G$ is the domestic money stock;
$F(G)$ is the foreign (domestic) money stock held by domestic

(foreign) residents, denominated in foreign (domestic) currency; and the other symbols were defined above in the text.

If domestic private residents are not net debtors in foreign currency, $F^{\mathrm{d}} > 0$ and an expected depreciation of the domestic currency increases the demand for domestic assets by foreign residents, with a decrease in the demand for domestic assets by domestic residents and an increase in the demand for foreign assets by foreign residents of the same amount. Thus, $f_\pi = -m_\pi$. Similarly, an increase in real wealth at home or abroad is distributed between the two assets so that $f_{\mathrm{A}} + m_{\mathrm{A}} = 1$.[28]

By (1) and (4), the desired private net nominal capital outflow in foreign currency, $(\dot{F}^{\mathrm{d}} - \dot{G}^{\mathrm{d}})/e$, is always equal to the actual capital outflow. Thus, substituting (3) in (1), differentiating the asset demand functions (1), (2) and (4) and rearranging, we get an expression for the nominal capital outflow (corrected for capital gains and losses owing to inflation at home and abroad) as a function of the proportional rate of real appreciation, the proportional change in the real money stocks and real outputs at home and abroad, and expectations changes, namely

$$\left[\dot{F} - \frac{\dot{G}}{e} - F\hat{P}^* - \frac{G}{e}\hat{P}\right](1 - f_{\mathrm{A}})$$
$$= -\left[F(1-f_{\mathrm{A}}) + \frac{G}{e}\right]\hat{e}_{\mathrm{r}} + f_{\mathrm{A}}\frac{M^{\mathrm{T}}}{e}\hat{\bar{M}}$$
$$-\eta^{\mathrm{f}}_{\mathrm{y}}F\hat{y} + \left(\eta^{\mathrm{f}}_{\pi}F + \eta^{\mathrm{g}}_{\pi}\frac{G}{e}\right)\hat{\pi} \qquad (5)$$

where

a caret (ˆ) over a variable denotes a proportional change;
$f_x = \partial f/\partial x$ denotes the partial derivative of f with respect to x;
$\eta_x = |f_x|x/f$ denotes the (positive) elasticity of f with respect to x; and
$\bar{M} = M^{\mathrm{T}}/P$ is the real money stock.

Balance of payments accounting implies that the difference between the real private excess supply of foreign currency from the current account surplus and the real private excess demand for foreign currency implied by the real capital outflow has to be equal to the change in the real stock of foreign assets of the central bank, or

$$(\bar{B} - \dot{\bar{F}} + \dot{\bar{G}})/e_{\mathrm{r}} \equiv \dot{\bar{F}}^{\mathrm{G}} \qquad (6)$$

where

$\bar{F} = F/P^*$;
$\bar{G} = G/P$;
$\bar{F}^G = F^G/P^*$ is the real stock of foreign assets of the central bank; and
$\bar{B}$ is the real current account surplus expressed in foreign currency.

From (6) the nominal current account, net of changes in the stock of foreign assets of the central bank (corrected for capital gains owing to foreign inflation) is equal to the corrected nominal capital outflow:

$$\bar{B}P^* - (\dot{F}^G - F^G\hat{P}^*) = \dot{F} - \frac{\dot{G}}{e} - \left(F\hat{P}^* - \frac{G}{e}\hat{P}\right). \quad (7)$$

From the balance sheet of the central bank, on the other hand, we can decompose the domestic money stock as:[29]

$$M^T = C + eF^G - K \quad (8)$$

where

C is domestic credit of the central bank system to the rest of the economy; and
K is the net worth of the central bank.

Assuming that changes in the valuation of foreign exchange reserves are not a source of money creation but rather are offset by changes in net worth, we can write real money growth as:

$$\hat{\bar{M}} = d + \phi \quad (8')$$

where

$d = \dot{C}/M^T - \hat{P}$ is real domestic credit creation as a proportion of the domestic stock; and
$\phi = e\dot{F}^G/M^T$ is the change in the 'foreign monetary base' as a proportion of the domestic money stock).

We now use (7) and (8′) in (5) and solve for the change in the real exchange rate:

$$\hat{e}_r = [\phi + f_A d - (1 - f_A)\, b]\, \mu - \eta\hat{y} + \psi\hat{\pi} \quad (9)$$

where

$b = e(\bar{B}P^* + F^G\hat{P}^*)/M^T$ is the current account, adjusted for capital losses owing to foreign inflation, as a proportion of the domestic money stock in foreign currency;

$\mu = M^{\mathrm{T}}/eI$;
$\eta = \eta_{\mathrm{y}}^{\mathrm{f}} F/I$;
$\psi = (\eta_{\pi}^{\mathrm{f}} F + \eta_{\pi}^{\mathrm{g}} G/e)/I$; and
$I = F(1 - f_{\mathrm{A}}) + G/e$ is the level of gross international investment weighted by the wealth propensities to hold domestic assets of domestic and foreign residents (respectively $1 - f_{\mathrm{A}}$ and 1).

Note that according to equation (9) an increase in central bank reserves as a proportion of gross (private) international investment has a one-to-one effect on the real exchange rate, because the effect via the domestic money supply is added to the effect via the capital account. The same effect would be obtained from a current account deficit and real domestic credit creation of the same magnitude ($-b = d$). Equation (9), on the other hand, can be simplified into various special cases that have been emphasized in recent models of exchange rate determination in a pure flexible exchange rate regime where $\phi = 0$. First, neglect wealth and income effects and assume that expectations are stationary ($f_{\mathrm{A}} = 0$, $\eta = 0$ and $\hat{\pi} = 0$). Then (9) expresses the 'acceleration hypothesis' mentioned above, adapted to a situation of inflation at home and abroad. Alternatively, assume that domestic and foreign assets are perfect substitutes on the demand side so that $f_{\mathrm{A}} = 1$ and (9) becomes a monetarist-type equation where, given expectations, the real exchange rate depreciates with real money growth (since $d = \bar{M}$ when $\phi = 0$) and appreciates with output growth (increase in the demand for domestic money). Finally, if purchasing power parity is also assumed, as in the usual monetarist model, then $\hat{e} = \hat{P} - \hat{P}^*$, where domestic inflation is given by nominal money growth less real output growth.

Suppose now that domestic residents are debtors in foreign currency, so that $F^{\mathrm{d}} < 0$. Then we have to have $f_{\mathrm{A}} < 0$ as well, but it still may be the case that $I > 0$ because $F(1 - f_{\mathrm{A}}) > G/e$. Then the sign of the effect of real output growth and real credit creation will be reversed, but assuming that $\eta_{\pi}^{\mathrm{f}}/\eta_{\pi}^{\mathrm{g}} > 1 - f_{\mathrm{A}}$, the signs of the effects of the other variables in (9) will remain the same. If $I < 0$, however, then the signs of the effects of ϕ and b will be reversed, while the sign of the effect of $\hat{\pi}$ may be reversed if $\eta_{\pi}^{\mathrm{f}}\eta_{\pi}^{\mathrm{g}} < 1 - f_{\mathrm{A}}$. Before we settle this empirical question, we will adapt equation (9) to a regime of currency inconvertibility.

If the domestic currency is inconvertible, equations (1) and (4) above describe stock demand and stock supply of foreign assets in the black market. Equation (7) still holds, provided there are no reported autonomous capital flows so that the right-hand side is simply the unreported (nominal) current account deficit in foreign currency.[30] Therefore the sum of the reported and unreported current accounts is equal to the change in central bank reserves. Equation (8), however, has to be modified because central bank reserves are valued at the official rate $\tilde{e}$. This also implies new definitions of the (reported) current account and the change in reserves as a proportion of the money stock. Then (9) becomes

$$\hat{e}_r = [(1-\tilde{f}_A)\,\tilde{\phi} - (1-f_A)\,\tilde{b}]\,\bar{\mu} + f_A \mu d - \eta\hat{y} + \psi\hat{\pi} \qquad (9')$$

where

$p = e/\tilde{e}$ is the black market premium;
$\tilde{b} = b/p$;
$\tilde{\phi} = \phi/p$;
$\tilde{f}_A = f_A(p-1)/p$; and
$\bar{\mu} = M^T/\tilde{e}I$.

To specify the expectations formation mechanism we choose a simple adaptive scheme,[31] such that

$$\pi = \pi(\bar{p}). \qquad (10)$$

According to (10), if the official rate depreciates the black market rate is expected to depreciate, but if the black market rate depreciates then it is expected to appreciate. This is of course equivalent to assuming extrapolative expectations with respect to the real official rate and regressive expectations with respect to the real black market rate, with the same elasticity, as a matter of convenience.

We now substitute the log differential of (10) into (9′) and rearrange to get an expression for the proportional rate of change of the black market rate:

$$\hat{e} = \hat{\tilde{e}} + [(1-\tilde{f}_A)\,\tilde{\phi} - (1-f_A)\,\tilde{b}]\,\tilde{\bar{\mu}} + f_A\tilde{\mu}d - (I/\tilde{I})\,\hat{\tilde{e}}_r - \tilde{\eta}\hat{y} \qquad (11)$$

where

$\tilde{I} = F(1-f_A+\eta^f_\pi\eta^\pi_p) + (G/e)(1+\eta^g_\pi\eta^\pi_p)$ is the level of gross international investment adjusted for expectations effects;
$\tilde{\mu} = M^T/e\tilde{I}$;
$\tilde{\bar{\mu}} = M^T/\tilde{e}\tilde{I}$; and
$\tilde{\eta} = \eta I/\tilde{I}$.

In equation (11) the current account is taken as exogenous, which is a simplification justified by our emphasis on the capital account. Similarly, neither domestic inflation – entering in the change in the real exchange rate, $\hat{\tilde{e}}_r$, and in real credit creation – nor real income, $\hat{y}$, would be exogenous in a more complete model. Another feature of (11) is that real official exchange rate depreciation reduces the black market premium directly rather than via the gain in competitiveness. The effect has an upper bound of 1, when the expectations elasticities in I are negligible. Clearly, if official exchange rate policy is based on a purchasing power parity rule, $\hat{\bar{e}}_r = 0$ and the real exchange rate has no effect on the black market premium.

Estimation

The main difficulty in estimating equation (11) has to do with the absence of data on black market transactions. As pointed out above, the reported current account of Portugal includes, via under-invoicing of exports and over-invoicing of imports, unauthorized capital flows, and there is also evidence of substantial capital flight during this period. The use of the reported current account net of change in the foreign assets of the banking system, while it underestimates the total capital account in so far as the exclusion of the faked current account transactions and capital flight is concerned, overestimates it in so far as foreign direct investment and long-term capital account transactions of the public sector are included. Since there are no gross data on short-term private capital flows, the use of the series on private long-term capital outflows to generate the stock of foreign assets does not allow for short-term borrowing in foreign currency by the private sector, even though this is believed to have taken place.

Concentrating on the case where $\tilde{I} < 0$, so that F, f_A and I are also negative, and taking ratios of stocks (and f_A) as positive parameters, we get the following equation for estimation.

$$\hat{e} = a_0\hat{\bar{e}} - a_1\tilde{\phi} + a_2\tilde{b} + a_3 d - a_4\hat{y} - a_s\hat{\bar{e}}_r. \tag{12}$$

If $a_0 \simeq a_1$, furthermore, we can collect, *à la* Girton and Roper (1977), the terms arising from the behaviour of the monetary authorities as measuring 'exchange rate pressure' in the official market, defined as $\omega = \hat{\bar{e}} - \tilde{\phi}$. Then we write (12) as

$$\hat{e} = a_0\hat{\bar{e}} - a_1\tilde{\phi} + a_2\tilde{b} + a_3 d - a_4\hat{y} - a_s\hat{\bar{e}}_r. \tag{12'}$$

According to equation (12′), the change in the end-of-period escudo–dollar black market rate in percentages per quarter ($\hat{e}$) is a linear function of the current account as a proportion of the money stock of the previous quarter, valued as the official rate ($\tilde{b}$); the measure of exchange rate pressure (obtained by subtracting from the change in the end-of-period official rate the balance on non-monetary transactions as a proportion of the money supply valued at the official rate, ω; and domestic credit creation as a proportion of the money stock less the domestic rate of inflation (d), the change in the real end-of-period official rate ($\hat{\bar{e}}_r$) and the change in industrial production as a proxy for real income ($\hat{y}$), both in percentages per quarter.

The results of the estimation of equation (12′) using ordinary least squares reported in table 6 confirm the assumed signs.[32] Note, however, that the relative size of the coefficients on d and b implies that the value of f_A may be about -1.8 if we use the sample mean of $p = 1.084$. This suggests the dangers of restoring convertibility and is a further argument for experimenting with a wider band. It also underscores the difficulties of estimation, so the results should be interpreted with some care.

A plot of the actual and fitted values from the regression can be found in figure 7. The drops in the black market rate in 1973(I), 1973(III); 1975(II) and 1976(I) are not captured by the model. The drops in 1973 are related to the appreciation of the official rate against the dollar after the devaluation of early March. The drop of 1975(II), just before the sample maximum of the 'hot summer' of 1975(III), can be explained by the fact that the deterioration of the current account following the 11 March leftist coup led to further restrictions on capital outflow and the levying of an import surcharge in May. Thus the capital outflow declined in 1975(II), but during 1975(III) it reached over $1 billion (from $0.3 billion), while the current account deficit declined from $230 million to $70 million. In 1976(I) the black market rate fell by about 16 per cent as the political situation stabilized. The official rate began to be actively

Table 6 Estimation of equation (12′) by ordinary least squares

Variable	*Coefficient*	*St. error*	*t*	*Mean*	*Aux.* R^2
$\tilde{b}$	4.24	1.05	4.03	−1.35	0.70
ω	2.81	0.57	4.92	3.62	0.92
d	2.53	0.57	4.43	0.03	0.60
$\hat{\bar{e}}_r$	−2.05	0.62	−3.31	−0.64	0.90
$\hat{y}$	−2.14	0.70	−3.05	1.29	0.51
$\hat{e}$				2.85	
Residuals				−0.24	

Statistics

R^2	R^2 adj	*DW*	*SER*	*F*	*(d.f.)*
0.68	0.62	2.29	6.98	10.8	(5.20)

Fig. 7 Actual and fitted values from table 6

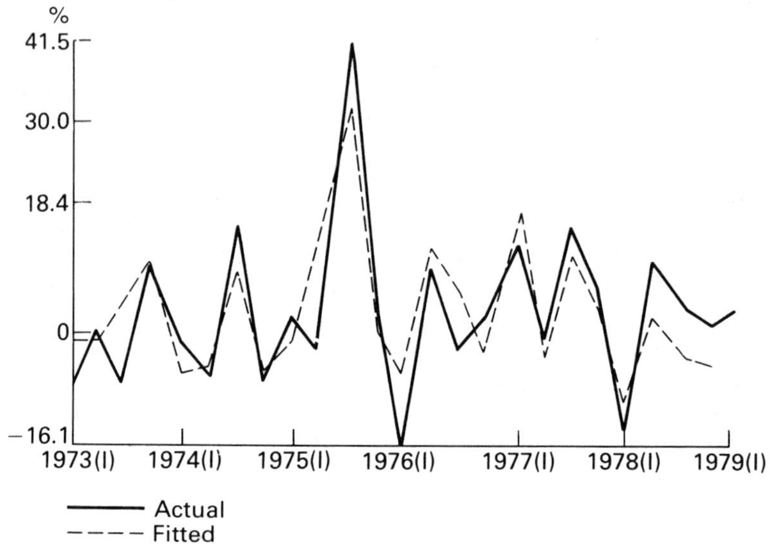

devalued (15 per cent in the two quarters), however, and the black market rate increased 9 per cent in 1976(II).

The increases in 1977(III) and 1978(II) are also underestimated by the model, since, given its enormous size, the increase of 1975(III) is fairly well predicted. The black market rate increased in the first quarter of 1977 but the premium declined. After the announcement of the crawling peg, however, the premium went up to 10 per cent in 1977(III) and 20 per cent in 1977(IV), also helped by the fact that the official rate was lower owing to the fall of the dollar in late 1977. In 1978(I), despite further deterioration in the current account, the black market rate declined by 13 per cent, to jump again by 10 per cent in the second quarter, possibly because the agreement with the IMF in May, while raising domestic interest rates substantially discontinued forward cover by the central bank. Between these two quarters the current and the capital account reversed from a deficit of $410 and $184 million respectively to a small surplus and an inflow of $400 million respectively.

Out-of-sample forecasts confirm, in any case, that the adoption of the crawling peg and the agreement with the IMF involved structural changes in the Portuguese exchange markets. We will focus here on the division of the sample into a period with a roughly fixed official exchange rate until the end of 1975, and a period with a depreciating official exchange rate thereafter. This division is somewhat arbitrary, because in the second half of 1976 and between the February 1977 devaluation and the adoption of the crawling peg, the official effective exchange rate was virtually fixed, and also because the loss in reserves was quite substantial in the second period. Nevertheless, as is evident from table 7, the size of the effects of changes in asset stocks is vastly different in the two subperiods. Thus the effect of the current account is 2.54 for the 'fixed rate' period, while it is 4.24 for the whole period. The size of the effect of exchange market pressure declines from 2.70 to 1.91, but the overall effect is 2.81. Real domestic credit creation, on the other hand, has a small and insignificant effect on the first period and an effect of 2.2 in the second. Over all, the fit is better in the first period, but there is less autocorrelation in the second (when the *DW* statistic is computed from a regression with a constant term), and the out-of-sample

Table 7 Forecasts and backcasts from table 6

	A 1973(I)–1975(IV)					*B* 1976(I)–1979(I)				
Variable	*Coefficient*	*St. error*	*t*	*Mean*	R^2	*Coefficient*	*St. error*	*t*	*Mean*	R^2
$\tilde{b}$	2.54	1.75	1.45	−0.37	0.70	3.92	2.04	1.92	−2.25	0.91
ω	2.70	0.67	4.01	1.02	0.84	1.91	1.11	1.71	6.02	0.98
d	0.43	1.36	0.32	−0.28	0.79	2.23	0.80	2.79	0.31	0.78
$\hat{\hat{e}}_r$	−1.33	0.85	−1.58	−2.43	0.88	−1.27	1.13	−1.13	1.01	0.96
$\hat{y}$	−0.89	1.38	−0.65	0.59	0.74	−0.29	1.24	−0.23	1.93	0.77
$\hat{e}$				3.49					2.27	
Residuals				−0.94					0.75	

Statistics

R^2 with constant (adj. d.f.)	0.87 (0.76)	0.75 (0.56)
R^2 alt.	0.84	0.73
DW (with constant)	2.43 (2.35)	1.40 (1.83)
SER	7.15	5.93
F (d.f.)	7.33 (5.7)	4.40 (5.8)
	1.1	3.2
	(1976(I)–1979(I)	*1973(I)–1975(IV)*
Forecast mean	7.62 (6.77)	2.82 (4.86)
Actual	2.27	3.48
Root m.s.e.	13.51 (15.37)	10.19 (10.99)
Theil's *U*	1.50 (1.71)	0.75 (0.81)

performance is better in terms of both the most mean square error (m.s.e.) and Theil's U. Not surprisingly, a comparison of the residuals and the prediction errors of the regression over the whole sample period, of the residual over the 'fixed rate' period and the respective forecast, and of the residual over the 'flexible rate' period and the respective backcast (figure 8) shows that the forecast underestimated the change in the black market rate whereas the backcast overestimated it.

Fig. 8 Fitted values, forecasts and backcasts from table 7

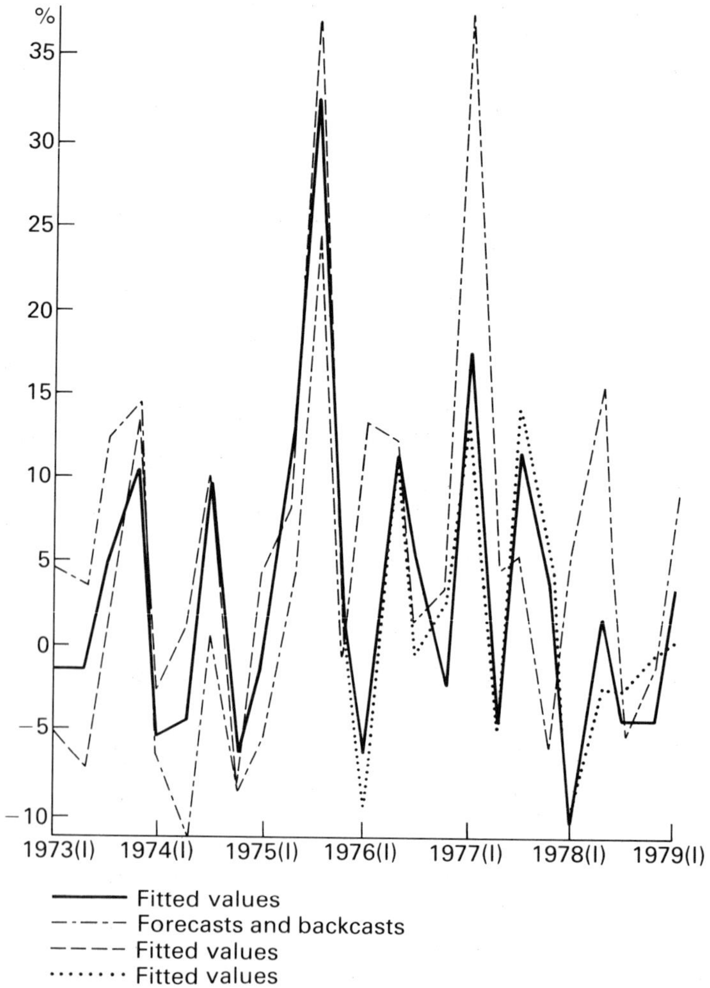

Sources: tables 6 and 7

Conclusion

This paper has attempted to put a simple portfolio balance model of the recent currency experience of Portugal in a macroeconomic and institutional perspective. Thus an overview of macroeconomic policy suggested that the IMF-inspired stabilization package of June 1978–March 1979 was successful because it changed the relative price of traded and non-traded goods, which was interpreted as the fundamental determinant of the exchange rate, and the interest differential at which the equilibrium relative price is discounted. On the other hand, the institutional perspective on the unofficial foreign exchange mechanisms showed that the traditional commitment to a fixed exchange rate was to a large degree circumvented by the private sector's wish to hold foreign assets.

The paper also contributes to the already sizeable analytical literature on the macroeconomic experience of Portugal in the 1970s by focusing on the determination of the black market rate under various official exchange rate regimes: an adjustable peg to the US dollar from December 1971 to August 1977, and a crawling peg in terms of a basket of currencies since then.

The motivation for taking into account the unofficial black and forward markets against the escudo was to assess the consequences of establishing convertibility of the escudo as part of the process of joining the European Economic Community. This was done by specifying and estimating an equation for the rate of change of the floating black market escudo–dollar rate. The results implied that the net stock of foreign assets unofficially held by the private sector was negative and therefore that the private sector wished to be debtor in foreign currency. As a consequence, the black market exchange rate depended positively on the reported current account surplus and negatively on a measure of pressure in the official foreign exchange market. The large estimated negative value of the real-wealth propensity to hold foreign assets suggests that a free (unified) foreign exchange market is likely to be unstable. This instability might be lessened if the feedback from the black market rate to the reported current account and the effect of claims to real capital and interest-bearing financial assets were not neglected in the specification of the model.

On the other hand, despite a rather poor out-of-sample performance, the precision of the estimates was remarkable, given severe data limitations and substantial structural changes.

One major implication of the econometric results is that the crawling peg regime is likely to be superior to a pure floating exchange rate. Nevertheless, the present discretionary crawl with tight controls on the access to the foreign exchange market is less informative about the consequences of establishing convertibility than a crawling peg with a wider band. Similarly, even though the rate of crawl was initially set to more than offset the inflation differential with major trading partners, we found a clear negative association between the annual rate of depreciation against the dollar and the current account surplus, except in 1973 and 1980.[33] As a consequence, it would seem preferable to actually use the expected current account as an indicator for the rate of crawl, with some weight given to the level of foreign assets of the banking system. This policy would make the exchange rate at which the current account is balanced the long-run equilibrium rate, but it would allow the capital account to determine the exchange rate in the short run and thus provide precious information about the type of convertibility that is best suited to facilitate the catching-up process with the EEC.

Notes

Earlier versions were presented at the European University Institute, Florence, on 12 March 1981, at the Fundacão Centro de Estudos do Comércio Exterior, Rio de Janeiro, on 27 July 1981, and at the University of Illinois in Champaign-Urbana on 2 December 1981. Comments from the participants and the members of my PhD committee are gratefully acknowledged. Errors are my own.

1 On the choice of a basket peg see Branson and Katseli (1981); on the choice of indicators see Branson and Macedo (1982).
2 This is discussed at length in Macedo (1981a, 1981c).
3 This emerges from the analysis in Macedo (1980a).
4 The structuralist view is very heterogeneous and encompasses *dependencia* extremes such as Murteira (1979) as well as the elasticity scepticism of the recent stances of Dornbusch (1980, 1981). A typical representative might be Stallings (1981). The elasticity optimists include Barbosa and Beleza (1979), Krugman and Macedo (1979), their discussants, Schmitt (1981) and Kouri (1981). A view in between is in Lopes (1980). This subsection draws on section I of Macedo (1981b). Further details in Macedo (1980a), and a discussion of the social science literature on Portugal since the Revolution in Macedo (1979d).
5 See, respectively, the memorandum to the 5th Provisional Government reproduced in Kolm (1977, pp. 53–5) and the report to the OECD by Dornbusch, Eckaus and Taylor in Gulbenkian (1977).
6 See Taylor (1979, chapter 4-2), drawing on Abel *et al.* (1977), Taylor in Gulbenkian (1977) and Krugman and Taylor (1978).
7 The index of the purchasing power of the escudo is defined as

$$Q_j = S_j \prod_{i=1}^{N} P_i S_i^{-\alpha_1}$$

where P_i = consumer price index in country i, and S_i = price of currency i in terms of dollars (annual average). See Macedo (1982a) for more details on the concept. This index has base = 1 in 1980 and in 1973 has the value of 4.76. Weighting schemes are discussed in Macedo (1981c), Appendix 1. The weights used here are: France 28, Germany 25, UK 26 and US 21.

8 See Kouri (forthcoming). Evidence on major countries is in Kouri and Macedo (1981); see also the econometric analysis of Branson *et al.* (1979) and Porter (1978).

9 See Macedo (1982a) for the method. The index described in note 7 with base 1973 = 100 would be 25 in 1979 and 21 in 1980.

10 Data on manufacturing, wages, consumer prices and industrial production from IMF *International Financial Statistics* and on employment from OECD *Main Economic Indicators*. OECD forecasts in December 1980 *Economic Outlook* were used for 1980. Portuguese data from Banco de Portugal, using the new manufacturing wage and continental consumer price index linked to the Lisbon index excluding rent from Instituto Nacional de Estatistica, *Boletim Mensual*, for the period before 1977. See quarterly indices and econometric evidence on exchange rate and wages in Macedo (1980c).

11 See Fry in Gulbenkian (1980), Macedo (1980b) and references therein.

12 The importance of relative prices is discussed at length in Beleza (1979). See also Barbosa and Beleza (1979) and Macedo (1979b).

13 Weekly escudo–dollar rates in the 'inland parallel market in bank notes' are quoted in *IR Statistical Market Letter*, and monthly rates are collected in *Pick's Currency Yearbook*. In the early 1950s, furthermore, a monthly 'free market rate' for escudo notes exchanged in Switzerland was reported in *IFS*. In the last *Currency Yearbook*, for 1977, Pick writes in characteristic style: 'the black market continued to boom, as banknote smuggling under the protection of diplomatic immunity became big business, with couriers carrying as many as esc. 7 million in bank notes in one shipment. Meanwhile, an efficient "Payments Lisbon" network was now operating, centered in New York, Brazil and Zurich' (p. 495). There are also regular reports on the escudo in *International Currency Review*.

14 The flow estimates are reported in J. A. Toscano (1978) from Lisbon experts on the unofficial market. The estimates from partner country data are in Barbosa and Beleza (1979).

15 See Macedo (1982b) for a model along these lines.

16 Einzig (1967) mentions occasional forward operations in escudos in London, but no regular quotes are recorded. Reuter and Samuel Montagu appear to report data on the escudo occasionally but the main source is International Reports Inc., New York. I am grateful to Ms Gail Weisgrau for making this data available. The weekly data have been interpolated for the weeks when no quotations were available. Thus 1975(II), 1976(I), 1976(II), 1976(III) are interpolated. After some experimentation, a spline of degree zero was used to interpolate the 53 missing observations in the sample from 3 January 1977 to 18 August 1978. There were no missing observations in the subsequent update to 26 December 1980. Further details on the data in Macedo (1979a).

17 The old argument about stabilizing or destabilizing speculation in the foreign exchanges hinges on where there is enough of it, as Machlup (1972) argued, or not, as defended by McKinnon (1979). Forward markets in non-

industrial countries have been described by Gerakis and Danker (1977), while Blejer and Khan (1981) have an empirical study of Singapore. A convincing explanation for the thinness of future markets, and a rejection of the 'strong efficient market hypothesis' when information is costly to acquire, is in Grossman and Stiglitz (1976).

18 Further details in section II of Macedo (1981b).

19 See discussion in Fry (1978).

20 See J. J. Toscano (1980), who uses the three-month Eurodollar and the six-month Portuguese deposit in covered interest differential calculations.

21 See Frenkel and Levich (1975 and 1977).

22 See Macedo (1980d) and references therein.

23 On the 'peso problem' see Krugman (1977), Frankel (1977) and Krasker (1979). In Portugal, the percentage of defaulted bills went up from about 3% of the amount of discounted bills in 1973, to 47% in 1975 and down to about 7% in early 1978. See Banco Português do Atlântico, *Conjuntura*, August 1978, figure 27.

24 In obvious notation, the covered differential is computed as

$$CD = \frac{R^* - R}{1 + R^*} + \frac{F^{\mathrm{b}} - S}{S}.$$

The rates would be adjusted for minimum deposit or reserve requirements. See Blejer and Khan (1981). For the computation of escudo yields on securities denominated in foreign currency using the actual depreciation of the escudo, see Barbosa and Beleza (1979), J. J. Toscano (1980), Lopes (1980), and the 1979 *Report* of the Bank of Portugal. The issue is discussed in Dornbusch Taylor (1977) and Dornbusch (1981), who, using the Brazilian experience, argue that the implied disincentive is small nevertheless.

25 See Macedo (1981c), Appendix 3.

26 If the constant a is different from zero, we would have another term

$$a \sum_{i=0}^{\tau-1} (\tau - i)\, b^i$$

which would diverge as $\tau \to \infty$. See Macedo (1979a).

27 See Kouri (forthcoming) and a two-country model in Macedo (1979c).

28 See Tobin (1969) and an extension to the open economy in Tobin and Macedo (1980).

29 Strictly speaking, this is high-powered money, but the model could be interpreted in terms of the banking system rather than the central bank as long as the money multiplier is exogenous.

30 See Macedo (1982b) for a theoretical model emphasizing that distinction.

31 A more complicated scheme can be found in Macedo (1979c).

32 These are in fact 'restricted' estimates from a more complete model where foreign variables and the correction for capital gains and losses of the central bank reserves turn out to be insignificant, and where $a_0 \simeq a_1$ as assumed in (12′). See Macedo (1979c, 1980c). Also, the fit improves slightly with an autocorrelation correction but the interpretation of the data is easier in terms of rate of exchange.

33 Macedo (1980a).

References

Abel, A., Beleza, L. M., Frankel, J., Hill, R. and Krugman, P. (1977), 'A economia portuguesa: evolucão recente e situacão actual'. In Gulbenkian Foundation... (1977), pp. 31-91.

Barbosa, M. and Beleza, L. M. (1979). 'External disequilibrium in Portugal: 1975-78; and R. Hill, 'Comment', *Economia*, October.

Beleza, L. M. (1979), 'Credit, wages and prices in a small, open economy: Portugal'. Unpublished PhD thesis, MIT.

Blejer, M. and Khan, M. (1981), 'The foreign exchange market in a highly-open developing economy: the case of Singapore'. IMF Departmental Memorandum, February.

Branson, W., Halttunen, H. and Masson, P. (1979), 'Exchange rates in the short run'. *European Economic Review*.

Branson, W. and Katseli, L. (1981). 'Exchange rate policies for developing countries'. In S. Grossman and E. Lundberg (eds), *The World Economic Order* (Macmillan, London).

Branson, W. and Macedo, J. (1982), 'The optimal weighting of indicators for a crawling peg', *Journal of International Money and Finance*, forthcoming.

Dornbusch, R. (1980), 'Comment on Barbosa and Beleza (1979)'. In Gulbenkian Foundation ... (1980).

Dornbusch, R. (1981), 'Portugal's crawling peg'. In Williamson (1981).

Dornbusch, R. and Taylor, L. (1977), 'Economic prospects and policy options in Portugal'. Unpublished, MIT.

Einzig, P. (1967), *The Theory of Forward Exchanges*, 2nd edn (Macmillan, London).

Frankel, J. (1977), 'All about flexible exchange rates'. Unpublished, MIT.

Frenkel, J. (1977), 'Transactions costs and interest arbitrage: tranquil versus turbulent periods'. *Journal of Political Economy*, vol. 85, no. 6, pp. 1209-26.

Frenkel, J. and Levich, R. (1975), 'Covered interest arbitrage: unexploited profits?' *Journal of Political Economy*, vol. 83, no. 2, pp. 325-38.

Fry, M. (1978), 'Deposits and deposit rates of interest'. *Economia*, May.

Gerakis, A. and Danker, D. (1977), 'Forward markets: a review of theory, practice and recent developments', IMF Department Memorandum, January.

Girton, L. and Roper, D. (1977). 'A monetary model of exchange market pressure applied to the postwar Canadian experience'. *American Economic Review*, pp. 537-48.

Grossman, S. and Stiglitz, J. (1976), 'Information and competitive price systems'. *American Economic Review*, vol. 66, no. 2, pp. 246-53.

Gulbenkian Foundation and German Marshall Fund of the United States (sponsors) (1977), *Conferencia Internacional Sobre Economia Portuguesa*, 2 vols (Lisbon).

Gulbenkian Foundation and German Marshall Fund of the United States (sponsors) (1980), *II Conferencia Internacional Sobre Economia Portuguesa*, 2 vols (Lisbon).

Kolm, S. C. (1977), *La Transition socialiste, la politique économique de gauche* (Cerf, Paris).

Kouri, P. (1981), 'The political economy of stabilization'. Comment on Stallings (1981).

Kouri, P. (forthcoming), 'The exchange rate and the foreign exchange market: a dynamic partial equilibrium approach'. In J. Bhandari and B. Putnam (eds),

The International Transmission of Disturbances under Flexible Exchange Rates, forthcoming.

Kouri, P. and Macedo, J. (1978), 'Exchange rates and the international adjustment process'. *Brookings Papers on Economic Activity*, no. 1.

Kouri, P. and Macedo, J. (1981), 'Perspectives on the stagflation of the 1970's'. In H. Giersch (ed.), *Macroeconomic Policies for Growth and Stability – the European Perspective* (J. C. B. Mohr, Tubigen).

Krasker, W. (1979), 'The "peso problem" in testing the efficiency of forward exchange markets'. *Journal of Monetary Economics*.

Krugman, P. (1977), 'Essays on flexible exchange rates'. Unpublished PhD thesis, MIT.

Krugman, P. and Macedo, J. (1979), 'The economic consequences of the April 25th revolution'; and J. Frankel, 'Comment'. *Economia*, October 1979.

Krugman, P. and Taylor, L. (1978), 'Contractionary effects of devaluation'. *Journal of International Economics*, vol. 8.

Lopes, J. Silva (1980), 'Contribution of external and internal factors to annual changes in the balance of payments on current account of Portugal'. Unpublished, IMF, October.

Macedo, J. (1979a), 'Foreign exchange market "efficiency"; the case of the Portuguese escudo and the US dollar'. EGC Discussion Paper no. 322, Yale University, October.

Macedo, J. (1979b), 'Monetarist models of exchange rate determination: the experience of Portugal'. EGC Discussion Paper no. 323, Yale University, October.

Macedo, J. (1979c), 'Exchange rates in Portugal 1973–78: a portfolio model of an inconvertible currency'. EGC Discussion Paper no. 324, Yale University, October.

Macedo, J. (1979d), 'Grandeza e Misérias dos Estudos Portugueses, Introduction to the Proceedings of a Panel on the Portuguese Economy', *Economia*, October.

Macedo, J. (1980a), 'Portuguese currency experience: an historical perspective'. In *Estudos em Homenagem ao Prof. Doutor Jose Joaquim Teixiera Ribeiro*, vol. IV (Boletim da Faculdade de Direito, Coimbra).

Macedo, J. (1980b), 'Comment on M. Fry'. In Gulbenkian Foundation... (1980).

Macedo, J. (1980c), 'Portugal and Europe: crawl or float?' Unpublished, Princeton University, January. A Portuguese version appeared in Trade Policy Research Center and Inteuropa (sponsors), *Portugal e o Alargamento da Comunidade Europeia* (Lisbon, 1981).

Macedo, J. (1981a), 'Portugal and Europe: the channels of structural interdependence'. In Macedo and Serfaty (1981).

Macedo, J. (1981b), 'Comment on R. Dornbusch', in Williamson (1981).

Macedo, J. (1981c), 'The recent currency experience of Portugal'. *International Finance Section Working Paper G-81-03*, Princeton University, October.

Macedo, J. (1982a), 'Portfolio diversification across currencies'. In R. Cooper, P. Kenen, J. Macedo and J. V. Ypersele (eds), *The International Monetary System under Floating Rates* (Ballinger, Cambridge, Mass.).

Macedo, J, (1982b), 'Exchange rate behavior with currency inconvertibility'. *Journal of International Economics*, February.

Macedo, J. (1982c), 'Portugal and Europe: the dilemmas of integration'. In T. Bruneau (ed.), *Underdevelopment, Emigration and Industrialization: The Case of Portugal.*

Macedo, J. and Serfaty, S. (eds) (1981), *Portugal since the Revolution: Economic and Political Perspectives* (Westview, Boulder, Colorado).

Machlup, F. (1972), *The Alignment of Foreign Exchange Rates* (Praeger, New York).

McKinnon, R. (1979), *Money in International Exchange: The Convertible Currency System* (Oxford University Press).

Murteira, M. (1979), 'The present economic situation: its origins and prospects'. In L. Graham and H. Makler (eds), *Contemporary Portugal, The Revolution and its Antecendents* (University of Texas Press, Austin, Texas).

Porter, M. (1978), 'Exchange rates and portfolio equilibrium'. Unpublished, Yale University, January.

Schmitt, H. (1981), 'Economic stabilization and growth in Portugal'. Unpublished, IMF Occasional Paper no. 2.

Stallings, B. (1981), 'Portugal and the IMF: the political economy of stabilization', and 'Comment' by P. Kouri; in Macedo and Serfaty (1981).

Taylor, L. (1979), *Macro Models for Developing Countries* (McGraw-Hill, New York).

Tobin, J. (1969), 'A general equilibrium approach to monetary theory'. *Journal of Money, Credit and Banking*, February.

Tobin, J. and Macedo, J. (1980), 'The short run macroeconomics of flexible exchange rates: an exposition'. In J. Chipman and C. Kindleberger (eds), *Flexible Exchange Rates and the Balance of Payments* (North Holland, Amsterdam).

Toscano, J. A. (1978), *Avaliacão economica de projectos segundo a metodologia do Banco Mundial, estimativa preliminar dos parametros nacionais* (Banco de Fomento Nacional, Lisbon).

Toscano, J. J. (1980), 'Diferenciais entre as remuneracões internas e externas'. Banco de Portugal, *Boletim Trimestral*, June.

Williamson, J. (ed.) (1981), *Exchange Rate Rules: The Theory, Performance and Prospects of the Crawling Peg* (Macmillan, London).

Index

Italic indicates a reference to a figure